Political Branding

This book demonstrates the progress that has been made on political branding research across international contexts. It focuses on the critical application of new concepts and frameworks, generating a deeper understanding of unexplored settings and positioning research from multiple perspectives.

It is important to consider different typologies of international political brands particularly as we have witnessed huge changes across political landscapes from Brexit, the rise of President Trump, the surge in populism and the development of sustainable-climate change movements. Given that there are many potential typologies and non-traditional political brands, this volume investigates different typologies and alternative political brands with the support of new and under-developed theoretical lens from multiple perspectives and contexts. These include Canada, Iceland, India, Indonesia and the United States of America. This book provides areas of reflection and explicit calls for further research, which in turn will advance insight into political brands and enhance our understanding of political marketing in action.

This is a must-read guide for setting out the implications of theory and practice for multiple stakeholders including political marketers, political scientists, politicians, political party organizers, brand managers and scholars across a wide range of social science disciplines.

The chapters in this book were originally published as a special issue of the *Journal of Political Marketing*.

Christopher Pich is senior lecturer in Marketing at Nottingham Business School, Nottingham Trent University, UK. Christopher is the Managing Editor for Europe of the *Journal of Political Marketing* and continues to publish articles in the *Journal of Business Research*, *European Journal of Marketing*, *International Journal of Market Research* and *Journal of Politics and Policy*. He focuses on topics such as political brand identity, image, reputation and co-branding in international settings.

Bruce I. Newman is Editor-in-Chief of the *Journal of Political Marketing* and author of several books and articles on political marketing, voter choice behavior and political strategy, including *The Marketing of the President* and most recently *Brand* (Kendall-Hunt Publishing, 2018).

Related Readings

Political Branding

More Than Parties, Leaders and Policies

Edited by
Christopher Pich and Bruce I. Newman

Routledge
Taylor & Francis Group

LONDON AND NEW YORK

First published 2021
by Routledge
2 Park Square, Milton Park, Abingdon, Oxon, OX14 4RN

and by Routledge
605 Third Avenue, New York, NY 10017

Routledge is an imprint of the Taylor & Francis Group, an informa business

Copyright © 2021 Taylor & Francis

All rights reserved. No part of this book may be reprinted or reproduced or utilised in any form or by any electronic, mechanical, or other means, now known or hereafter invented, including photocopying and recording, or in any information storage or retrieval system, without permission in writing from the publishers.

Trademark notice: Product or corporate names may be trademarks or registered trademarks, and are used only for identification and explanation without intent to infringe.

British Library Cataloguing-in-Publication Data
A catalogue record for this book is available from the British Library

ISBN 13: 978-0-367-49227-4 (hbk)

Typeset in Garamond
by codeMantra

Publisher's Note
The publisher accepts responsibility for any inconsistencies that may have arisen during the conversion of this book from journal articles to book chapters, namely the inclusion of journal terminology.

Disclaimer
Every effort has been made to contact copyright holders for their permission to reprint material in this book. The publishers would be grateful to hear from any copyright holder who is not here acknowledged and will undertake to rectify any errors or omissions in future editions of this book.

Contents

Citation Information   vi
Notes on Contributors   viii

1   Evolution of Political Branding: Typologies, Diverse Settings and Future Research   1
    Christopher Pich and Bruce I. Newman

2   Understanding the Magic of Credibility for Political Leaders: A Case of India
    and Narendra Modi   12
    Varsha Jain and Ganesh B. E.

3   Moderators and Mediators of Framing Effects in Political Marketing:
    Implications for Political Brand Management   30
    Andrzej Falkowski and Magdalena Jabłońska

4   Scripted Messengers: How Party Discipline and Branding Turn Election
    Candidates and Legislators into Brand Ambassadors   50
    Alex Marland and Angelia Wagner

5   Exploring Personal Political Brands of Iceland's Parliamentarians   70
    Guja Armannsdottir, Stuart Carnell, and Christopher Pich

6   Why Cryptocurrencies Want Privacy: A Review of Political Motivations and
    Branding Expressed in "Privacy Coin" Whitepapers   103
    John Harvey and Ines Branco-Illodo

7   The Emergence of Science as a Political Brand   132
    Todd P. Newman

8   Symbolic Political Communication, and Trust: A Young Voters' Perspective of
    the Indonesian Presidential Election   148
    *Ihwan Susila, Dianne Dean, Raja Nerina Raja Yusof,
    Anton Agus Setyawan and Farid Wajdi*

Index   171

Citation Information

The chapters in this book were originally published in the *Journal of Political Marketing*, volume 19, issue 1–2 (May 2020). When citing this material, please use the original page numbering for each article, as follows:

Chapter 1
Evolution of Political Branding: Typologies, Diverse Settings and Future Research
Christopher Pich and Bruce I. Newman
Journal of Political Marketing, volume 19, issue 1–2 (May 2020) pp. 3–14

Chapter 2
Understanding the Magic of Credibility for Political Leaders: A Case of India and Narendra Modi
Varsha Jain and Ganesh B. E.
Journal of Political Marketing, volume 19, issue 1–2 (May 2020) pp. 15–33

Chapter 3
Moderators and Mediators of Framing Effects in Political Marketing: Implications for Political Brand Management
Andrzej Falkowski and Magdalena Jabłońska
Journal of Political Marketing, volume 19, issue 1–2 (May 2020) pp. 34–53

Chapter 4
Scripted Messengers: How Party Discipline and Branding Turn Election Candidates and Legislators into Brand Ambassadors
Alex Marland and Angelia Wagner
Journal of Political Marketing, volume 19, issue 1–2 (May 2020) pp. 54–73

Chapter 5
Exploring Personal Political Brands of Iceland's Parliamentarians
Guja Armannsdottir, Stuart Carnell, and Christopher Pich
Journal of Political Marketing, volume 19, issue 1–2 (May 2020) pp. 74–106

Chapter 6
Why Cryptocurrencies Want Privacy: A Review of Political Motivations and Branding Expressed in "Privacy Coin" Whitepapers
John Harvey and Ines Branco-Illodo
Journal of Political Marketing, volume 19, issue 1–2 (May 2020) pp. 107–136

Chapter 7

The Emergence of Science as a Political Brand
Todd P. Newman
Journal of Political Marketing, volume 19, issue 1–2 (May 2020) pp. 137–152

Chapter 8

Symbolic Political Communication, and Trust: A Young Voters' Perspective of the Indonesian Presidential Election
Ihwan Susila, Dianne Dean, Raja Nerina Raja Yusof, Anton Agus Setyawan and Farid Wajdi
Journal of Political Marketing, volume 19, issue 1–2 (May 2020) pp. 153–175

For any permission-related enquiries please visit:
http://www.tandfonline.com/page/help/permissions

Contributors

Guja Armannsdottir Marketing Department, Nottingham Business School, Nottingham Trent University, United Kingdom.

Ines Branco-Illodo Marketing and Retail Division, Stirling Management School, University of Stirling, Scotland, UK.

Stuart Carnell Marketing Department, Nottingham Business School, Nottingham Trent University, United Kingdom.

Dianne Dean Sheffield Business School, Sheffield Hallam Business School, UK.

Andrzej Falkowski Department of Psychology, SWPS University of Social Science and Humanities, Warsaw, Poland.

Ganesh B. E. MICA, Ahmedabad, Gujarat, India.

John Harvey N/LAB, Nottingham University Business School, University of Nottingham, UK

Magdalena Jabłońska Department of Psychology, SWPS University of Social Science and Humanities, Warsaw, Poland.

Varsha Jain Marketing Department, MICA, Ahmedabad, Gujarat, India.

Alex Marland Department of Political Science, Memorial University of Newfoundland, St. John's, Canada.

Bruce I. Newman Department of Marketing to DePaul University, Chicago, USA.

Todd P. Newman Department of Life Sciences Communication, University of Wisconsin-Madison, USA.

Christopher Pich Marketing Department, Nottingham Business School, Nottingham Trent University, United Kingdom.

Anton Agus Setyawan Department of Management, Universitas Muhammadiyah Surakarta, Indonesia.

Ihwan Susila Department of Management, Universitas Muhammadiyah Surakarta, Indonesia.

Angelia Wagner Department of Political Science, University of Alberta, Edmonton, Canada.

Farid Wajdi Department of Management, Universitas Muhammadiyah Surakarta, Indonesia.

Raja Nerina Raja Yusof Faculty of Economics and Management, Universiti Putra Malaysia, Serdang, Malaysia

Evolution of Political Branding: Typologies, Diverse Settings and Future Research

CHRISTOPHER PICH

BRUCE I. NEWMAN

Political branding has developed into an established and vibrant sub-discipline of political marketing. Indeed, political branding research continues to push boundaries by critically applying consumer based branding theories, concepts and frameworks to the political environment. Recently, political branding scholars have segmented research into different categories such as corporate, candidate, leader, local-regional, internal or external in orientation. Despite this development, there continues to be limited research on alternative or different typologies of political brands. This study reaffirms political branding as a distinct area of research and discusses how political brands can be conceptualised and operationalised. Further, drawing on seven empirical and conceptual papers, which focus on different typologies of political brands from a range of international contexts including Canada, USA, Iceland, Indonesia and India, we reflect on the current political branding environment. We conclude that there are multiple relationships and numerous interconnected political brands, which represent an intricate environment or ecosystem. This study offers academics and political actors guidance on how to conceptualise political brands and provides a starting point to map out the ecosystems of political brands. Finally, this study provides explicit calls for further research in political branding.

INTRODUCTION

This is the second special issue of a journal devoted entirely to research on the application of branding concepts, theories and frameworks to politics. Furthermore, this special issue builds on the first special issue devoted to political branding facilitated by Needham and Smith (2015). Indeed, Needham and Smith (2015) discussed advancements in the sub-discipline of political branding and presented explicit gaps for further research. Since then, progress has been made on political branding research focusing on the critical application of new concepts and frameworks, generating a deeper understanding of unexplored contexts and settings and positioning research from multiple perspectives (Billard 2018; Meyerrose 2017; Nai and Martinez 2019; Simons 2016). Despite the development of political branding, existing work continue to focus on the party *leader* or *party* political brands particularly in traditional political systems (Husted et al. 2018; Meyerrose 2017; Nielsen 2016). Given there are many potential typologies and nontraditional political brands, this grounds an area for future research. Therefore, this special issue investigates different typologies and alternative political brands with the support of new and under-developed theoretical lens from multiple perspectives and in contexts ranging from Canada, Iceland, India, Indonesia and the United States of America.

POLITICAL BRANDING – *A DISTINCT AREA OF RESEARCH*

Political branding has developed into a distinct area of research within the discipline of political marketing (Scammell 2015). Taking a step back, political branding can be simply defined as the critical application of traditional branding concepts, theories and frameworks to politics in order to provide differentiation from political competitors and identification between citizens and political entities (Harris and Lock 2010; Needham and Smith 2015). Further, the conceptualization and investigation of political brands has developed significantly over the last twenty year since the seminal work of Lock and Harris (1996). For example, there is a shared understanding that political parties [local–regional, national and international], pressure groups, movements, politicians, candidates and campaigns can be conceptualized as 'political brands' (Ahmed, Lodhi, and Ahmad 2017; Billard 2018; Meyerrose 2017; Nai and Martinez 2019; Simons 2016; Scammell 2015; Smith 2009; Speed, Butler, and Collins 2015).

In addition, investigating how political brands are positioned by political actors and how they are understood in the minds of citizens continues to be a topical area of study across national–international jurisdictions (Baines et al. 2014; Nielsen 2016). This insight allows political entities to develop long-term strategies and processes to develop and manage their brands (Pich, Armannsdottir, and Spry 2018). Recently, political branding research has started to segment into different categories such as corporate, candidate, leader, local–regional, internal or external in orientation. In fact, the case has been made that a political brand is an extension of research carried out in the for-profit and nonprofit sectors, where the citizen/voter in the political marketplace can be viewed in a similar context as a consumer in the commercial marketplace (Newman and Newman 2018). Despite these developments, there continues to be limited research on *alternative* political brands, *nontraditional* political brands, *new* political brands and political brands in *different settings* and *contexts*. Further, there still seems to be very few pragmatic models-frameworks that can be used by political brands to assess their identity, image, reputation or position that will ultimately support the development of strategy and political brand management. This in turn is supported by broader explicit calls for further research on political branding (Billard 2018; Husted et al. 2018; Marland 2016; Nai and Martinez 2019; Nielsen et al. 2016).

POLITICAL BRANDING – *CONCEPTUALISATIONS AND OPERATIONALIZATION*

Political brands are multifaceted and often complex entities designed to differentiate from competition (Lock and Harris 1996; Phipps, Brace-Govan, and Jevons 2010; Pich, Armannsdottir, and Spry 2018). Further, political brands are often difficult to operationalize. Nevertheless, political brands can be considered a trinity of elements including the *party, leader* and *policy* (Butler et al. 2011; Davies and Mian 2010; O'Cass and Voola 2011; Smith 2008; Smith and French 2009; Speed, Butler, and Collins 2015) (Figure 1). This simple approach allows us to 'make sense' of different types of political brands and serves to ground studies, followed by the adoption of a theoretical lens. It is

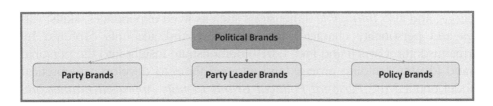

FIGURE 1. The political brand trinity.

encouraging to see that political marketing research continues to broaden its scope and consider different typologies of political brands beyond party leader, party and policy. For example, existing research has focused on the investigation of party leader brands (Jain and Ganesh 2019), parliamentarians (Armannsdottir, Carnell and Pich 2019), and candidates and legislators (Falkowski and Jabłońska 2019; Marland and Wagner 2019). However, recently, we have witnessed work on political brand communities (Newman 2019), cryptocurrencies [policy brands] (Harvey and Branco-Illodo 2019) and political brand communications (Susila et al. 2019) (Figure 1).

More specifically, Jain and Ganesh (2019) focused on the importance of *credibility* of party leader brand image in the context of India's Prime Minister Narendra Modi. Their work investigated used secondary research to investigate how social media marketing is often utilized to build a credible, authentic yet personal political brand image. Indeed, Jain and Ganesh (2019) argued that party leaders should periodically consider the strategy of crisis management along with the adopting a collaborative co-constructed multi-stakeholder approach to develop political brand image in the mind of voters. Furthermore, they maintain that in order to create a credible, consistent political brand image, practitioners and politicians should not only embrace a professional persona but also communicate humility, personal characteristics and relatable personality. Despite that Jain and Ganesh's (2019) study was grounded on secondary research, they conclude that future work should conduct longitudinal research on the credibility of political brand image in other contexts and adopt different methodological approaches.

The exploration of the personal characteristics of political brands is proving a popular topic area within political marketing-branding. For instance, Armannsdottir, Carnell and Pich (2019) investigated the personal political brand identities created and developed by Icelandic Parliamentarians from a brand creator [politician] perspective. Armannsdottir, Carnell and Pich (2019) framed their exploration with the concept of *personal branding* – a strategy grounded within the impression management literature designed to allow individuals to actively manage a positive identity and communicate desired impressions (Johnson 2014). Indeed, Armannsdottir, Carnell and Pich (2019) argued that personal political brands need to project an authentic character and distinct identity, structured around *tangible* dimensions such as physical appearance, style, online and offline communication tools and actions, and also *intangible* dimensions such as lived experiences, skills, values and personality characteristics. The first-hand accounts captured by Armannsdottir, Carnell and Pich (2019) demonstrate insight into the personal brand identity building process and allowed them to develop a theoretical model entitled the *Personal Political Brand Identity Appraisal Framework*, which could be used to periodically audit current identity and develop desired personal political brands of politicians and other political actors.

Similarly, Marland and Wagner (2019) and Falkowski and Jabłońska (2019) continued with the typology of candidates and legislators as political brands. Indeed, Marland and Wagner (2019) examined the link between personal political brands and party *discipline*. Furthermore, their qualitative study contextualized in the political party system of Canada highlighted that candidates are often characterized as brand ambassadors or brand champions of the corporate 'party' brand. Political brand ambassadors must adhere to party message and stick to the approved script in order to communicate a coherent position and for the brand to be deemed authentic. In addition, candidates can be considered a 'franchise' of the corporate party and will be disciplined and potentially expelled from the corporate party if they are not 'on message'. Corporate parties must strike a fine balance between party 'authority and individual authenticity' (Marland and Wagner 2019) in order to minimize tensions and misalignment. Therefore, discipline and maintaining the mantra of being 'on message' can stifle individuality and highlights the difficulty of developing personal political brands (Marland and Wagner 2019). Being 'on message' is only one aspect of the political brand management process. Indeed, successful political messages, campaigns and policies need to be made relevant, clearly communicated and 'framed' in order to capture and maintain the interests of voters (Falkowski and Jabłońska 2019). Falkowski and Jabłońska (2019) assessed the *priming, framing* and *agenda setting* by political parties as a means of developing persuasive messages and contributing to the management of candidate political brand image. Furthermore, Falkowski and Jabłońska (2019) argued that framing messages, creating favorable associations and desired imagery is strategic in nature and part of an ongoing process of political brand management. Therefore, they suggested that successful candidate image can improve voting intention for the candidate [and party] as long as messages, policies and campaigns are made relevant and appealing to voters. Thus framing involves clearly communicating the implications of policy in action (Falkowski and Jabłońska, 2019). Finally, Falkowski and Jabłońska (2019) continue to call for more research into the political brand management process and specifically call for more insight into the use of artificial intelligence [AI] in political marketing.

Nevertheless, understanding how political brands communicate and engage with voters continues to be a core area of research within political marketing. Likewise, Susila et al. (2019) examined this topic area in an under-researched context and interestingly from a young voter perspective. More specifically, Susila et al. (2019) explored how young voters understand *symbolic communication* created and expressed by politicians and government and assessed how it related to the acceptance and engagement with political brands. Indonesia was used to contextualize the study as it is 'both secular and the world's largest Muslim democracy' (Susila et al. 2019:

2). Susila et al. (2019) revealed the important role of political communication in building trust and ensuring that political brands are considered believable and authentic. Indeed, they highlighted that trustworthy political brands can mobilize citizens and lead to participation in the electoral process by communicating an array of signals ranging from intangible, symbolic, value-laden cues and tangible elements such as appearance of candidates in terms of apparel and style. Just like the work of Armannsdottir, Carnell and Pich (2019) and Jain and Ganesh (2019), Susila et al. (2019) developed a systematic framework for academics, practitioners and politicians. Their framework can be used as a mechanism to generate a greater understanding of the cultural antecedents of trust in political brand communications (Susila et al. 2019). Furthermore, the systematic frameworks demonstrate the development of political marketing-branding discipline and raises the gantlet for further academic research and highlights the practical implications of research in action (Armannsdottir, Carnell and Pich 2019; Jain and Ganesh 2019; Susila et al. 2019).

Nonetheless, returning to Susila et al. (2019), it reminds us that it is important that political brands in all shapes and sizes from parties, governments, politicians, policies, campaigns, movements or nationals/regions need to routinely understand how they communicate and position their brands as this will reveal if they are clearly differentiated from competitors and provide citizens rationale for identification. Indeed, Newman (2019) highlighted there is limited insight into how political brands utilize 'science' and 'science related issues' as a means of differentiation and creation of political brand communities within the political environment of the United States of America. Furthermore, Newman (2019) demonstrated that the emergence of different typologies of political brands such as political brand communities and their use of 'science' as a unique selling point reinforced the importance of a clear, coherent identity. The use of the 'science brand' fused as part of a politician's or party's' identity may strengthen the levels of trust in the mind of citizens as this will enhance the authority and credibility of political brands (Newman 2019). This in turn reminds political marketers that strong political brands are supported and created by a collaborative community or wide eco-system of stakeholders.

The emergence of alternative and different typologies of political brands continues to highlight the numerous gaps that continue to exist within the academic literature. For example, Harvey and Branco-Illodo (2019) challenge the existing boundaries of political brands and reconceptualise a new style of political brand in the form of *cryptocurrencies*. Cryptocurrencies are digital currencies used by political, public and private groups and individuals as an online monetary community that utilize cryptography for robust security procedures and anti-counterfeiting in nature

(Harvey and Branco-Illodo 2019). Looking back at the existing studies that tend to be grouped via the trinity of elements [party, leader and policy], is difficult to categorize cryptocurrencies as political brands in relation to the existing trinity conceptualization. Harvey and Branco-Illodo (2019) argue that cryptocurrencies often referred to as 'privacy coins' provide the user with a degree of confidentiality and anonymity and questions the political motivations of this digital currency. Further, they highlight the growing interest yet limited understanding of cryptocurrencies and propose that they often position themselves as political brands pointing to alignment with political philosophies and ideologies. Therefore, Harvey and Branco-Illodo (2019) present a theoretical-conceptual paper not only raising the proposition that cryptocurrencies can be conceptualized as political brands but identify the ethical tensions present within the communities of people calling for the adoption of privacy coins. This paper raises an interesting point in that we should continually challenge the conceptualization of political brands, be prepared to reconceptualise and accept that there are many typologies of political brands. This reveals many areas of future research.

POLITICAL BRANDING – *A MULTIFACETED ENVIRONMENT*

As we reflect on the recent articles published on political brands, it reminds us that political brands are complex, multifaceted and there continues to be many areas which remain under-developed and under-researched. On the one hand, it is important to adopt a critical perspective and *revisit* concepts, theories and frameworks that have already been applied to political marketing-branding to develop, build on and challenge in different settings and contexts. For example, concepts such as engagement, identity, image, reputation, equity and positioning. Alternatively, there are many concepts, theories and frameworks that have yet to be extended to political marketing-branding such as brand communities, value co-creation, brand architecture and event branding to name but a few and deserve a first visit. This demonstrates numerous opportunities for political branding research particularly as traditional political systems face turbulent times and constitutional crises and new political systems emerge.

As we have identified different typologies and the complex nature of political brands, it is important to start to map out the political branding environment as political brands go beyond the *party, leader* and *policy*. Building on the trinity of elements (Bulter et al. 2011; Davies and Mian 2010; O'Cass and Voola 2011; Smith 2008; Smith and French 2009), we put forward the start of an updated environment of elements (Figure 2).

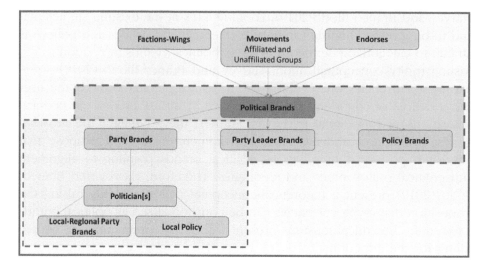

FIGURE 2. The political branding environment.

The environment of elements highlight the overlapping yet distinct nature of political brands. For example, party political brands can also be divided into a sub-trinity. Politicians or Members of Parliament will be the leader of their local party/constituency, which will include local supporters, activities and party members. The politician or Member of Parliament could also have localized policies, which could be distinct from party policy. This represents a sub-political brand, which again needs a degree of alignment with the party political brand. Likewise, there are many different types of sub-political brands which can be affiliated [and unaffiliated] or factions within party political brands such as political groups, movements, endorses and can be seen as political brands in their own right. Therefore, this suggests that there are multiple relationships and numerous interconnected political brands, which represents an intricate environment or ecosystem. This represents the starting point for further research in political brands.

CONCLUSION AND FUTURE RESEARCH

This article not only highlights the diversity of political branding research often in different contexts and settings but also reveals that there are many under-researched and under-developed areas of study. Indeed, despite significant progress in this area including in this special issue, there remains many under-developed areas. Ideology [values], campaigns outside election periods, political movements, comparative and longitudinal studies, ecosystems, nationals/destinations, events, sub-groups/wings, movements, political groups, endorses and populism. In addition, further research should adopt a multidiscipline approach and consider using theoretical lens [concepts, theories and frameworks] from other disciplines across marketing, psychology and social sciences. Therefore, the special issue of the Journal of Political Marketing suggests several considerations for future research that will demonstrate theoretical and managerial relevance and impact including:

- Alternative political brands – [beyond corporate and local-individual]
- Sub-political brands
- Political collaborative consumption
- Comparative research
- Longitudinal research
- Contemporary issues
- Additional frameworks
- Multi-discipline approach
- Ecosystems
- Irregular settings and contexts – [new democracies, under-researched jurisdictions and island communities for example]
- New political brands – [such as Bitcoin, Crypto-Currencies, Foodbanks, political movements, trade unions etc.]
- Online political brand communities [virtual political market places]
- Radical movements – grassroots groups
- The rise of alternative economies
- Pop-up political brands – [Vote Leave and Vote Remain – UK Referendum for example]
- Long-term engagement and participation

REFERENCES

Ahmed, M. A., A. S. Lodhi, and Z. Ahmad. 2017. "Political Brand Equity Model: The Integration of Political Brands in Voter Choice." *Journal of Political Marketing* 16 (2):147–179. doi: 10.1080/15377857.2015.1022629.

Armannsdottir, G., S. Carnell, and C. Pich. 2019. "Exploring Personal Politic Brands of Iceland's Parliamentarians." *Journal of Political Marketing* 19 (1, 2)

Baines, P., I. Crawford, N. O'Shaughnessy, R. Worcester, and R. Mortimore. 2014. "Positioning in Political Marketing: How Semiotic Analysis Adds Value to Traditional Survey Approaches." *Journal of Marketing Management* 30 (1–2): 172–200. doi: 10.1080/0267257X.2013.810166.

Billard, T. J. 2018. "Citizen Typography and Political Brands in the 2016 US Presidential Election Campaign." *Marketing Theory* 18 (3):421. doi: 10.1177/1470593118763982.

Butler, P., N. Collins, and R. Speed. (2011). "The Europeanisation of the British political marketplace." *Journal of Marketing Management* 27 (7-8):675–690. doi: 10.1080/0267257X.2011.593540.

Davies, G., and T. Mian. (2010). "The Reputation of the Party Leader and the Party being Led." *European Journal of Marketing* 44 (3-4):331–350. doi: 10.1108/03090561011020453.

Falkowski, A., and M. Jabłońska. 2019. "Moderators and Mediators of Framing Effects in Political Marketing. Implications for Political Brand Management." *Journal of Political Marketing* 19 (1, 2). doi: 10.1080/15377857.2019.1652221.

Harris, P., and A. Lock. 2010. "Mind the Gap: The Rise of Political Marketing and a Perspective on Its Future Agenda." *European Journal of Marketing* 44 (3/4): 297–307. doi: 10.1108/03090561011020435.

Harvey, J., and I. Branco-Illodo. 2019. "Why Cryptocurrencies Want Privacy: A Review of Political Motivations and Branding Expressed in 'Privacy Coin' Whitepapers." *Journal of Political Marketing* 19 (1):2. doi: 10.1080/15377857.2019.1652223.

Husted, E., M. Fredriksson, M. Moufahim, and J. Gronbaek Pors. 2018. "Political Parties: Exploring the Inner Life of Party Organisations." *Theory and Politics in Organisation*, 1–7. ISSN 1473-2866, 1-7

Jain, V., and Ganesh B. E. 2019. "Understanding the Magic of Credibility for Political Leaders: A Case of India and Narendra Modi." *Journal of Political Marketing* 19 (1):2. doi: 10.1080/15377857.2019.1652222.

Johnson, K. 2014. "The Importance of Personal Branding in Social Media: Educating Students to Create and Manage Their Personal Brand." *International Journal of Education and Social Sciences* 4 (1):1–8.

Lock, A., and P. Harris. 1996. "Political Marketing – Vive la Difference!." *European Journal of Marketing* 30 (10/11):14–31. doi: 10.1108/03090569610149764.

Marland, A. 2016. *Brand Command: Canadian Politics and Democracy in the Age of Message Control.* Vancouver: UBC Press.

Marland, A., and A. Wagner. (2019). "Scripted Messengers: How Party Discipline and Branding Turn Election Candidates and Legislators into Brand Ambassadors." *Journal of Political Marketing* doi: 10.1080/15377857.2019.1658022.

Meyerrose, A. M. 2017. "It Is All about Value: How Domestic Party Brands Influence Voting Patterns in the European Parliament." *Governance* 24 (2): 1–18. doi: 10.1111/gove.12327.

Nai, A., and F. Martinez. 2019. "The Personality of Populists: Provocateurs, Charismatic Leaders, or Drunken Dinner Guests?" *West European Politics* 42 (7):1337. doi: 10.1080/01402382.2019.1599570.

Needham, C., and G. Smith. 2015. "Introduction: Political Branding." *Journal of Political Marketing* 14 (1–2):1. doi: 10.1080/15377857.2014.990828.

Newman, T. 2019. "The Emergence of Science as a Political Brand: USA." *Journal of Political Marketing* 19 (1):2. doi: 10.1080/15377857.2019.1652225.

Newman, B. I., and T.P. Newman. 2018. *Brand.* Dubuque, IA: Kendall Hunt Publishing Co.

Nielsen, S. W. 2016. "Measuring Political Brands: An Art and a Science of Mapping the Mind." *Journal of Political Marketing* 15 (1):70–95.

O'Cass, A., and R. Voola. (2011). "Explications of Political Market Orientation and Political Brand Orientation using the Resource-Based View of the Political

Party." *Journal of Marketing Management* 27 (5-6):627–645. doi: 10.1080/0267257X.2010.489831.

Phipps, M., J. Brace-Govan, and C. Jevons. 2010. "The Duality of Political Brand Equity." *European Journal of Marketing* 44 (3/4):496–514. doi: 10.1108/03090561011020552.

Pich, C., G. Armannsdottir, and L. Spry. 2018. "Investigating Political Brand Reputation with Qualitative Projective Techniques from the Perspective of Young Adults." *International Journal of Market Research* 60 (2):198. doi: 10.1177/1470785317750817.

Scammell, M. 2015. "Politics and Image: The Conceptual Value of Branding." *Journal of Political Marketing* 14 (1–2):7–18. doi: 10.1080/15377857.2014.990829.

Simons, G. 2016. "Stability and Change in Putin's Political Image during the 2000 and 2012 Presidential Elections: Putin 1.0 and Putin 2.0." *Journal of Political Marketing* 15 (2–3):149. doi: 10.1080/15377857.2016.1151114.

Smith, G. (2008). "Politically Significant Events and Their Effect on the Image of Political Parties." *Journal of Political Marketing* 4 (2-3):91–114. doi: 10.1300/J199v04n02_05.

Smith, G. 2009. "Conceptualising and Testing Brand Personality in British Politics." *Journal of Political Marketing* 8 (3):209–32. doi: 10.1080/15377850903044858.

Smith, G. and A. French. (2009). "The Political Brand: A Consumer Perspective." *Marketing Theory* 9 (2):209–226. doi: 10.1177/1470593109103068.

Speed, R., P. Butler, and N. Collins. 2015. "Human Branding in Political Marketing: Applying Contemporary Branding Thoughts to Political Parties and Their Leaders." *Journal of Political Marketing* 14 (1–2):129–51. doi: 10.1080/15377857.2014.990833.

Susila, I., D. Dean, R. Nerina Raja Yusof, and A. A. Setyawan. 2019. "Symbolic Political Communications and Trust: A Young Voters' Perspective of the Indonesian Presidential Election." *Journal of Political Marketing* 19 (1, 2). doi: 10.1080/15377857.2019.1652224.

Understanding the Magic of Credibility for Political Leaders: A Case of India and Narendra Modi

VARSHA JAIN

GANESH B. E.

The field of political marketing has majorly benefited from the use of social media platforms. This has been true both for eastern and western contexts. The primary areas in political marketing that have majorly benefited from the social media usage have been the political leader and the evaluations of the leader by the voters. In the Indian context too, the use of social media techniques has been hailed as the Holy Grail of political marketing. This estimation is quite apposite. Nevertheless, what must not be forgotten is that the complexities of the bonding between political leaders and voters are not only premised primarily on the efficacy of social media techniques but also include other key dimensions. Thus, this article focuses on the importance of credibility as a key dimension. This dimension is inevitable to make social media techniques as effective as they are in political marketing. To substantiate this, we have comprehensively engaged with the fields such as traits of political leaders, crisis management and collaboration. These deliberations have been contextualized to the case of Narendra Modi, the prime minister of India. Further, these deliberations culminate in an effective framework. Academicians and practitioners of political marketing can extensively utilize this framework.

INTRODUCTION

The development of a strong image for a political leader is premised on a key dimension: credibility. Credibility is a continual development and not an end target. Greater the credibility, the more effective the image of the political leader. Thus, this article is an attempt at understanding the connection between credibility and the image of the political leader. Before commencing in-depth discussions on the connection between credibility and the image, we would need to comprehend the necessary underlying patterns. The first pattern is the bond between the voters and the political leader. Here, the voters are considered as consumers. The second pattern is the importance of reducing the distance between the voters and the political leader. Voters can be engaged with in the same fashion as the consumers and their synchronization with the political leader can be premised on the following focus areas: political information, interest and attention (Bartle and Griffiths 2002). The area of political information is one of the first requirements to reduce the distance between the voters and the political leader.

This political information will be able to incite the interest of the voters, if the political leader premises it on the needs and aspirations of the voters. After the interest is generated, the attention of the voters can be sustained when the leader uses the interest developed and the information therein "to reduce complexity in an environment of proliferating choice and information" (Needham 2006, 184).

Based on the overview above, we can summarize that credibility is an important dimension in reducing the distance between the voters and the political leader. Credibility as seen above can be expanded further. The first operational explication of credibility is based on relevance. Relevance refers to positioning the political leader and the communication thereof in terms of the electoral audience's prioritization. Here, the communication becomes synonymous with the leader who is communicating. This is because unlike products and services, political leaders do not have directly empirically verifiable metrics. Rather, relevance would play a huge role in that the political leader positions the needs and demands of the voters as touch points of evaluation.

This is because voters with strong views and prioritizations tend to support when the political leader is in line with their views and evaluations. Supplementing this, Scammell (2015) has emphasized on leveraging concerns and agendas in the context of maximized interaction between political parties and voters. To summarize, credibility of political leader is important in political marketing. However, there is very little work in this area. There are papers that focus on the dimensions of political leaders (Serazio 2015) political leaders and trust (Diers-Lawson and Donohue 2013) and leaders influencing policies (Guzmán, Paswan, and Van Steenburg 2015). However, there are no papers aiming at credibility of the political leader, primarily in the eastern context. Thus, this article studies this concept and develops a conceptual framework, which comprehensively explains the credibility of political leader. Credibility in terms of relevance is an important requirement for the political leader to maximize the bonding with the voters. To develop a more engaged comprehension of political leader and political marketing with due importance on credibility, the next section will be dedicated to an explication of the same.

POLITICAL LEADER AND POLITICAL MARKETING

Political leaders have a significant role (Speed, Butler, and Collins 2015) and strong influence on marketing approaches related to their leadership and party. They use relevant marketing communications to influence the voters. Further, there are symbolic and interactive elements in political marketing that has to be managed strategically by the political leader (Pich and Dean 2015; Scammell 2015). The hedonic dimensions develops the long-term loyalty (Needham 2006) that connects the political leaders with the voters more emotionally. These dimensions and connections of the political leaders are important for the eastern context and young voters. These voters use social media extensively and thus, the political leaders uses this platform (Jain et al. 2017) to establish their credibility.

Political leaders use political marketing approaches for sharing information, developing interest and seeking attention especially via social media. Political leaders create their own value by humility, tenacity, and accuracy (Jain et al. 2018) and reflect their personality (Jain et al. 2018; Kim et al. 2018) to become more credible (Milewicz and Milewicz 2014). Thus, to develop the strong connect with the voters credibility of the political leader is very important (Dumeresque 2012). The credibility attributes are to be aligned with the political marketing for voters' high engagement. This area is always important as it establishes connect of the political leader with the voters. While developing the connect credibility of the political leader is imperative (Jain et al. 2017) there are no conceptual frameworks primarily from the eastern context, which will be addressed by this article. The subsequent sections would extensively explain the credibility and the various elements associated with credibility of the political leader, which is the core objective of this article.

A CONCEPTUAL GROUNDING OF CREDIBILITY

The concept of credibility can be segued into the field of political marketing and branding. Credibility has been understood in light of the interpretation and perception of a political leader and her messages.

Credibility also serves a key role in political branding and marketing as it involves synchronizing the connections between the intended audience and the realities being portrayed by the political leader. The realities that are portrayed become the means by which the leader is interpreted. The portrayal and the interpretation are integral to credibility (Cwalina, Falkowski, and Newman 2014). This is because the political leader and the credibility allow the voters to weave a continuous flow of interpretation. In addition, at the heart of credibility is accessibility to the information that the political leader conveys.

Thus, credibility is based on the degree of accessibility and applicability (Cohen 2008). Greater the degree of accessibility and applicability, stronger can be the credibility of the political leader. Finally, credibility is not restricted only to the value systems, interpretation and contexts of the individual voter. Credibility includes the context in which the message was delivered. In the context of political branding and marketing, credibility is even more complex as it is based on the politicization of the issue (Arceneaux 2012). Further, the credibility of the political leader has five main sub-elements: traits of the political leader, image of political leader, performativity of political leader, protection of political leader, and reduction of distances between the political leader and the voter, which will be explained in the subsequent sections. The next section will deal with the concept of credibility and the traits of the political leader.

Traits of the Political Leader

The credibility of the political leader can be further understood in the following manner. Political parties and leaders have to engage with a specific possibility. This specific possibility is that, credibility can be affected by their ability to strengthen the bond between them and the voters. Thus, we can operationalize credibility as a strong bond between the political leaders and the voters. The development of credibility can be further substantiated by anticipating the contingencies that might beset the political leader. Thus, the political leader would need to be constantly ready and anticipate crises. This anticipation could be best achieved in terms of locus of control, which means that the political leaders' chances of bonding with the voters would be higher if they attribute routes of their decision making to the voters' needs and priorities.

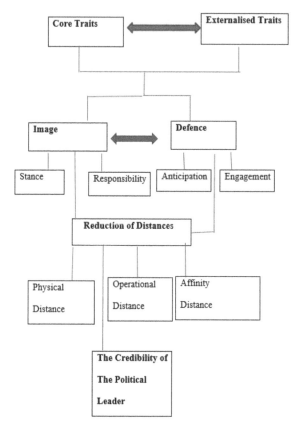

FIGURE 1. Framework explaining the credibility of a political leader.

Going on, voters experience a lesser degree of alienation when the political leaders maintain a base where the local and immediate requirements of the voters are attended to with the highest degree of consideration. This alacrity would act as a stronger base of credibility for the political leader.

We have thus contextualized the nature of credibility as illustrated in Figure 1. This contextualization can be further strengthened by supplementing it with the traits of the political leader. The traits of the political leader have two parts; core traits and externalized traits. These dimensions deeply influence the credibility of the political leader. Core traits of the political leader are more functional in nature. The externalized traits are based on image perception and communication. These core traits help us understand the functioning of the personality of the individual very effectively as they connect very well with the person of the political leader.

These traits of the leader are primarily the dimensions driven by consistency in terms of prioritization, plans, and actions (Serazio 2015).

The externalized traits act as heuristic representation of the aspirations of the voters and trans-situational objectives.

Both the core and externalized traits are related to the development of credibility (Schneider and Samkin 2010). Both forms of traits represent enduring dispositions and objectives, which the voters consider most important. The dispositions and objectives are based on the frequency and intensity at which the voters assess an individual or organization. In addition, this assessment is often prioritized. These priorities are defined as being positive and negative.

Thus, both core and externalized traits are related to the choices and actions that the political leaders embrace. Subsequently, the expression and communication of the political leaders are seen to be coordinated with values that the voters and the larger society to which they belong to hold high. Thus, we can see that the core and individual traits become modes of connection and modes of self-regulation. Therefore, when the political leader decreases the discrepancies between the core and externalized traits, greater will be the connection with the voters (Heino, Ellison, and Gibbs 2010).

IMAGE OF POLITICAL LEADER

One of the most important means of strengthening the connection with the voters is to show how important the goals and objectives of the voters are for them. This process facilitates the political leader in communicating to voters. These individuals perceive their own image based on the priorities and traits that political leaders reflect in their policies, actions, and communication (Guzmán, Paswan, and Van Steenburg 2015). We have seen so far that the connection between the political leader and the voters can be strengthen by the former synchronizing their core and externalized traits with the values and aspirations of the voters (Park and John 2010).

If there is a disjuncture between the core and externalized traits, the political leader is not able to bring forth the traits that are at the core. Therefore, this means that the political leader is not undertaking decisions, which reflect core traits. This disjuncture is more critical when the voters have trusted the leader based on certain externalized traits. The criticality becomes clear when the voters realize that the externalized traits are merely a cover or empty surfaces. Hence, the core trait of the political leader influence credibility and here is the first proposition based on this key insight.

P1. The core and externalized traits should match each other in order to maximize the credibility of the political leader

Political Leader and Performativity

The credibility of the political leader is in itself a connecting medium between the political leader and the voters. There are reciprocal associations between the credibility and the performativity of the political leader. The performativity of the political leader reinforces the identity of the voters and the integrity of the leader. The voters asses the political leader based on the words and promises made by the political leader vis-à-vis performances based on the promises. The other attributes of the political leader are trust, respect, accountability, and fairness (Diers-Lawson and Donohue 2013). Political leaders are also assessed after the challenges and the tests that they undergo. This means that the talks about integrity and patience by the political leader will not suffice to win over the voters, as the real test is through their actual, decisions and actions.

There must be consistency between the words and the actions of the political leaders. This consistency not only maintains their reputation but also the reputation of their political party. Political leaders must be purpose driven. Moreover, the voters should perceive the leaders as genuine individuals worthy of the position. The internal and external stakeholders always observe political leaders keenly. Thus, the authentic political leader is led by the conviction and purpose, which is credible, and woven with the personal values. Their actions are based on strong values and trustworthy belief systems that lead to high levels of integrity (Casteltrione 2015). The next section will deal with the modes of protecting the credibility of the political leader.

Political Leader and the Protection of Credibility

Credibility, as seen earlier, is not a one-point target. Rather, a continuum, which needs to be protected from diminution. The credibility of the political leader can be protected based on two important premises; image and defense. Here, image is defined as the perceptions of the agency that is communicated and shared by an audience (Wilcox and Cameron 2006). In our context, the agency is the political leader. These perceptions are experienced as the results of the words and deeds of the communicative entity, the political leader. The second premise, defense, refers to maintaining and modulating the audience perception and head off attacks on the credibility of the political leader.

Further, there is a proportional link between the extent of damage to credibility and the level to which the person is held responsible. Therefore, the more the political leader is able to integrate his/her credibility on the aspirations and goals as defined by the voters, more secure is the reputation from attacks (Cameron, Pang, and Jin 2008). Thus, the political leader could identify and influence a set of public perceptions that are based on facts, values, or policy (Heath 1997). It is quite evident from the previous sections that the protection of the leader's credibility is based only on information transfer. Rather, reputation is more important for maintaining the quality of the social relationship between the political leader and external audiences (Palenchar and Heath 2002).

This maintenance is based on stance, which is dynamic and changes based on the situation. It also dependent on to which degree the political leader is considered responsible for acts and results. This responsibility is better understood in terms of organization and situational factors. Here, the leader's credibility is compromised when the responsibility of the acts and results is within the space of the organization (Gilpin and Murphy 2006). Further, the necessity of protecting the credibility of the political leader is so high that politics is often characterized as a political conflict model (Seeger 2002). Such an ever-ready state about challenges to credibility is a fundamental requirement for political leaders. This state can be maintained by instituting the following principles: assume the worst-case scenario: everything that can go wrong will go wrong; act based on a disaster scenario: all potential problems that might affect reputation are considered; do not miss time: establish safeguards against potential devaluation. Therefore, ability of the political leader to anticipate crises can enhance the credibility of the political leader especially in terms of the image, which leads to second proposition.

P2. The ability to anticipate and engage with crises leads to enhancement in the credibility of the political leader

P2a. The ability of the political leader to maintain a strong defence in terms of image leads to enhancement in the credibility of the political leader

Political Leader and the Reduction of Distances

Understanding the nature of credibility in its relevant dimensions has helped us engage with it. The previous section provided dimensions and factors that were necessary to understand the nature of the credibility of the political leader. The current section deals with the extension and consolidation of the dimensions of the credibility of the political leader. Here, Brake (2015) offers a functional lever necessary for the same.

The reason for the same is that the framework is centralized on the conception of collaboration. This effective conception is based on a two-point operationalization of collaboration. Moreover, it allows the political leader to maximize the effectiveness of their credibility. The two-point operationalization of collaboration is structured collaboration and emergent collaboration. The first is formal and synchronized. It is characterize by expected outcome, defined roles, and scope of action, established time-frames, and standard processes.

Supplementing the same is emergent collaboration. This form is unstructured, flexible, and spontaneous. Formal collaboration is already instituted with the purpose of achieving specific objectives. Emergent collaboration develops even as the structured collaboration is set in place. Thus, the credibility of the political leader would become stronger by integrating both forms of collaboration. This is because optimal improvements in the ability to collaborate are directly linked to increased improvements in credibility. This is made possible by the ability of collaboration to reduce three distances; physical distance: caused by separation owing to geography and time zones; operational distance: created by a sense of disconnect caused by communication challenges which leads to a sense of isolation; affinity distance: caused by an excessive lack of commonality amongst shareholders due to a missing shared vision.

This leads to a lack of development of the specific nature of relations that meet the specific social needs of the voters. These three distances enhance certain impediments to building a strong bond between the voters and the political leaders. The impediments are isolation, referring to the fact of minimal or non-existent contact, fragmentation of affiliation and minimal attention paid to guiding and structuring of efforts at improving the bond between voters and the political leader. In summation, we can see that isolation, fragmentation, and confusion are key factors that affect the credibility of the political leader. Importantly, reduction of distance elevates the credibility of political leader, which leads to the third proposition.

P3. Reduction of distances (i.e., physical distance, operational distance, and affinity distance) enhances the credibility of the political leader

Based on the propositions and deliberations, please find the framework developed to enhance the credibility of the political leader in Figure 1.

VOTER ENGAGEMENT IN INDIA

There are significant changes in the current patterns of voter engagement in India. The citizens are more engaged with the political leadership. Earlier, the voters were participants who were involved only in the voting process. Today, the voters in India demand stability. This stability has become very necessary to promote voter turn around. One of the most important aspects of this prevention is maximizing the credibility of the political leader. This credibility and the prevention of voter turnaround are especially relevant in the Indian context as the electoral volatility is very high in India as compared to other countries in the world (Pal 2015).

Credibility, in the context of the political leader, could be seen as a continuum. This is very relevant in the Indian context. India is the largest democracy in the world and has different political leaders who possess significant influence on the voters' engagement. Thus, it is imperative that the political leader in the Indian context realize that the momentum of political strategies in India has changed. It was earlier based on class structures, caste divisions, and religious affiliations. This trend was operational from 1947 to late 1990. Post 1990, with the rise of regional voting blocs (Hallin and Mancini 2004) and technological changes in communication, the focus of political campaigns in India has undergone serious changes.

One of the most visible changes has been the projection of market-led development and liberalization as one of the prime electoral promises. Another hallmark in the Indian context has been the favoring of the middle class (Fernandes 2006). Concomitantly, the ersatz Gandhi-Nehru legacy and value have now come to be associated with an inability in law enforcement, muzzling of corruption, and fostering crony capitalism (Karnik and Lalvani 2012). Another important aspect that would need to be considered is the importance of the credibility of the leader vis-à-vis the credibility of the political party. It could be surmise that the political party's provenance and record of accomplishment play an important role in the development of credibility.

Here, the Indian political context has the first-past-the-post form of electoral result decisions. This primarily means that if a political candidate gains even one more vote than the competing political candidate, the first candidate is declared a winner. On the other hand, if political leaders could adopt a more proportional representation logic of electoral decision-making, they could have a greater advantage. This advantage is that the voters could favor a political candidate who does not belong to a winning party but enjoys popularity. The predilection of voters to favor political leaders who might be from a different political party is higher. It can therefore be surmised that credibility of the political leader surpasses the credibility of the political party (McDonnell and Cabrera 2019). Thus, the charts and direction for the development of the credibility of the political leader in India are set. We could now contextualize the deliberations vis-à-vis the case of Narendra Modi.

NARENDRA MODI – BACKGROUND

Before considering the background of Narendra Modi, we could consider key cases of political leaders. This consideration would allow this study to understand the links between credibility and political leaders. One of the first cases we could consider is that of the former American President, Franklin Delano Roosevelt (F.D.R). FDR's communication and actions were exemplars for the development of credibility. The reason for the same was that his politicization of key issues were backed up by the prioritization of the voters' issues.

Another important factor of FDR, which allow us to understand credibility, was his inclusion of diverse interest groups. It was even surmise that later presidents from the Republican Party in the United States emulated the credibility developed by FDR by his inclusive politics. Another example that could help understand credibility further is the former Chancellor of West Germany, Konrad Adenauer (Adenauer). Adenauer's case helps understand credibility through other key dimensions. The first key dimension was Adenauer's ability to connect with the grass roots of West Germany. It is surmised that Adenauer's grass root appeal became a strong point that protected him against perceptions of elitism and high handedness.

Another important dimension that could be understood in the context of Adenauer and credibility was his focus on the economic and technological strengthening of West Germany. One of the most important dimension of Adenauer that could help us understand credibility further was his acknowledgement of Israel's demand for reparations in the 1950s. In light of these dimensions and leaders, we can contextualize the nature and context of credibility in the context of Narendra Modi. When Narendra Modi was chosen by the BJP as the 16th prime ministerial election in India in 2014, this was the world's largest election (Pal 2015). Before this, Modi had made his debut in the country's mainstream election in 1987 (Chandra 2013). He was actively involved in the RSS and campaigned in his young days (BBC News 2014). Subsequently, Modi became the Chief Minister of Gujarat state with 13 years of tenure, longest in the history of the country, 2001 to 2014 (Pathak 2014).

He developed the state with the key focus on prosperity, progression, and economic development (Dwivedi and Kapoor 2015). This penchant for development was one of the first motifs he used to consolidate his credibility. Thus, in one stroke, he minimized both operational distance and the geographical distance between the voters and himself. His official webpage highlighted the Gujarat development model that was used in this state. This page received worldwide recognition and used latest technology to link issues related to agriculture, industry, and services (Kaur 2015).

He further established his credibility by creating a status of stability and growth by maintaining the locus of achievements close to his governance (Sen 2016). One of the first examples of the same was decreasing poverty primarily among the Muslim community, decrease in child malnutrition, and enhancement in the education level in the state of Gujarat. Thus, Modi had an overwhelming victory in the general election. If the above was a case in point of reducing distances of affiliation, Modi also displayed panache in crisis management.

The political opponents accused that Modi played a key role in staging the 2002 Gujarat communal riots, which happened while he was the chief minister of the Gujarat (India Today Web Desk 2018). The riots led to the burning of the trains and killing of more than 60 Hindu pilgrims and 1000–2000 Muslims (Jaffrelot 2015). Modi's government was blamed for not preventing the riots while he was the chief minister. This blame was transferred to the political leadership of Modi as well (India Today Web Desk 2018. The first means of shifting the locus from his leadership, Modi (Human Rights Watch 2019), issued a series of press notes on this riot. He stated that this episode was related with the Pakistan's proxy war and terrorism against the state (Krishnan and Roche 2014).

Modi's balancing the weight of right wing fundamentalism substantiated this shift of locus and the development of a pragmatic leader dedicated to development and growth. Simply, Modi's raison d'être was development sans ideological limitations. The economic agenda of the party was not visible earlier as the aim was only on Swadeshi (own country). Modi changed the agenda to growth and development under his leadership (Price 2015). His government was able to publicize the events that were related to commerce and business. The next section will deal with the means by which Narendra Modi established his credibility further.

NARENDRA MODI: EXTENSION AND ESTABLISHMENT OF CREDIBILITY

To gain credibility, Modi developed communication aimed at the core and externalized traits, which affected image, defense, and reduction of distance between the voters, as reflected in Figure 1. This section would provide insights to understand how Modi has used seven approaches to establish credibility among the voters. First, the central message that Modi used to engage with the voters was the #acchedin (good days) story. Modi projected his image very effectively and successfully as an action-oriented leader. He positioned himself as almost the only political leader who was capable of bringing good times to the common people living in the country. To do so, he used hash tags as #achche din that appeared more frequently as compared to #Namo from the twitter handle of Modi (@narendramodi). This meant that "good times" and the image of Modi were closely integrated with each other. The success of "good times" affected the image of Modi and vice a versa. Second, Modi also adopted a globalized language along with good governance and growth model, which was understood by the investors, policy makers and voters who live in India and abroad. There was an internal consensus about these key dimensions within the party. Hence, there were lesser challenges for the political leader. The whole idea was to attract like-minded people (Kaur 2015). The sartorial fashion of the political leader was also crafted accordingly. His "Modi Kurta" (shirt with short sleeves) became popular. This attire reflected the simplicity of the leader (Sardesai 2014). This fashion attire was made popular with the help of television that reflected his 'masculinity'. Voters were able to connect with the political leader not only because of his image but also by his "Kurta." Many voters started wearing this Kurta and felt connected to Modi. This was one of the most effective means of maximizing the credibility of the political leadership of Narendra Modi. Third, to understand this, we can see the approval and likes leveraged by providing the Modi masks to the voters. These voters used the masks and supported Modi very effectively. In addition, the feeling was developed which mentioned, "We are all Modi." By this strategy, Modi had ingrained the aspirations of the voters with his core, externalized traits, and melded them with the aspirations of the voters. Capping all these modes of maximizing the credibility of his leadership, Modi launched a new campaign known as Namo based on the first two letters of his first and last names. Fourth, he conducted a series of virtual public meetings. Modi's 3D hologram appeared on the stage across locations (Baishya 2015). Voters were engaged by Modi's speeches. With these digital initiatives, he also used conventional approaches such as rallies. For instance, he addressed more than 125 rallies in the first 15 days and 10 meetings in a day during the days ahead of election. The 3D technology developed powerful images of the political leader and 132 holographic shows connected him with the large number of voters (Verma 2014). One of the most important gleanings from the means of maximizing the credibility of Narendra Modi as a political leader was that social media is a lever and not the lynchpin. It is evident that social media connections reduce the distance between the political leader and the voters. Fifth, this reduction made possible only if the leader has already synchronized the core traits and externalized traits as explicated in the context of Narendra Modi. What is more important is to note that the credibility of the leadership of Narendra Modi was the main hub around which the spokes of social media usage functioned effectively. Case in point of this was enabling the voters to send their queries to the political leader easily via social media platforms. These social media based approaches helped Modi escalate from regional branding (related to State) to the national level branding of prime minister. This was done again by keeping the aspirations and needs of the voters in mind (Jungherr 2016). Sixth, his speeches in multiple languages were also posted on the website, which was highly appreciated by the voters. Many voters joined as citizens for accountable governance. These voters were from the premier institutions of the country and young tech savvy individuals. There were more than two million people from different fields such as information technology, marketing, media, and finance. They carried out live conversations with Modi through these social media networks (Ghatak and Roy 2014). The other campaigns on the social media platforms were Namo4Pm, Pledge4Modi, and Modi4PM. Thus, despite elevating his campaign from a regional level to a national level, Modi's credibility as a political leader was narrow-casted with the use of the relevant regional languages. Seventh, slogans infusing high energy among the voters for the political leader were used. Another catchy phrase was "Achche Din Aane Wale Hain" (good days are coming). This infusion again helped instill a sense in the voters that they were contesting in the 2014 elections. It must also be noted here that social media and technological interventions do not fully translate into tangible advantages for political branding. The reason for the same is that technological interventions cannot substitute for close personalized contact between the political leaders and the voters. More so, the presence of technological interventions is often consider, as a comprehensive be all solution to issues of credibility. In fact, technological interventions can often act as a means for top down communication rather than bottom up communication, which is more inclusive. The reason for the same is that technological interventions often accelerate and magnify the information transfer from the political leader to the voters.

IMPLICATIONS

This study has attempted to understand the importance of credibility as a central conception for political branding. Further, the study has understood credibility in terms of the distances that could affect the proximity of political leaders and voters. This study has also tried to develop a framework that can be contextualized and used by political leaders and practitioners for political branding. Finally, this study has attempted to juxtapose core traits and externalized traits in the development of the credibility of the political leader.

It endeavors to serve scholars and professionals consolidate a deep understanding of the construct and applicability of credibility and its wide-ranging implications for political leaders. Scholars could develop sharpened and nuanced theoretical insights. Analogously, industry professionals could develop strategies to leverage credibility and achieve their goals. This conception of credibility shifts away from a certain deification of social media. Thus, credibility is a continuum, which influences the effectiveness of the political leader's ability to bond with the voters. Similarly, the political leader's ability to bond with the voters influences the credibility of the leader.

Keeping this in mind, social media usage should be undertaken by the political leader. Additionally, political leaders can clearly realize that the most effective social media platform can only function well if they can leverage the credibility of the political leader.

SCOPE FOR FUTURE RESEARCH

Future studies can employ empirical verification to consolidate the salience of the most relevant variables. These studies can be conducted in newly emergent democracies with young and digitally oriented consumers. Political parties and leaders can understand the dynamics of impression management. They can also understand the dynamics of impression man-agement in the rural sectors for leaders and parties. Very importantly, this study acts as a base for Artificial Intelligence and Machine Learning enhancement of political branding. Further, studies could focus on the importance of crisis management on a long- term basis. Additionally, future studies can study the means of modeling and charting a cyclical under-standing of the credibility of the political leader. Research dedicated to the interchange and exchange between the credibility of the political leader and the full potential of the word of mouth developed by voters. Longitudinal studies can understand if there are any differences between the development of the credibility of male political leaders and female political leaders. In addition, future studies could investigate the political leader's values in specific cases such as human rights, democracy, equality, etc. as possible sources of credibility. Greater attention could be paid to the role of deep learning and machine learning in the development of credibility. The area of credibility in political branding could also be enriched by studying the nature of ethnic belief systems.

REFERENCES

Arceneaux, K. 2012. "Cognitive Biases and the Strength of Political Arguments."*American Journal of Political Science* 56 (2):271–285. doi:10. 1111/j.1540-5907.2011.00573.x.

Baishya, A. 2015. "Selfies|# NaMo: The Political Work of the Selfie in the 2014 Indian General Elections." *International Journal of Communication* 9 (15): 1686–1700.

Bartle, J., and D. Griffiths. 2002. "Social-Psychological, Economic and Marketing Models of Voter Behaviour Compared." In *The Idea of Political Marketing*, edited by N. J. O'Shaughnessy and S. C. Henneberg, 19–37. Connecticut: Praeger.

BBC News. 2014. "Narendra Modi's early life." *BBC*, May 26. https://www.bbc. com/news/world-asia-india-27514601.

Brake, T. 2015. *Borderless Collaboration: Creating Value Together in the New World of Work*. Guilford: Transnational Management Association.

Cameron, G. T., A. Pang, and Y. Jin. 2008. "Contingency Theory: Strategic Management of Conflict." In *Public Relations: From theory to Practice*, edited by Tricia Hansen-Horn and B. Dostal Neff, 132–156. Boston: Pearson.

Casteltrione, I. 2015. "The Internet, Social Networking Web Sites and Political Participation Research: Assumptions and Contradictory Evidence." *First Monday* 20 (3):1–17. doi:10.5210/fm.v20i3.5462.

Chandra, R. 2013. "The Rise and Rise of Narendra Modi." *India Today*, September 23. https://www.indiatoday.in/featured/story/narendra-modi-modi-as-pm-bjp-gujarat-210885-2013-09-13.

Cohen, J. E. 2008. *The Presidency in the Era of 24-Hour News*. Princeton: Princeton University Press.

Cwalina, W., A. Falkowski, and B. O. Newman. 2014. "Persuasion in the Political Context: Opportunities and Threats." In *The Handbook of Persuasion and Social Marketing*, edited by D. W. Stewart, 61–128. Santa Barbara, CA: Praeger.

Diers-Lawson, A. R., and J. Donohue. 2013. "Synchronizing Crisis Responses after a Transgression: Analysis of BP'S Enacted Crisis Response to the Deepwater Horizon Crisis in 2010."*Journal of Communication Management* 17 (3):1–18. doi:10.1108/JCOM-04-2012-0030.

Dumeresque, D. 2012. "The Net Generation: Its Impact on the Business Landscape." *Strategic Direction* 28 (9):3–5. doi:10.1108/sd.2012.05628iaa.003.

Dwivedi, Y. K., and K. K. Kapoor. 2015. "Metamorphosis of Indian Electoral Campaigns: Modi's Social Media Experiment." *International Journal of Indian Culture and Business Management* 11 (4):496–516. doi:10.1504/IJICBM.2015.072430.

Fernandes, L. 2006. *India's New Middle Class: Democratic Politics in Era of Economic Reform*. Minneapolis, MN: University of Minnesota Press.

Ghatak, M., and S. Roy. 2014. "Did Gujarat's Growth Rate Accelerate under Modi?" *Economic and Political Weekly* 49 (15):12–15.

Gilpin, D., and P. Murphy. 2006. "Refraining Crisis Management through Complexity." In *Public Relations Theory II*, edited Carl Botan and Vincent Hazleton, 329–344. Mahwah, NJ: Lawrence Erlbaum.

Guzmán, F., A. Paswan, and E. Van Steenburg. 2015. "Self-Referencing and Political Candidate Brands: A Congruency Perspective." *Journal of Political Marketing* 14 (1–2):175–199. doi:10.1080/15377857.2014.990837.

Hallin, D., and P. Mancini. 2004. *Comparing Media Systems*. Cambridge: Cambridge University Press.

Heath, R. L. 1997. *Strategic Issues Management: Organizations and Public Policy Challenge*. Thousand Oaks. CA: Sage Publications.

Heino, R. D., N. B. Ellison, and J. L. Gibbs. 2010. "Relationshopping: Investigating the Market Metaphor in Online Dating." *Journal of Social and Personal Relationships* 27 (4):427–447. doi:10.1177/0265407510361614.

Human Rights Watch. 2019. "IV. Overview of the Attacks Against Muslims." *Human Rights Watch*. Accessed July 11, 2019. https://www.hrw.org/reports/2002/india/India0402-03.htm#P690_124297.

India Today Web Desk. 2018. "Supreme Court to hear plea challenging Gujarat riots clean chit to Modi on Monday." *India Today,* November 13. https://

www.indiatoday.in/india/story/narendra-modi-gujarat-riots-clean-chit-supreme-court-zakia-jafri-1387481-2018-11-13

Jaffrelot, C. 2015. "The Modi-Centric BJP 2014 Election Campaign: New Techniques and Old Tactics." *Contemporary South Asia* 23 (2):151–166. doi:10.1080/09584935.2015.1027662.

Jain, V., M. Chawla, B. E. Ganesh, and C. Pich. 2018. "Exploring and Consolidating the Brand Personality Elements of the Political Leader." *Spanish Journal of Marketing - ESIC* 22 (3):295–318. doi:10.1108/SJME-03-2018-0010.

Jain, V., C. Pich, B. E. Ganesh, and G. Armannsdottir. 2017. "Exploring the Influences of Political Branding: A Case from the Youth in India." *Journal of Indian Business Research* 9 (3):190–211. doi:10.1108/JIBR-12-2016-0142.

Jungherr, A. 2016. "Twitter Use in Election Campaigns: A Systematic Literature Review." *Journal of Information Technology & Politics* 13 (1):72–91. doi:10.1080/19331681.2015.1132401.

Karnik, A., and M. Lalvani. 2012. "Growth Performance of Indian States." *Empirical Economics* 42 (1):235–259. doi:10.1007/s00181-010-0433-0).

Kaur, R. 2015. "Good Times, Brought to You by Brand Modi." *Television & New Media* 16 (4):323–330. doi:10.1177/1527476415575492.

Kim, P., H. Chang, R. Vaidyanathan, and L. Stoel. 2018. "Artist-Brand Alliances to Target New Consumers: Can Visual Artists Recruit New Consumers to a Brand?" *Journal of Product & Brand Management* 27 (3):308–319. doi:10.1108/JPBM-02-2017-1412.

Krishnan, U., and E. Roche. 2014. "Modi slams Pakistan for 'proxy war of terrorism'." *Livemint*, August 12. https://www.livemint.com/Politics/5vKctlKh7JFhJOXanwMPdP/Narendra-Modi-slams-Pakistan-for-proxy-war-against-India.html.

McDonnell, D., and L. Cabrera. 2019. "The Right-Wing Populism of India's Bharatiya Janata Party (and Why Comparativists Should Care)." *Democratization* 26 (3):484–501. doi:10.1080/13510347.2018.1551885.

Milewicz, C. M., and M. C. Milewicz. 2014. "The Branding of Candidates and Parties: The US News Media and the Legitimization of a New Political Term." *Journal of Political Marketing* 13 (4):233–263. doi:10.1080/15377857.2014.958364.

Needham, C. 2006. "Special Issue Papers Brands and Political Loyalty." *Journal of Brand Management* 13 (3):178–187. doi:10.1057/palgrave.bm.2540260.

Pal, J. 2015. "Banalities Turned Viral: Narendra Modi and the Political Tweet." *Television & New Media* 16 (4):378–387. doi:10.1177/1527476415573956.

Palenchar, M. J., and R. L. Heath. 2002. "Another Part of the Risk Communication Model: Analysis of Communication Processes and Message Content." *Journal of Public Relations Research* 14 (2):127–158. doi:10.1207/S1532754XJPRR1402_3.

Park, J. K., and D. R. John. 2010. "Got to Get You into my Life: Do Brand Personalities Rub off on Consumers?" *Journal of Consumer Research* 37 (4):655–669. doi:10.1086/655807.

Pathak, M. 2014. "Narendra Modi bids farewell to Gujarat, says state's model key to BJP win." *Livemint*, May 22. https://www.livemint.com/Politics/5NZ8zKXRcr7PubYoGDfF8L/Anandiben-Patel-to-be-new-Gujarat-chief-minister.html.

Pich, C., and D. Dean. 2015. "Political Branding: Sense of Identity or Identity Crisis? An Investigation of the Transfer Potential of the Brand Identity Prism to the UK Conservative Party." *Journal of Marketing Management* 31 (11–12): 1353–1378. doi:10.1080/0267257X.2015.1018307.

Price, L. 2015. *The Modi Effect: Inside Narendra Modi's Campaign to Transform India*. London: Hodder Books.

Sardesai, R. 2014. *The Election that Changed India*. New Delhi: Penguin India.

Scammell, M. 2015. "Politics and Image: The Conceptual Value of Branding." *Journal of Political Marketing* 14 (1–2):7–18. doi:10.1080/15377857.2014. 990829.

Schneider, A., and G. Samkin. 2010. "Accountability, Narrative Reporting and Legitimation: The Case of a New Zealand Public Benefit Entity." Accounting, Auditing & Accountability Journal 23 (2):256–289.

Seeger, M. W. 2002. "Chaos and Crisis: Propositions for a General Theory of Crisis Communication." *Public Relations Review* 28 (4):329–337. doi:10.1016/S0363-8111(02)00168-6.

Sen, R. 2016. "Narendra Modi's Makeover and the Politics of Symbolism." *Journal of Asian Public Policy* 9 (2):98–111. doi:10.1080/17516234.2016.1165248.

Serazio, M. 2015. "Branding Politics: Emotion, Authenticity, and the Marketing Culture of American Political Communication." *Journal of Consumer Culture* 17 (2):1–17. doi:10.1177/1469540515586868.

Speed, R., P. Butler, and N. Collins. 2015. "Human Branding in Political Marketing: Applying Contemporary Branding Thought to Political Parties and Their Leaders." *Journal of Political Marketing* 14 (1–2):129–151. doi:10.1080/ 15377857.2014.990833.

Verma, L. 2014. "RSS Magazine Defends Jat Youth, Blames Akhilesh Govt." *The Indian Express*, January 6. http://archive.indianexpress.com/news/rss-maga-zine-defends-jat-youths-blames-akhilesh-govt/1215885/.

Wilcox, D. L., and G. T. Cameron. 2006. *Public Relations Strategies and Tactics*. 8th ed. Boston: Pearson.

Moderators and Mediators of Framing Effects in Political Marketing: Implications for Political Brand Management

ANDRZEJ FALKOWSKI AND MAGDALENA JABŁOŃSKA

*Due to its important practical implications, there has been a grow-
ing number of studies on framing conducted by scholars from
various research domains. There has been, however, no paper that
would provide a comprehensive overview of various moderators
and mediators of the effect. The aim of this paper is to address this
research gap, concentrating on psychological moderators and
mediators of framing characteristic for political marketing. The
paper consists of three parts. In the first part, the concepts of framing, priming and agenda-setting as well as the similarities and
differences between them are presented in order to resolve common
terminological inconsistencies. In the second, we discuss the
moderating role of such variables as knowledge, trust in media
and values on framing effect. In the third section, psychological
mechanisms that underlie framing and priming are reviewed.
Here, cognitive mediators such as accessibility and applicability
effects are presented, followed by the discussion of the moderating
and mediating role of emotions in framing effects, with special
attention given to positive-negative asymmetry observed in the
evaluation of political candidates and events. Finally, implication
for political brand management are discussed. Our findings can
be relevant for politicians, specialists dealing in political brand
image and scholars studying framing effects.*

INTRODUCTION

Framing effects have a significant impact on the formation and management of the image of a political brand. In their origins, priming and framing effects were the subject of interest of psychologists, with numerous studies conducted by John Bargh (e.g. Bargh and Chartrand 1999) and Kahneman (2011), respectively. Although the use of framing in political marketing has been shown to have a significant effect on the image of political candidates (Falkowski and Jabłońska, 2019), launch of unpopular reforms (Cwalina and Falkowski, 2018), the presentation of political campaigns (Schuck et al., 2013) and election manifestos (Wüst, 2009), there has not been an integrated analysis of the circumstances in which these effects are most likely to be effective as well as the underlying psychological mechanisms. Therefore, the aim of this paper is to provide a comprehensive review of moderators and mediators that are most relevant in political marketing.

Additionally, in our paper, we will briefly address the differences between framing, priming and agenda-setting and provide evidence showing that in addition to the cognitive side of framing and priming effects, their emotional dimension is also important, in which the negativity effect plays an important role. Finally, we will discuss practical implications of the research on framing effects suggesting that a proper use of framing and priming in a marketing strategy allows for the creation of effective persuasive messages which can strengthen or weaken the image of politicians or support for communicated causes. Finally, we will show that effective management of a political brand depends to a large extent on controlling these effects, especially framing, both from the cognitive and emotional side.

DEFINING THE TERMS: FRAMING, PRIMING AND AGENDA – SETTING

Chong and Druckman (2007, 109), one of leading researchers in the field of framing in politics, noted that "frames in communication matter". Indeed, scientists have amassed plethora of evidence showing that often small changes in the presentation of an issue lead to unexpectedly large changes of opinions. Frames have been shown to affect beliefs, attitudes and behavior of its recipients and as such they are a powerful communication tool and an interesting research subject for media specialists, psychologists, sociologists, economists and political scientists.

The aim of the following paper is to present a concise review of most common moderators of framing effects along with the mediators responsible for the effect. We concentrate on psychological cognitive and affective mechanisms underlying framing and priming in political communication, with special attention given to the role of emotions in shaping political evaluations.

The essence of frame theory was well explained by Minsky (1975) who said:

> "When one encounters a new situation (or makes a substantial change in one's view of a problem), one selects from memory a structure called a frame. This is a remembered framework to be adapted to fit reality by changing details as necessary" (Minsky 1975, 212).

Understood in such a way, a frame can be defined as a as a mental construction of a representation of an object or event on the basis of memory schemata and previous experience (Cwalina, Falkowski, and Newman 2015). Of course, a person does not have only one particular representation of for instance a political candidate that is held in his or her memory. Instead, numerous schemata are available and serve as possible reference points that can shape the perception and interpretation of a given person or event. As such, framing can be understood as the "process of culling a few elements of perceived reality and assembling a narrative that highlights connections among them to promote a particular interpretation" (Entman 2007, 164).

The political, social and economic reality we live in is complex and subject to numerous interpretations. For instance, the same problem of cutting expenditures on unemployment benefits for those who are not actively looking for employment can be presented, depending on the frame adopted, as an inhumane act against those who are already worse off or an economically sound decision to make (or even a beneficial one for those affected if presented as an encouragement to search for work). Hence, framing consists of selecting a particular angle at which a problem should be perceived. As defined by Gamson and Modigliani (1987) framing is a "central organizing idea or story line that provides meaning to an unfolding strip of events, weaving a connection among them" (143). By activating some concepts, values or emotions rather than others, framing changes the underlying considerations used in one's evaluation, leading the audience to arrive at more or less predictable conclusions (Chong and Druckman 2007; Price, Tewksbury, and Powers 1997).

It is needless to say that due to its power to affect people's opinions, framing has been a subject of numerous studies in psychology (Tversky and Kahneman 1981), media communication (Entman 2007) and political marketing (Cwalina, Falkowski, and Newman 2015). The effect of framing has been very often analyzed together with priming. Although the two concepts are related and sometimes even used interchangeably (Chong and Druckman 2007), they rely on different psychological mechanisms. Miller and Krosnick explain the difference between the two, saying: "framing and priming are substantively different effects – the former deals with how changes in the *content* of stories on a single issue affect attitudes toward a relevant public policy, the latter with how changes in the *number* of stories about an issue affect the ingredients of presidential performance evaluations" (in Druckman 2001, 1043–1044; italics in original).

Priming, however, is not restricted solely to changes in the amount of information used for judgment. From psychological perspective, priming pertains to "the effects of prior context on the interpretation of new information" (Fiske and Taylor 2008, 60) and it has been shown to affect cognition, emotions and behavior. Contrary to framing, which changes the relevance of information, priming increases the accessibility of some concepts in memory, making them more available than others. Although the accessibility effect has been questioned in media priming (Miller and Krosnick 2000), cognitive research shows that when making decisions people rarely take into consideration all available information. Instead, being cognitive misers (Taylor 1981), they rely on a limited subset of evidence, most likely the one which is easily accessible from memory. Recently activated primes can temporarily increase the accessibility of a concept, whereas frequent primes make the construct chronically accessible long after the exposure to the message (Cwalina, Falkowski, and Newman 2015).

Although the effectiveness of priming seems to depend on the accessibility of the concept, framing is more likely to affect its applicability, that is construct's importance for a matter discussed. The more accessible and the more applicable the construct is, the more likely it is to lead to attitude change. Accessibility and applicability effects are, however, a matter of degree and as suggested by Miller and Krosnick (1996), "there might be a gradient of priming effects, decreasing in strength as attitudes become more and more remote from those being directly activated by a story" (82). Similarly, the relationship between priming and framing effects is also a matter of degree: although priming typically has an effect on the content of the news (i.e. the "what"), and framing effects tend to affect the way in which the topic is evaluated (the "how"), there is also an area in which the two effects overlap. One of the examples of such a situation is affective priming in which activation of positive and negative emotions or concepts makes these concepts not only more available but also serves as an important source of information that may lead to attitude change.

The distinction between framing and priming is not the only terminological inconsistency. Similarly, there is an overlap between the concepts of framing and agenda-setting which both analyze how the selection and presentation of public policy issues in the news affects the perception of these issues by the public (Semetko and Valkenburg 2000). As explained by Pan and Kosicki (1993, 70, emphasis in the original) framing "expands beyond agenda-setting research into *what* people talk or think about by examining *how* they think and talk about issues in the news". As such the aim of framing is to provide news frames that are "conceptual tools which media and individuals rely on to convey, interpret and evaluate information" (Neuman, Just and Crigler 1992, 60). Using salient attributes of a message such as content selection (agenda-setting), its internal organization, or thematic structure, framing renders "particular thoughts applicable, resulting in their activation and use in evaluations" (Price, Tewksbury, and Powers 1997, 486). Readers interested in a further analysis of the distinctions between framing, priming and agenda-setting may find helpful articles by Scheufele and others (Scheufele 2000; Scheufele and Tewksbury 2006; Maher 2001; or Weaver 2007). A more thorough discussion of different news frames, on the other hand, can be found in Semetko and Valkenburg (2000). In the next section of the paper, we will discuss more thoroughly the relationship between cognitive and emotional moderators and mediators of framing effects.

MODERATORS OF FRAMING IN POLITICAL MARKETING

A number of factors moderating the effectiveness of framing such as values (Nabi 2003), previous knowledge and interest in politics (de Vreese 2010), source credibility (Druckman 2001) as well as trust in media (Miller and Krosnick 2000) have been identified.

Previous knowledge and interest in politics seem to be one of the most extensively studied moderators of the effectiveness of framing. Although scholars have amassed a sizeable amount of evidence on the impact of the level of knowledge on these effects, the findings seem to point to two contradictory effects. Experiments conducted by Miller and Krosnick (2000) suggested that the effect is more likely to take place among people with substantial knowledge about politics. Similar results were found also earlier by Krosnick and Brannon (1993) and Nelson, Oxley, and Clawson (1997) who showed that high levels of political knowledge enhanced attitude change. According to the authors, the effect can be explained with the fact that more knowledgeable individuals are able to process information better, making it more accessible and relevant in decision making. Such a finding runs contrary to conventional wisdom regarding susceptibility to framing which views those who are influenced by it as oblivious "victims". Miller and Krosnick (2000) explain this non-intuitive result, stating:

> "People who evidence priming appear not to be unknowing victims of a powerful and manipulative force. Rather, they are political experts, who apparently *choose* to rely on a source they trust to help them sort through the wealth of information they have obtained in order to make political judgments".
> (Miller and Krosnick 2000, 312).

Other researchers, however, have come to contrary results. Considerable body of evidence suggests that the changes in the way a problem was presented or the issue was formulated has a stronger effect on less knowledgeable individuals (Krosnick and Kinder 1990; Haider-Markel and Joslyn 2001; Schuck and de Vreese 2006). It seems that in the case of less knowledgeable people the accommodation of new information into knowledge schemata is much easier than for people who have more extensive knowledge in the topic and who rely on accumulated information (Kinder and Sanders 1990). Chong and Druckman (2007) explain these contradictory results, pointing to prior attitudes as a moderator of the relationship between knowledge and framing, stating, "after controlling for prior attitudes, knowledge enhances framing effects because it increases the likelihood that the considerations empathized in a frame will be available or comprehensible to the individual" (112).

Apart from previous knowledge, the effectiveness of framing depends also on other individual predispositions such as values and partisan loyalties. Research has shown that strong opinions about a certain issue, especially if it pertains to morality or ethics, are less likely to be influenced by frames that contradict such values. For instance, Brewer (2003) analyzed how political knowledge and values such as traditional morality and egalitarianism affected American public opinion about gay rights. The study showed that strong attitudes about gay rights shaped the evaluation of other gay rights frames, making individuals less likely to change their prior opinions. The effect, however, was moderated by political knowledge, once again showing that those who have more knowledge are also more likely to be change their opinion.

Trust in media has been identified as yet another important moderator of the effectiveness of framing and priming. Even though the trust for public media has considerably decreased over last years among general audience (Cohen 2008), those who still find mass media as a credible source of information are more likely to be affected by the manipulations in the way information is presented. For instance, research conducted by Miller and Krosnick (2000) showed that exposure to stories about drugs and immigration presented by trusted national media networks increased the importance of that issue in judgments of presidential job performance. Here again, however, the effect was noticeable only in people who had good political knowledge and trusted media.

Framing effects are restricted not only by individual differences among people such as strong predispositions, values, knowledge or trust in media but also may depend on situational context in which the message was delivered and the message itself. Considerable evidence suggests that the effectiveness of framing depends also on the level of politicization of an issue. AnalysingAnalyzing opinions of Danish citizens on the government's performance and comparing them with media content in the time of the study, Togeby (2007) found that the more the issue was contentious in the conflicts between the ruling party and the opposition, the stronger was the effect of framing. Such a finding is not surprising, taking into consideration psychological studies on the relationship between emotion and message persuasiveness showing that the more emotional the content is, the more likely people are to process information superficially and be affected by framing (Gross 2008; Nabi 1998).

Having discussed the main moderators of framing, in the next section, we move on to the review of cognitive and affective mechanisms that mediate framing effects.

COGNITIVE MEDIATORS OF FRAMING

From the cognitive perspective, two mechanisms – accessibility and applicability – have been often quoted as likely mediators of the framing effect. Framing understood as the outcome of accessibility effects has been often described as a memory process that makes a particular information more cognitively accessible (Iyengar in de Vreese 2010; Iyengar and Kinder 2010). Here, the argument follows that when people come across a political topic, they are likely to use the criteria and interpretation of a particular event that has been most frequently or recently presented in the media. As it has been previously discussed in the section on the differences between priming and framing, such an understanding, however, seems to be more related to the former than the latter (de Vreese 2010). Furthermore, there is some empirical evidence showing no effect of framing on cognitive accessibility of information covered in the news and the effect itself has been questioned (Nelson, Oxley, and Clawson 1997).

The rise in salience is another mechanism that may explain cognitive processes involved in framing. Framing as an applicability effect assumes that a particular frame is effective not because its message is easily retrieved from memory and cognitively accessible but because it is perceived as important and relevant in the matter discussed. Such an understanding of framing has been propagated by Nelson and coauthors who stressed the importance of the weights attributed to considered beliefs (Nelson and Oxley 1999; Nelson, Oxley, and Clawson 1997). Having analyzed the relationship between the two processes, de Vreese (2010) concludes that both mechanisms – accessibility and applicability – can take place independently thus "selectively enhancing the psychological importance and *weight* given to specific beliefs can be accomplished without accessibility of these concepts in memory" (195; italics in original). Both processes, however, may also coincide so that "framing effects occur via a combination of applicable constructs, accessible constructs, and what has been labeled 'other factors'" (de Vreese 2010, 195).

Price and Tewksbury (1997) attempted to integrate accessibility and applicability effects in a one coherent model based on their temporal activation. Using earlier distinction into framing and priming, framing is seen as an applicability effect, whereas priming is regarded as an accessibility effect. Both effects are activated at different stages of information processing. Applicability effects take place early on, when salient attributes of the news activate certain criteria or ways of looking at the issue, which are used as immediate reference points for further judgments and decisions. Applicability effects are conceptualized as first-order effects. On the other hand, accessibility is a second-order effect and takes place in later stages, when a certain frame is accessible due to a temporary residual excitation or high baseline levels of excitation.

When analyzing the differences between framing and priming and their underlying cognitive mechanisms, it is also worth considering persuasion which is another type of attitude change. Conceptually different from framing and priming, the effectiveness of persuasion rests upon belief change (Nelson, Oxley, and Clawson 1997). Contrary to two aforementioned effects, persuasion leads to opinion change by providing new information about the matter which has not been previously known, that is it was not a part of the recipient's belief structure. Framing and priming, on the other hand, do not add new knowledge but rely on the information already present in the recipient's knowledge structure, by making it more relevant or accessible (Nelson, Oxley, and Clawson 1997).

The distinction into persuasion, framing and priming sheds new light on the moderating role of previous knowledge in attitude change, which has been already discussed in the previous section. As it has been mentioned, contrary to common knowledge, research showed that people with extensive knowledge were more likely to be affected by framing. Taking into consideration that the process relies on the activation of information already stored in the recipient's mind, such a result, however, is not so surprising, as more knowledgeable people have accumulated more concepts which can be responsive to framing manipulation. Furthermore, the distinction can be also used to explain why in some cases people are more impervious to attitude change. For instance, Price and Na (2000 in Chong and Druckman, 2007) showed that when participants were allowed to deliberate on a given matter before being presented with a particular message, the frame impact was limited. Similarly, if people were allowed to discuss the matter with others, especially people holding conflicting perspectives, framing effectiveness was significantly reduced (Druckman and Nelson 2003). In situations such as these, when the respondents have more time to critically process information, attitude change, or its lack as in the discussed studies, relies on a more conscious examination of the problem and is a result of a belief change.

AFFECTIVE MODERATORS AND MEDIATORS OF FRAMING

Framing effects have been also studied with reference to emotions. Although initially more attention was given to cognitive processing of news content, the amount and intensity of emotions being communicated every day in the media could not be overlooked and led to more research in this area. Soon, the importance of emotions in framing effects was recognized. In this section, we present a comprehensive review on the relationship between emotion and framing.

The effect of emotions on frames is diverse. As noted by Druckman and McDermott (2008), "emotion can provide a foundation upon which the framing of particular options can be based or constructed, thus influencing decision prior to choice, as well as during choice itself" (316). First, previously induced affective states may change the way in which a frame is perceived as relevant or accessible. This approach is well explained by Nabi (2003) who compares emotions to frames, stating that "repeated pairing of certain emotions with particular ideas or events eventually shapes the way in which one interprets and responds to those events that in turn affect one's worldview" (227). The effect relies on the interplay between cognitive and affective processes which has been an area of numerous psychological studies showing that emotions, similarly to frames, affect the way in which information is gathered, stored in memory, recalled and used to as relevant criteria for judgment (Dolan 2002; Izard 1992; Schwarz 2000).

It is needless to say that various emotions elicit different responses. Hence, the moderating effect of affective states on framing has been researched with regard to different models of emotions. The valence model of emotions differentiates affective states into two broad categories, positive and negative affect. As expected, numerous studies have shown that positively framed news leads to positive attitudes (Brader 2005; Gross, Brewer, and Aday 2009), whereas unpleasant emotions influence opinions in a negative way (Arceneaux 2012). The comparison of the effect of positive and negative emotions almost invariably provides evidence for a more prominent role of unpleasant stimuli. For instance, the experience of negative emotions such as anger and fear led to higher political participation (measured as a willingness to engage in such activities as wearing a campaign button, volunteering for a campaign, attending a rally and donating money) than positive emotions (Valentino et al. 2011). Similar results were also found by Druckman and McDermott (2008) who analyzed the moderating effect of various affective states on the susceptibility to frames. The results of their study showed that enthusiasm reduced the impact of framing, whereas distress amplified it. Furthermore, the impact of emotions depended not only on the valence of emotions but also problem domain, with the effects being stronger in life and death decisions and insignificant with regard to financial problems (Druckman and McDermott 2008).

Numerous other instances in which negative information works stronger than its positive counterpart can be found with regard to framing effects, in particular previously discussed agenda setting. For instance, the research on news coverage about foreign nations showed that the more negative the news was, the more likely respondents were to think unfavorably about the country. Positive information had, however, no influence on public perceptions (Wanta, Golan, and Lee 2004). Similar results were also found with regard to economic news, where it was found that such news were more often framed in a negative rather than positive manner. Additionally, such negative coverage was a significant predictor of consumer expectations about the future of the economy, but positive news had no such an effect (Hester and Gibson 2003).

Another type of framing, intensively studied in the field of economy but also relevant in political settings, is equivalency framing. It manifests itself when two logically equivalent statements make people change their preferences, depending on the way in which the content is presented (Tversky and Kahneman 1986). Taking a well-known example of an unusual, very dangerous Asian disease which is expected to kill a certain number of people, the same information may be presented in a positive (the number of people saved) or negative light (the number of people who will die if a given option is selected). Almost invariably, participants decide to opt for the positive variant, despite the fact that it may lead to suboptimal decisions (Kahneman and Tversky 1979; see also Druckman and McDermott 2008). The effect, called loss aversion, is one of the most important findings of prospect theory, which describes and explains various instances in which negative information has more impact on judgments and decisions than its positive counterpart. Drawing on the same psychological principle, Cwalina and Falkowski (2018) showed that news frames which present the consequences of unpopular reforms together (that is bundling them into one message) lead to more favorable evaluation of these reforms than when the reforms are presented individually. In a similar vein, research on framing tax increases conducted by Risner and Bergan (2016) delivered evidence suggesting that the presentation of the same value in terms of items results in a higher support for the reforms than when the value is displayed in terms of a yearly or weekly amount.

In political setting, Jabłońska and Falkowski (2018) analyzed the moderating role of the reference point on candidate evaluation and voting intention, looking on how the comparisons to an ideal and bad politician influenced the perception of the candidate. In a way, a reference point may be perceived as a frame used for the interpretation of the observed reality. The results of the study showed that when the candidate was juxtaposed with a bad politician, his affective evaluation and intention to vote for him were higher than when the reference point was positive. Furthermore, negative framing resulted in an increase in the preference for the candidate (compared to the initial measurement), whereas juxtaposition of the candidate with the image of an ideal politician had no effect on attitude change. Similar findings were also reported by Bizer and Petty (2005) who showed that participants who were asked to conceptualize their political preferences as being against a candidate were more resistant to a counterattitudinal message than were the participants who thought about themselves as supporters of their candidate.

So far, we have presented numerous accounts of the ways in which positive and negative emotions (the valence model of emotions) moderate framing effects. Another approach to the study of emotions is a discrete emotion model which differentiates between various affective states of the same valence. Although the two-dimensional perspective may be in some cases sufficient and literature presents a large number of studies using combined measures of positive and negative emotions (Brader, Valentino, and Suhay 2008; Rahn, Kroeger, and Kite 1996), there is a plethora of evidence suggesting that different positive and negative emotions vary with regard to approach-avoidance tendencies (Crigler and Just 2012) and thus a more in-depth analysis of discrete emotional states is recommended (Druckman and McDermott 2008).

For instance, from four emotions tested (enthusiasm, contentment, anger and fear) only anger and enthusiasm turned out to moderate the effect of framing and resulted in attitude change (Lecheler, Schuck, and de Vreese 2013). The findings may be interpreted with higher approach tendencies and low avoidance behavior which are characteristic for both emotions. Moreover, the effect may be further mediated by deep information processing which is promoted by higher arousal as suggested by Valentino et al. (2011). Other studies on the relationship between emotion and cognition with regard to framing found a similar pattern. Lecheler, Schuck, and de Vreese (2013) as well as Nabi (1999) found that whereas anger led to confrontational behavior and a more careful analysis of information, fear resulted in retreat and low cognitive processing.

The negativity effect and the relationship between framing and a cognitive process of similarity judgments was also investigated by Falkowski and Jabłońska (2018) who analyzed how adding positive and negative features to candidate profiles affects candidate evaluation. In their research, they focused on two issues: the valence of features (positive and negative features) and the valence of the referents for similarity judgments (comparisons to an ideal politician or a bad politician). The results of the study showed that additional unfavorable traits had a stronger negative effect on similarity to an ideal candidate than positive features, the effect of which, although positive, was much weaker. Such findings yet again give support to the negativity effect by showing that negative characteristics of a political candidate tarnish his or her image much more than positive traits make it more attractive. Interestingly, however, the effect disappeared in negative framing condition, that is in the situation in which the candidate was compared with a bad politician. Further analyses showed that these differences in the results can be explained with the mediating role of affective evaluation of the candidate, which turned out to be more relevant in attitudes framed negatively.

IMPLICATIONS FOR POLITICAL BRAND MANAGEMENT

The previously discussed differential effect that positive and negative information items and affective states have on the perception of political candidates are examples of a much broader concept of positive-negative asymmetry. Another instance of this asymmetry is negative comparative advertising, in which framing mechanism relies on comparison judgments where one candidate is juxtaposed against his/her better or worse alternative. Although the effectiveness of negative political ads has been called into question (Lau et al. 1999), there is a convincing body of evidence showing that negative comparisons can actually lead to brand image depreciation. One of such examples is Kaid's (1997) study on negative comparative advertising. During the presidential campaign of 1996, in which Bill Clinton and Bob Dole were competing for the presidency, Lynda Lee Kaid conducted an experimental research on advertising spots that distorted candidate images. Different groups of participants watched original negative spots of Dole and Clinton where distorted pictures were used or the same ads with distortions removed. Figure 1 presents the effect that negative advertisements prepared by Dole's election team had on Clinton's resulting evaluation and participants' intention to vote for him. A comparable effect was observed also for advertisements that distorted Dole's image.

The results show an interesting effect. Unsurprisingly, research showed that negative advertising tarnishes the image of an attacked candidate and reduces the intention to vote for him or her. More importantly, however, it also increases the chances of the opposing candidate whose campaign prepared these spots. The effect is corroborated in the research by Faber, Tims, and Schmitt (1990) who showed negative ads to be more likely to cause target-partisans to strengthen support for the target candidate, and source-partisans to strengthen support for the ad sponsor.

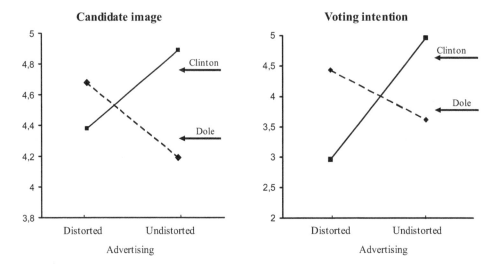

FIGURE 1. The effect of distorted stimuli in the ads presented by the Dole Campaign on Candidate Image and Vote Intention. The evaluation was the mean of 12 seven-point scale of semantic differential, developed in order to measure the candidate's image and the intention was measured on 1 seven-point scale. Source: Cwalina, Falkowski and Newman, 2015, 114.

Kaid's (1997) study bears some similarity to Bizer and Petty's (2005) research on valence framing in which participants were framed to think either in terms of support for their candidate or opposition towards the other candidate. Similarly, distorted advertisements in Kaid's experiment made potential voters think in "anti-Clinton" and "anti-Dole" categories. As shown by these two studies, framing voters in terms of opposition led to their stronger preference for the favored candidate, higher resistance to attitude change (Bizer and Petty 2005) as well as higher preference for the candidate who used negative advertisements (Kaid, 1997).

Summing up, it can be stated that negative information about a candidate has a much more detrimental effect on politician's image compared to positive information of comparable strength. Thus electoral campaign staff members should be especially alert to negative attacks from opposing candidates and concentrate on designing marketing strategies aimed at neutralizing the impact of negative advertising. As presented, current knowledge and research on the negativity effect show that such strategies are more effective in protection of brand image than strategies aimed at presenting and strengthening positive features of a brand.

CONCLUSIONS AND DIRECTIONS FOR FURTHER RESEARCH

The aim of the following paper was to present a brief overview of most important studies on framing effects. In the first section, we have established that although priming and framing are to some extent similar and often coincide, they are based on different psychological mechanisms. Priming seems to lead to higher accessibility of a concept, whereas framing makes a certain issue or idea more relevant and applicable in attitude formation process. Later, we have discussed moderators of framing effects such as previous knowledge, values, trust in media and politicization of an issue. Here, we concluded that the level of knowledge about the topic is a very strong variable affecting the effectiveness of framing. Furthermore, although contradictory results can be found, it seems that more knowledgeable people are more likely to be influenced by framing, a finding which runs against common knowledge. Finally, we have presented cognitive and affective mechanisms that explain framing effects, with more attention given to positive-negative asymmetry.

The presented review of contemporary studies on framing effects points to two important conclusions in the area of political marketing research. Firstly, framing rests upon one of the most fundamental rules of behavior, that is the dependence on the reference point. There are no absolute evaluations – a judgment is always relative and context-based. It can change depending on the changes in the environment and the way the problem was formulated, which has been stressed in Kahneman and Tversky's research on preference formation and decision-making process (Kahneman 2011; Tversky and Kahneman 1986). The comparisons that one makes – whether to a particular situation or to one's expectations about it – are the essence of psychological judgments that take place in a competitive environment.

The second observation pertains to positive-negative asymmetry which has been noticed in research on positive and negative framing. The witnessed negativity effect has important practical implications for controlling attitudes towards various political and social issues. For instance, the way in which a question is formulated may unconsciously strengthen or weaken such an attitude, depending on the positive or negative point of reference which was used in the question. When asked about an attitude towards abortion, a person is likely to be more socially engaged if the question is formulated as an anti-abortion statement (negative framing) than a pro-life position (positive framing). Finally, the research can be also applied to social behavior as it explains well the mechanism behind attitude formation, depending on the way in which an issue was presented. Based on the findings of numerous studies, it may be stated that it is better to present oneself so that one is compared to a negative point of reference, for instance one's competitor, than to promote one's positive features. This result explains also well the effectiveness of negative political comparative advertising which has shown that negative comparisons and pointing to opponent's weaknesses have a positive influence on the image of the attacking candidate. The phenomenon – known as the negativity effect – has important implications for the management of political brand image.

The review suggests also that cognitive framing, which is dependent upon such variables as previous knowledge, interest in politics, trust as well accessibility and applicability effects, is often separated from affective framing. Positive and negative emotions fit very well the positive-negative asymmetry observed in evaluations as shown by Öhman, Lundqvist, and Esteves (2001) who found that people have much higher sensitivity for negative emotions than positive ones. Probably no one would challenge the contention that political behavior is a result not only of a cognitive evaluation of politicians and political parties but also emotions that they evoke. Future studies on moderators and mediators of framing should aim at integrating cognitive and emotional processes into one coherent model which can be used in the analysis of political behavior and political brand image management in a way that is closer to the observed reality.

Other path of research worth pursuing is the use or artificial intelligence and machine learning in the analysis of large scale data such as digital media by making automatic content analysis much faster, less expensive and more comprehensive (Burscher et al. 2014). Finally, so called frame, understood as "a data-structure for representing a stereotyped situation" (Minsky 1975, 211) was the basis for frame language used for knowledge representation in artificial intelligence. According to Russell and Norvig (2010), these structural representations assemble facts about particular object and event types into large taxonomic hierarchies analogous to a biological taxonomy. If non-congruent information is encountered, a frame is modified to fit a particular situation. This operation pertains to learning processes which may in future consider the nature of artificial intelligence and machine learning as producers of frame modifiers.

ACKNOWLEDGMENTS

The authors contributed equally to the research.

FUNDING

The research was funded by a grant sponsored by the National Science Center, Poland, grant number 2015/19/N/HS6/00767.

REFERENCES

Arceneaux, Kevin. 2012. "Cognitive Biases and the Strength of Political Arguments." *American Journal of Political Science* 56 (2):271–285. doi: 10.1111/j.1540-5907.2011.00573.x.

Bargh, John A., and Tanya L. Chartrand. 1999. "The Unbearable Automaticity of Being." *American Psychologist* 54 (7):462–479. doi: 10.1037/0003-066X.54.7.462.

Bizer, George Y., and Richard E. Petty. 2005. "How we Conceptualize Our Attitudes Matters: The Effects of Valence Framing on the Resistance of Political Attitudes." *Political Psychology* 26 (4):553–568. doi: 10.1111/j.1467-9221.2005.00431.x.

Brader, Ted. 2005. "Striking a Responsive Chord: How Political Ads Motivate and Persuade Voters by Appealing to Emotions." *American Journal of Political Science* 49 (2):388–405. doi: 10.1111/j.0092-5853.2005.00130.x.

Brader, Ted, Nicholas A. Valentino, and Elizabeth Suhay. 2008. "What Triggers Public Opposition to Immigration? Anxiety, Group Cues, and Immigration Threat." *American Journal of Political Science* 52 (4):959–978. doi: 10.1111/j.1540-5907.2008.00353.x.

Brewer, Paul R. 2003. "Values, Political Knowledge, and Public Opinion about Gay Rights: A Framing-Based Account." *Public Opinion Quarterly* 67 (2):173–201. doi: 10.1086/374397.

Burscher, Björn, Daan Odijk, Rens Vliegenthart, Maarten De Rijke, and Claes H. De Vreese. 2014. "Teaching the Computer to Code Frames in News: Comparing Two Supervised Machine Learning Approaches to Frame Analysis." *Communication Methods and Measures* 8 (3):190–206. doi: 10.1080/19312458.2014.937527.

Chong, Dennis, and James N. Druckman. 2007. "Framing Public Opinion in Competitive Democracies." *American Political Science Review* 101 (4):637–655. doi: 10.1017/S0003055407070554.

Cohen, Jeffrey E. 2008. *The Presidency in the Era of 24-Hour News*. Princeton, NJ: Princeton University Press.

Crigler, Ann N., and Marion R. Just. 2012. "Measuring Affect, Emotion and Mood in Political Communication." In *The Sage Handbook of Political Communication*, edited by Holli A. Semetko and Margaret Scammell, 211–224. Thousand Oaks, CA: Sage Publications.

Cwalina, Wojciech, and Andrzej Falkowski. 2018. "Crisis Management: Government Strategy in Framing Reform Proposals and Communications." *Journal of Political Marketing* 17 (2):122–136. doi: 10.1080/15377857.2018.1447754.

Cwalina, Wojciech, Andrzej Falkowski, and Bruce O. Newman. 2015. "Persuasion in the Political Context: Opportunities and Threats." In *Persuasion and Social Marketing*, edited by David W. Stewart, 61–128. Santa Barbara, CA: Praeger.

de Vreese, Claes H. 2010. "Journalistic News Frames." In *Doing framing analysis: Empirical and Theoretical Perspectives*, edited by Paul D'Angelo and Jim A. Kuypers, 187–214. New York: doi: Routledge.

Dolan, Raymond J. 2002. "Emotion, Cognition, and Behavior." *Science* (New York, N.Y.) 298 (5596):1191–1194. doi: 10.1126/science.1076358.

Druckman, James N. 2001. "On the Limits of Framing Effects: Who Can Frame?" *The Journal of Politics* 63 (4):1041–1066. doi: 10.1111/0022-3816.00100.

Druckman, James N., and Rose McDermott. 2008. "Emotion and the Framing of Risky Choice." *Political Behavior* 30 (3):297–321. doi: 10.1007/s11109-008-9056-y.

Druckman, James N., and Kjersten R. Nelson. 2003. "Framing and Deliberation: How Citizens' Conversations Limit Elite Influence." *American Journal of Political Science* 47 (4):729–745. doi: 10.1111/1540-5907.00051.

Entman, Robert M. 2007. "Framing Bias: Media in the Distribution of Power." *Journal of Communication* 57 (1):163–173. doi: 10.1111/j.1460-2466.2006.00336.x.

Faber, Ronald J., Albert R. Tims, and Kay G. Schmitt. 1990. "Accentuate the Negative? The Impact of Negative Political Appeals on Voting Intent." In *Proceedings of the American Academy of Advertising*, 10–16. Austin: University of Texas at Austin.

Falkowski, Andrzej, and Magdalena Jabłońska. 2018. "Positive–Negative Asymmetry in the Evaluations of Political Candidates. The Role of Features of Similarity and Affect in Voter Behavior." *Frontiers in Psychology* 9:213. doi: 10.3389/fpsyg.2018.00213.

Fiske, Susan T., and Shelley E. Taylor. 2008. *Social Cognition: From Brains to Culture*. New York: McGraw-Hill.

Gamson, William A., and Andre Modigliani. 1987. "The Changing Culture of Affirmative Action." *Research in Political Sociology*, edited by Richard D. Braungart, 137–177. Greenwich, CT: JAI Press.

Gross, Kimberly. 2008. "Framing Persuasive Appeals: Episodic and Thematic Framing, Emotional Response, and Policy Opinion." *Political Psychology* 29 (2):169–192. doi: 10.1111/j.1467-9221.2008.00622.x.

Gross, Kimberly, Paul R. Brewer, and Sean Aday. 2009. "Confidence in Government and Emotional Responses to Terrorism after September 11, 2001." *American Politics Research* 37 (1):107–128. doi: 10.1177/1532673X08319954.

Haider-Markel, Donald P., and Mark R. Joslyn. 2001. "Gun Policy, Opinion, Tragedy, and Blame Attribution: The Conditional Influence of Issue Frames." *The Journal of Politics* 63 (2):520–543. doi: 10.1111/0022-3816.00077.

Hester, Joe Bob., and Rhonda Gibson. 2003. "The Economy and Second-Level Agenda Setting: A Time-Series Analysis of Economic News and Public Opinion about the Economy." *Journalism & Mass Communication Quarterly* 80 (1):73–90. doi: 10.1177/107769900308000106.

Iyengar, Shanto, and Donald R. Kinder. 2010. *News that Matters: Television and American Opinion*. Chicago, IL: University of Chicago Press.

Izard, Carroll E. 1992. "Basic Emotions, Relations among Emotions, and Emotion-Cognition Relations." *Psychological Review* 99 (3):561–565. doi: 10.1037/0033-295X.99.3.561.

Jabłońska, Magdalena, and Andrzej Falkowski. 2019. "Framing in Political Evaluations. An Empirical Study on the Role of Positive and Negative Comparisons in Affect and Preference Construction." *Journal of Political Marketing*, Submitted.

Kahneman, Daniel. 2011. *Thinking Fast and Slow*. New York: Macmillan.

Kahneman, Daniel, and Amos Tversky. 1979. "Prospect Theory: An Analysis of Decisions under Risk." *Econometrica* 47 (2):263–291. doi: 10.2307/1914185.

Kaid, Lynda Lee. 1997. "Effects of the Television Spots on Images of Dole and Clinton." *American Behavioral Scientist* 40 (8):1085–1094. doi: 10.1177/0002764297040008009.

Kinder, Donald R., and Lynn M. Sanders. 1990. "Mimicking Political Debate with Survey Questions: The Case of White Opinion on Affirmative Action for Blacks." *Social Cognition* 8 (1):73–103. doi: 10.1521/soco.1990.8.1.73.

Krosnick, Jon A., and Donald R. Kinder. 1990. "Altering the Foundations of Support for the President through Priming." *American Political Science Review* 84 (2):497–512. doi: 10.2307/1963531.

Krosnick, Jon A., and Laura A. Brannon. 1993. "The impact of the Gulf War on the ingredients of presidential evaluations: Multidimensional effects of political involvement." *American Political Science Review* 87 (4):963–975.

Lau, Richard R., Lee Sigelman, Caroline Heldman, and Paul Babbitt. 1999. "The Effects of Negative Political Advertisements: A Meta-Analytic Assessment." *American Political Science Review* 93 (4):851–875. doi: 10.2307/2586117.

Lecheler, Sophie, Andreas R.T. Schuck, and Claes H. de Vreese. 2013. "Dealing with Feelings: Positive and Negative Discrete Emotions as Mediators of News Framing Effects." *Communications* 38 (2):189–209.

Maher, T. Michael. 2001. "Framing: An Emerging Paradigm or a Phase of Agenda Setting?" In *Framing Public Life, Perspectives on Media and our Understanding of the Social World*, edited by Stephen D. Reese, Oscar Gandy and August E. Grant, 83–94. Mahwah, NJ: Erlbaum.

Miller, Joanne M., and Jon A. Krosnick. 1996. "News Media Impact on the Ingredients of Presidential Evaluations: A Program of Research on the Priming Hypothesis." In *Political Persuasion and Attitude Change*, edited by Diana Carole Mutz, Paul M. Sniderman, and Richard A. Brody, 79–100. Michigan: University of Michigan Press.

Miller, Joanne M., and Jon A. Krosnick. 2000. "News Media Impact on the Ingredients of Presidential Evaluations: Politically Knowledgeable Citizens Are Guided by a Trusted Source." *American Journal of Political Science* 44 (2):301–315. doi: 10.2307/2669312.

Minsky, Marvin. 1975. "A Framework for Representing Knowledge." In *The psychology of Computer Vision*, edited by Patrick Henry Winston, and Berthold Horn, 211–277. New York: McGraw-Hill.

Nabi, Robin L. 1998. "The Effect of Disgust-Eliciting Visuals on Attitudes toward Animal Experimentation." *Communication Quarterly* 46 (4):472–484. doi: 10.1080/01463379809370116.

Nabi, Robin. L. 1999. "A Cognitive-Functional Model for the Effects of Discrete Negative Emotions on Information Processing, Attitude Change, and Recall." *Communication Theory* 9 (3):292–320. doi: 10.1111/j.1468-2885.1999.tb00172.x.

Nabi, Robin. L. 2003. "Exploring the Framing Effects of Emotion: Do Discrete Emotions Differentially Influence Information Accessibility, Information Seeking, and Policy Preference?" *Communication Research* 30 (2):224–247. doi: 10.1177/0093650202250881.

Nelson, Thomas E., and Zoe M. Oxley. 1999. "Issue Framing Effects on Belief Importance and Opinion." *The Journal of Politics* 61 (4):1040–1067. doi: 10.2307/2647553.

Nelson, Thomas E., Zoe M. Oxley, and Rosalee A. Clawson. 1997. "Toward a Psychology of Framing Effects." *Political Behavior* 19 (3):221–246. doi: 10.1023/A:1024834831093.

Neuman, W. Russell, Marion R. Just, and Ann N. Crigler. 1992. *Common Knowledge*. Chicago: University of Chicago Press.

Öhman, Arne, Daniel Lundqvist, and Francisco Esteves. 2001. "The Face in the Crowd Revisited: A Threat Advantage with Schematic Stimuli." *Journal of Personality and Social Psychology* 80 (3):381–396. doi: 10.1037/0022-3514.80.3.381.

Pan, Zhongdang, and Gerald M. Kosicki. 1993. "Framing Analysis: An Approach to News Discourse." *Political Communication* 10 (1):55–75. doi: 10.1080/10584609.1993.9962963.

Price, Vincent, and David Tewksbury. 1997. "News Values and Public Opinion: A Theoretical Account of Media Priming and Framing." In *Progress in Communication Sciences: Advances in Persuasion*, edited by George A. Barett and Franklin J. Boster, 173–212. Greenwich, CT: Ablex.

Price, Vincent, David Tewksbury, and Elizabeth Powers. 1997. "Switching Trains of Thought: The Impact of News Frames on Readers' Cognitive Responses." *Communication Research* 24 (5):481–506. doi: 10.1177/009365097024005002.

Rahn, Wendy M., Brian Kroeger, and Cynthia M. Kite. 1996. "A Framework for the Study of Public Mood." *Political Psychology* 17 (1):29–58. doi: 10.2307/3791942.

Risner, Geneviève, and Daniel E. Bergan. 2016. "Say It with Candy: The Power of Framing Tax Increases as Items."*Journal of Political Marketing* 15 (1):22–44. doi: 10.1080/15377857.2014.959685.

Russell, Stuart J., and Peter Norvig. 2010. *Artificial Intelligence: A Modern Approach*. 2nd ed. Upper Saddle River, NJ: Prentice Hall.

Schuck, Andreas R. T., Rens Vliegenthart, Hajo G. Boomgaarden, Matthijs Elenbaas, Rachid Azrout, Joost van Spanje, and Claes H. de Vreese. 2013. "Explaining Campaign News Coverage: How Medium, Time, and Context Explain Variation in the Media Framing of the 2009 European Parliamentary Elections." *Journal of Political Marketing* 12 (1):8–28. doi: 10.1080/15377857.2013.752192.

Semetko, Holli A., and Patti M. Valkenburg. 2000. "Framing European Politics: A Content Analysis of Press and Television News." *Journal of Communication* 50 (2):93–109. doi: 10.1111/j.1460-2466.2000.tb02843.x.

Scheufele, Dietram A. 2000. "Agenda-Setting, Priming, and Framing Revisited: Another Look at Cognitive Effects of Political Communication." *Mass Communication and Society* 3 (2–3):297–316. doi: 10.1207/S15327825MCS0323_07.

Scheufele, Dietram A., and David Tewksbury. 2006. "Framing, Agenda Setting, and Priming: The Evolution of Three Media Effects Models." *Journal of Communication* 57 (1):9–20. doi: 10.1111/j.0021-9916.2007.00326.x.

Schuck, Andreas R. T., and Claes H. De Vreese. 2006. "Between Risk and Opportunity: News Framing and Its Effects on Public Support for EU Enlargement." European Journal of Communication 21 (1):5–32. doi: 10.1177/0267323106060987.

Schwarz, Norbert. 2000. "Emotion, Cognition, and Decision Making." *Cognition & Emotion* 14 (4):433–440. doi: 10.1080/026999300402745.

Togeby, Lise. 2007. "The Context of Priming." *Scandinavian Political Studies* 30 (3):345–376. doi: 10.1111/j.1467-9477.2007.00184.x.

Taylor, Shelley E. 1981. "The Interface of Cognitive and Social Psychology." In *Cognition, Social Behavior, and the Environment*, edited by John H. Harvey, 189–211. Hillsdale: Lawrence Erlbaum.

Tversky, Amos, and Daniel Kahneman. 1981. "The Framing of Decisions and the Psychology of Choice." *Science* (New York, N.Y.) 211 (4481):453–458. doi: 10.1126/science.7455683.

Tversky, Amos, and Daniel Kahneman. 1986. "Rational Choice and the Framing of Decisions." The Journal of Business 59 (S4):S251–S278. doi: 10.1086/296365.

Valentino, Nicholas A., Ted Brader, Eric W. Groenendyk, Krysha Gregorowicz, and Vincent L. Hutchings. 2011. "Election Night's Alright for Fighting: The Role of Emotions in Political Participation." *The Journal of Politics* 73 (1):156–170. doi: 10.1017/S0022381610000939.

Wanta, Wayne, Guy Golan, and Cheolhan Lee. 2004. "Agenda Setting and International News: Media Influence on Public Perceptions of Foreign Nations." *Journalism & Mass Communication Quarterly* 81 (2):364–377. doi: 10.1177/107769900408100209.

Weaver, David H. 2007. "Thoughts on Agenda Setting, Framing, and Priming." *Journal of Communication* 57 (1):142–147. doi: 10.1111/j.1460-2466.2006.00333.x.

Wüst, Andreas M. 2009. "Parties in European Parliament Elections: Issues, Framing, the EU, and the Question of Supply and Demand." *German Politics* 18 (3):426–440. doi: 10.1080/09644000903055849.

Scripted Messengers: How Party Discipline and Branding Turn Election Candidates and Legislators into Brand Ambassadors

ALEX MARLAND

ANGELIA WAGNER (iD)

Political parties with strict party discipline are well-placed to demand that their election candidates and legislators promote the party brand. The franchise-franchisee relationship causes representatives to relinquish individual expression in exchange for centralized party messaging. This article looks at how a strategic desire for party unity combines with internal brand management to turn lower-ranking politicians in a parliamentary system into party brand ambassadors. Our Canadian case study draws on in-depth interviews with party leaders, Members of Parliament, political staff, candidates for office and prospective candidates. The implications for representative democracy in a Westminster system are considered, including the representational constraints for racial and sexual minorities.

Political parties devote considerable resources to developing, refining and promoting a political brand they hope voters will support by voting them (back) into office or by endorsing their policies. Much political marketing scholarship thus focuses on parties and/or party leaders (e.g., Needham 2005; Pich, Dean, and Punjaisri 2016; Scammell 2001; Speed, Butler, and Collins 2015), paying particular attention to how they use marketing techniques such as branding to sell voters on their political product. This emphasis on party elites, however, tends to ignore the part that election candidates and legislators play in the diffusion of party messaging. The role of local party representatives is especially crucial in parliamentary systems where party discipline dictates that they publicly support the party leader. The popular image of low-ranked politicians is usually one of trained seals. It is a perception that fails to recognize their importance to the party's political communication objectives and glosses over the complex ways in which they view this function.

In this article, we reconceptualize the branding role of election candidates and legislators in parliamentary systems where parties are strong and party discipline is stronger. We argue that candidates and backbenchers in a political system with strict party discipline are conditioned to act as messengers who stick to an approved script. This mentality is heightened if the party leadership espouses a brand orientation that urges the repetition of talking points to amplify the leader's message and promote communications congruity. Diverging opinions are vocalized in private settings with the understanding that those who freelance in public will be sanctioned. Individual politicians—already in a tug of war between representing party interests or those of constituents, and wrestling with personal convictions—are constrained in their ability to build their own brand. From the moment they apply to represent the party, candidates begin their transformation into brand ambassadors, which is to say they enter into a brand contract to prioritize the representation of party interests. Some brand ambassadors embrace the role, and are natural communicators. Others robotically repeat party message lines word-for-word and lack authenticity. Partisans who are independent-minded learn that a branding mantra requires their public subservience to the party leadership.

To explore the concept of low-ranking politicians as information conduits, we conduct a qualitative examination of the localized realities of party branding. We divulge the ways that party personnel coordinate messaging among election candidates and legislators to unify communication into a cohesive whole. We seek to identify the strategic rationale for these efforts, bringing to life compelling reasons for a strong party brand while identifying what this means for those on the front lines of democracy. In the process we explicitly link two concepts—branding and party discipline—normally treated as distinct and demonstrate how they feed into each other in the party's political communication process. Our conceptualization of party brand ambassadors offers a theoretical starting point from which to empirically explore branding dynamics in party-centered political systems. This study also contributes to our understanding of political representation in today's media environment; about the ferocity of branding in political parties, elections, legislatures and governance; and about how message control can limit individual public expression in politics.

We begin with a brief review of representative democracy, party discipline and branding before introducing the idea of party brand ambassadors. We situate our case study and outline the research method, drawing generalized insights from 170 in-depth interviews with party leaders, legislators, political staff, election candidates and prospective candidates in Canada. Our qualitative findings are presented in a generic manner to facilitate theory-building and application to other jurisdictions.

CONCEPTUALIZING BRAND AMBASSADORS IN PARTY POLITICS

The desire of party elites to synchronize all communication aggravates longstanding debates about the nature of representative democracy (e.g., Downs 1957; Eulau et al. 1959; Pitkin 1967). Most discussion focuses on the Burkean dichotomy of delegate and trustee types of representational styles. Delegates are elected representatives who govern according to the wishes of their constituents, while trustees make decisions based primarily on their own views. Some politicians project a home style to develop a personal vote, communicating to electors that they are a strong representative in the capital city, or alternatively emphasizing their deep connections with the local community (e.g., Cain, Frejohn, and Fiorina 1987; Fenno 1978; Gulati 2004). Then there are styles of representation that emphasize party responsibilities, such as the work of party builders who actively promote the party brand or the party soldiers who have a more passive role as a member of a partisan team (Bernhard and Sulkin 2018; Karlsson 2013). There are many reasons for this shift, among them the professionalization of political parties since Britain's Edmund Burke was a Member of Parliament in the 18th century, including the phenomena of permanent campaigning, political marketing, digital politics and so on.

Most politicians do not neatly fit into any particular style. Rather, they combine elements of some or all aspects in their representational practice. This is especially true when politicians must deal with controversial issues, such as those involving religion and morality. Further debate surrounds the nature and effectiveness of descriptive representation (e.g., Beckwith 2007; Childs and Krook 2009; Mansbridge 1999). Some scholars argue that members of a legislative assembly should approximate the socio-economic characteristics of the population, especially in terms of gender, race, class, and sexuality (Carnes 2018; Mansbridge 1999). Yet others challenge the assumption that a social group's physical presence in legislatures will automatically translate into government policies favorable to that group (Childs and Krook 2009; Trimble 2008). Political parties, institutional structures, public opinion and other factors limit the ability of individual representatives to shape policy (e.g., Haider-Markel 2010; Och and Shames 2018). These tensions can be flashpoints in western liberal democracies.

The influence of the party and its leader is particularly vibrant in Westminster systems with strong party discipline. Historically, party discipline foremost concerns what happens within the legislative precinct. Representatives deliberate policy in closed-door caucus meetings and emerge with a united front. They socialize as a team and develop relationships with like-minded people. Each party's whip pressures representatives to toe the party line in legislative committees, debate on bills and especially votes (Jackson 1968; Jones 2016). After all, in a parliamentary system the government can fall on a confidence issue, such as a budget bill, if it fails to secure a majority of legislators' votes. Incentives and punishments are dangled, such as travel junkets and speaking time, supported by the general promise of climbing the political career ladder. It follows that most research about party cohesion and discipline examines legislators' voting records (e.g., Bowler and McElroy 2015; Carrubba, Gabel, and Hug 2008; Kam 2009; Olson 2003). Such studies of legislative behavior overlook the strategic relationship between party discipline and message discipline in a brand-centric environment. We argue that branding can further explain why so many representatives now subscribe to unwavering unity outside the legislature and act as party brand builders and soldiers regardless of the context.

Party unity is necessary for governing and for those seeking to form government. It is difficult, and sometimes impossible, to advance a political agenda amidst the drama, negativity and turmoil that accompanies news of internal conflict. Consistency and cohesion are therefore integral to the party's image, its popularity and its electoral success. On both the campaign trail and during governance, the leader wants to be publicly supported by everyone affiliated with the party, through all media touchpoints. Strong party discipline provides a formidable foundation for party branding.

In many respects, political parties are like franchise organizations that bring local franchisees into the fold (Carty 2002, 2004; Marland 2003). Franchisees are authorized to be affiliated with the main brand provided that they reasonably follow the same playbook. They use the brand name and logo; benefit from centralized communications such as advertising and media relations; offer a menu of choices designed by the corporate head office; and have a bit of flexibility to respond to the local market (e.g., King, Grace and Weaven 2013; Marsh and Fawcett 2011). The franchisor and franchisee cooperate on reputation management and exchange information through private channels. The franchisee is a local presence for the brand, as are party candidates and legislators who have their own digital brand personality (Lilleker 2015) and politicians with their own localized campaign networks (Karlsen and Skogerbø 2015). A noteworthy difference between the private and political sectors is that in business a franchisee gives money to the franchisor for the contractual right to sell branded goods and/or services in a regional market (e.g., Shane 1998). They only set up shop where there is market demand. By comparison, major political parties are pressed to field candidates in all electoral districts, including those where there is no party infrastructure and low public support. Parties sometimes urge people without a public profile or political experience to put their name on the ballot in an unwinnable electoral district. A further demarcation is that a franchisee is unlikely to have their personal history scoured by opponents or be the target of horrible comments from social media trolls. These issues aside, all types of franchisees enter into a relationship that permits them to be affiliated with the corporate brand, provided that they uphold certain conditions.

Evidence is mixed about whether branding is good or bad for democracy and governance (e.g., Eshuis and Klijn 2012, 135–148; Marland 2016, 350–379; Marsh and Fawcett 2011; Scammell 2015). Brands are foremost communications constructs. They are "clusters of functional and emotional values making promises about unique experiences" (Vallaster and de Chernatony 2005, 183). Among the many benefits of branding are that it improves public awareness, market differentiation, customer loyalty, price premiums and shareholder value. Political strategists espouse branding because it simplifies information searches and adds value to communications. Candidates and legislators benefit from centralized resource supports. Approved messages offer time savings and career safety in both campaigns and governance. During campaigns, party candidates receive talking points, have access to party machinery, can lean on the party platform, and are offered templates for signage, brochures and website design. During governance, party staff provide legislators with content for media interviews, news releases, speeches, social media shareables, newsletters and so forth.

Yet branding has its critics. Branding distracts and deceives audiences (Bertilsson and Rennstam 2018). Organizations prioritize an intangible brand construct and their public image over improving the tangible product or the lives of employees (Klein 2000). In politics, the party leader is the face of the brand, and policy details are cast aside in favor of images and symbols. Image management is relentless, and the segmentation of audiences into target groups polarizes the electorate. Branding constrains the freedom of constituents' representatives to speak up publicly, which increases the power of the party leader's inner circle, weakens public trust in elected officials and reduces confidence in representative democracy. It is manifested in attempts to control citizen interactivity, such as structuring social media forums so that participants use the same keywords as party leaders, a practice that is most difficult with civil rights and religion (Freelon 2017). At its worst, political branding can be used for vile and sinister purposes (O'Shaughnessy 2009). Consequently, the conformity of party branding both helps and hinders democracy, with practical implications for local representation in political environments where rigorous party discipline invites the heavy hand of the brand.

Of interest to us is that human elements play a formative role in branding and franchising (King, Grace, and Weaven 2013). A single interaction with a representative of the brand can affect a customer's cognitive, emotional and social attachments to it (Crouch et al. 2016). For representatives to humanize the brand, facilitate emotional connections, and build affection and trust, they must "treat customers in a way that is consistent with the brand promise [that] the organization conveys through its public messages" (Morhart, Herzog, and Tomczak 2009, 123). Managing the interactions of frontline personnel who interact with the public is therefore fundamental to the branding of a service organization.

Among the variants of the franchisee analogy are brand ambassadors, brand champions, brand advocates and corporate ambassadors. The labels all refer in some manner to messengers who promote brand values in exchange relationships (Fisher-Buttinger and Vallaster 2008) and who enrich the brand image by advocating the brand at work and after hours (Löhndorf and Diamantopoulos 2014). Their behavior aligns with the brand promise, brand identity and customer expectations (Xiong, King and Piehler 2013). No consensus exists in the literature about whether brand ambassadors are exclusively high-ranking corporate representatives, all of an organization's employees or even all citizens of a community who are identity avatars. Where there is agreement is that internal brand management and internal communications are crucial to brand success.

Ensuring that employees embody the brand and adopt it as part of their lifestyle is part human resources function and part strategic marketing. Personnel who identify with the brand are motivated to participate in brand-building efforts that generate positive word of mouth (Löhndorf and Diamantopoulos 2014) and in turn improve employee productivity (Men 2014). Internal brand management begins with recruitment and hiring (Al-Shuaibi, Mohd Shamsudin, and Aziz 2016). A psychological commitment is nurtured among employees to foster an evangelical passion. Nurturing a brand from the inside-out requires that an organization's leadership articulate a vision and develop a brand-centric organizational culture (Vallaster and de Chernatony 2005), such as by sharing information about decisions, events and policies through personal interactions, email and social media

(Men 2014). These are some of the many facets of internal brand management hidden from public view.

However, brand ambassadors are human beings, not a fleet of robots. They have different aptitudes and interests. Those who are enthusiastic about the brand will be frustrated without a strong understanding of their role or clear management direction (Rehmet and Dinnie 2013). The risk of brand dissonance is high in party politics. Candidates and legislators may be deliberative thinkers who disagree with their party. They may feel that message consistency pushed from a capital city by the party leadership is disconnected from the grassroots and local regions (Pich, Dean, and Punjaisri 2016, 108). The potential to either enhance or damage the leader's image and the party brand means that political brand ambassadors need to be managed. They are viewed by the party leadership as both a communications vehicle and a potential threat.

The challenge for individual candidates is to reconcile their own political brand with that of their party. Brandidates are candidates with strong personal brands (Kaneva and Klemmer 2016). Brandidates exist where there is institutional flexibility to brand individual personas even when doing so clashes with the party's brand values. There must be weak party discipline or else the individual has extraordinary authority. Thus, brandidates are party leaders, members of weak opposition parties and independent candidates, and are generally more prevalent in presidential systems. They draw upon their own unique mix of attributes, personality and values to construct a public image that conveys authenticity and credibility (Guzmán and Sierra 2009; Speed, Butler, and Collins 2015). Brandidates use their personal political brand to get elected and advance their political careers. In systems with heavy party discipline, a brandidate affiliated with a major party operates within the contours of the party brand and leader's brand, and must choose between being viewed as foremost a brand ambassador or a rebel. Star candidates with a public profile and fresh faces new to the political arena will be confronted with this communications reality.

The difficulty that every aspiring politician faces in a party-centered political system is that their personal brand is indelibly connected with a party's brand (Speed, Butler, and Collins 2015, 142). Whatever is known or perceived to be true about that party brand is used to understand and/or interpret the actions of every candidate who runs under that banner (Loat and MacMillan 2014, 164). The party brand typically reflects the party's longtime ideological position, track record in government or opposition, and the interests and characteristics of current and past party leaders. Candidates are treated as soldiers on the electoral battlefield, expected to loyally parrot the party message, and must wear a party uniform of campaign materials that have a consistent look and feel. The individuality of

the party soldier is of little consequence to those in the party command center.

This type of human branding in a party-centered system puts a new
twist on age-old dilemmas of representation. On the one hand, the party
leader must have brand authority, and the ability to deliver on campaign
promises. On the other, individual representatives must have brand
authenticity, and nurture their own political persona that challenges party
positions from time-to-time (Speed, Butler, and Collins 2015). Party discipline is designed to eliminate this tension by handing message control over
to the party leader. This limits who can or wants to be affiliated with
a party.

Canada is an excellent case for exploring candidates as brand ambassadors. Leaders are selected by the membership at large and exercise considerable authority over their caucus. Discipline is so vigorous that a
governing party can pass major policies with limited caucus consultation
(Malloy 2006, 121) and even minor votes are treated as confidence motions
(Aucoin, Jarvis, and Turnbull 2011). For instance, under Prime Minister
Justin Trudeau, Liberal Members of Parliament (MPs) are required to vote
with their party on traditional confidence matters, on everything concern-
ing the party's election platform, and on all constitutionally protected civil
liberties issues. Major political parties are gatekeepers over who gets to sit
in Parliament because minor party candidates and independents are rarely
elected. Leaders wield the ultimate power of deciding whether to sign a
candidate's nomination papers, including those of an incumbent. During a
campaign, a candidate is quickly replaced if unsavory comments from
years before become public, something that opponents work to unearth.
During governance, legislators who make controversial remarks abruptly
vanish from public view, and those who vote against the party on a
whipped vote are demoted. The threshold for ejecting a sitting MP, especially a party stalwart, is considerably higher than it is for cutting ties with
a no-name candidate during the heat of a campaign. In short, the internal
conflict over brand identity and lack of buy-in for message consistency that
occurs elsewhere (e.g., Pich, Dean, and Punjaisri 2016) stands in contrast
with the brand-centric philosophy of major political parties in Canada.
Parties on the political left (McGrane 2019), political center (Nimijean
2006) and political right (Marland 2016) all follow a leader-driven brand.

DATA

To explore the role of lower-ranking politicians as brand ambassadors, we
administered in-depth interviews with 170 Canadians between 2016 and
2018. The data were collected for two separate projects. The first phase

(n = 101) was part of a project examining perceptions of political candidacy. Approximately half of those research participants are former candidates for federal, provincial, and/or municipal office. The other half were citizens identified by third-party informants as possessing the qualities and qualifications desirable in a political candidate. Participants represent a range of gender identities, racial/ethnic backgrounds, sexual orientations, and party affiliations to facilitate the development, rather than the testing, of theory regarding the challenges involved with political candidacy for different groups of citizens (Eisenhardt and Graebner 2007). The interview protocol included a question about the respondent's expectations and/or experiences with political parties: "What do (did) you think the challenges would be in terms of dealing with your preferred political party?" This question, as well as a general discussion of the benefits and drawbacks of running for elected office, provide the data for this study. MAXQDA, a qualitative data analysis software, was used to systematically code these interview transcripts and identify themes in the data.

The second phase (n = 69) was part of a project examining the intersection of party discipline and message coordination. Interviews were conducted in summer 2018 with 13 former party leaders including two past prime ministers, a sitting provincial premier, 19 sitting MPs, six former MPs, three former federal candidates, three sitting provincial politicians and 24 national-level political staff ranging from chiefs of staff to communications managers. Participants were drawn from across the country and major political parties, including some party whips. They were asked for their thoughts about party discipline and cohesion; how political parties coordinate messaging during campaigns and governance; the nature of forums where legislators and candidates can speak freely; and the implications for politicians who go off message. The concept of brand ambassador was discussed with many of them.

Interviews are ideal for exploring the interaction between political branding and party discipline because they allow research participants to provide insights into otherwise hard-to-research phenomenon (Kvale 2007). Interviews were administered in-person or by telephone for between 20 minutes to 2½ hours. Participants were recruited through a combination of purposeful sampling whereby we developed a grid and contacted people we did not personally know; convenience sampling whereby we interviewed people in our personal networks, such as those physically located close to our institutions; and snowball sampling whereby some participants and some political elites we know vouched to potential respondents on our behalf. Participants were provided with background information about the project, a consent form and a discussion guide. Approximately a quarter of people we approached declined to participate for reasons that we hypothesize include lack of interest and anxiety about disclosing internal party secrets. Almost all participants agreed to be audio recorded. Further information about the methodology is available from the authors upon request. The next section outlines research participants' perspectives on the interaction between political communication, branding and party discipline in electoral politics.

FINDINGS

In Canada, a political party's brand ambassadors convey national messages locally and relay local concerns back to the national party apparatus. Any internal politicking and lobbying are treated as private business matters. Candidates and legislators are encouraged to use digital megaphones to repeat messages of the day and generally cheer the leader. Websites and social media are platforms for engaging in democratic deliberations with constituents as long as those discussions promote the party line. Anonymity no longer exists: public remarks are monitored by party staff who practice rapid response. Loyal soldiers are rewarded with role promotions and resources; a brand ambassador who freelances is required to apologize and is ostracized by the leadership. Those whose public behavior seriously threatens the brand are dropped as candidates or evicted from the party caucus. This concept of an ambassador is in line with the concept of a party brand builder or soldier, who generally puts the party before constituents or personal conviction.

Talking about political communication with politicians and political staff in Canada quickly turns to a conversation about party discipline. It is evident that the underlying principles of that longstanding organizational philosophy permeate party politics irrespective of branding. We want to unpack to what extent branding bolsters that mentality and becomes a strategic objective in its own right. It appears to us that it is impossible to completely disentangle them: the Canadian case suggests that party discipline and party branding are now fused. Branding ranks near the top of the list of reasons evoked by senior party personnel about why candidates and legislators should toe the party line.

Proponents of party discipline make a persuasive argument when they couch their control agenda within the strategic benefits of brand strategy. There is a sense of urgency about communications cohesion. Social media, smartphones, proto-journalists and opponents practicing black arts mean that anyone with an official role in the party is a potential liability. A single individual affiliated with a political party can destabilize and damage the hard-won image of the party and the leader. From the perspective of those in the party center, candidates and legislators must be actively managed to avoid being thrust into crisis communications. Keeping them on brand is a constant priority. Likewise, many candidates and legislators are anxious that they will be on the wrong side of the social media mob. They find protection by sticking to message lines or saying nothing. Moreover, being an active brand ambassador is thought to be a route to obtain privileges and rewards from the party leadership.

Party leaders, many legislators and especially party staff are emphatic about the need for party unity. They present this in different ways. Some remark on the media turmoil that occurs without cohesion. Some insist that caucus is the place to voice concerns. Some, particularly staff as well as legislators, talk about the party brand. To them, party discipline is more of a political science and news media concept, and is terminology that is seen as too heavy handed. Instead, almost all partisans talk about the team and teamwork, with many using sports analogies to explain their approach to party politics. The leader is the coach, everyone on the team plays a contributing role, and they collectively make sacrifices in order to win as a group.

People who want to be an MP begin their transformation into a brand ambassador at the moment they apply to represent the party as a candidate. A Canadian who wishes to seek the local nomination must complete pages of paperwork and be interviewed by party officials. They must confirm in writing that they support the party's values and that they will publicly support its platform. The national party conducts a rigorous background check that encompasses criminal records to social media histories. A good-conduct monetary deposit may be required. A green-light committee determines whether there are grounds to deny participation and any serious red flags are brought to the attention of a designated national-level party official. The basis for rejecting a prospective candidate seems to revolve around whether controversy will ensue and disrupt the national campaign. The reasons are not publicly disclosed; even the rejected nominee must guess. The human resources function of internal brand management and party discipline are underway.

Aspiring candidates have some flexibility during the local nomination campaign to propose policy solutions for local issues. Participants can publicly challenge party thinking within the boundaries of their written agreement to support party principles. It is the last time that freewheeling commentary will be tolerated. Sometimes an upstart surprises the party establishment and wins the nomination over a party insider. Other times a candidate wins by acclamation, particularly in places where the party is weak or when the leader reappoints an incumbent MP as the candidate. In rare cases, the party leader may reject the local nominee, such as if new concerns emerged or there is a stated intention to ensure candidate diversity (e.g., more women, non-whites, LGBTQ). They must all publicly fall in line from this point forward. The next phase of brand management is about to begin.

A party's nominated candidates participate in campaign training schools where the leader's staff impresses the urgency of message discipline. Candidates are informed that local efforts will account for just five to 10 percent of the votes they receive; the rest will come from the national campaign, party affiliation, impressions of the leader and the overall brand. Any public deviation from the party risks distracting from communicating a national agenda that requires copious planning. Candidates learn that they are all expected to publicly support every aspect of the party platform and to keep quiet otherwise. They are told to not take public positions that contradict the leader or the party, especially under the microscope of an election campaign. They lack authority to make a local policy pledge. They must promote the platform and, on local matters, may simply promise to fight on behalf of constituents. A commitment for general advocacy projects a strong local image of representation without boxing in the party. During the campaign it is common for candidates who bring the party brand into disrepute to be quickly replaced with another candidate. Social media skeletons missed during screening and controversial new social media posts are a common culprit.

The brand mentality persists once the election campaign is over. Staying on message publicly is a means to an end that is slightly different than bloc voting in the legislature. At legislator training sessions they learn about the power and authority of the leadership, cabinet (if applicable), the house leader and the party whip. It is through constant contact with colleagues and political staff, including their own parliamentary precinct staff, that legislators are reminded about conformity. They are provided with the message of the day, receive approved messaging for national media interviews, are praised at caucus by the leader for promoting the brand, and are given talking points for committee and legislative chamber debates. Party consultants and senior communications personnel occasionally deliver caucus presentations to impress the strategic value of branding.

Once in office, politicians learn to lobby and negotiate internally, and to work with the party whip if there is a policy issue that they disagree with. During governance the shackles of message discipline are loosened slightly and the leadership team attempts to nurture a culture of brand commitment. For example, encouraging legislators to voluntarily repeat messages generate buy-in by treating them with respect, whereas ordering them around is an irritant. They are urged to voice concerns in caucus where the party leader will listen. They can and do engage in vigorous conversations with senior officeholders, such as ministers, and with their peers. But the quid pro quo is that in public they must present an image of brand symmetry. This is good for the party leader and the brand—to a point. Complicity brings a loss of authenticity and local representation. The party deals with this by asking brand ambassadors to rephrase key messages and use their own words. Moreover, as long as the party values are maintained as guiding principles, the national party is unconcerned when representatives talk publicly about local issues without obtaining clearance. As with any franchisor-franchisee relationship, there will suddenly be considerable interest if localized commentary rockets through cyberspace and becomes a national story.

The fusion of party discipline and brand strategy has implications for political recruitment and representation. Prospective candidates are aware of the electoral costs of a lack of party unity. They give considerable thought to whether they believe in the political product enough to be effective brand ambassadors. Their values must closely align with that of the political party before seeking to run for a party's nomination. A lack of strong partisan alignment keeps some individuals from entering partisan politics despite intense interest in public affairs. Sharp conflict between personal opinion and official policy makes it nearly impossible for some people to be effective party brand ambassadors. They simply do not believe enough in the political product to try to sell it to voters.

Most candidates and legislators express little philosophical difference with the party for which they chose to run. Of all the potential drawbacks to electoral politics that they list, disconnect between personal and party views is not usually one of them, though there are exceptions. On occasions when low-ranking politicians or candidates disagree with party policy, they often look at the bigger picture in terms of what is best for their community or country as a whole, or they determine to stay quiet rather than damage the party brand. Abortion is a case in point. On this contentious issue most are prepared to defer to the policy preferences of their party and, by extension, their constituents. The assumption is that the party's policy has wide public support and thus meets the expectations of representative democracy.

Racial and sexual minorities, in particular, struggle to believe in party brands they view as too narrow in focus. They are concerned their candidacies would be little more than a symbolic attempt by parties to descriptively, but not substantively, represent the country's diversity. Political parties, in their view, are preoccupied with candidates who tick off social diversity boxes in terms of gender, race, sexuality, and disability. The parties display far less interest in incorporating into the party platform the perspectives, values and interests of these candidates or the social groups they represent. Racial and sexual minorities are reluctant to become candidates and, by extension, brand ambassadors for a political party they view as non-responsive to the interests of their respective communities.

A one-size-fits all approach to party messaging creates additional difficulties for minority candidates who run in ethnically diverse ridings. In these cases, there is a desire to highlight aspects of the candidate's background that might appeal to different voters, and to downplay those that do not. Voters in one neighborhood might be responsive to a candidate's racial identity, while voters in another might be more receptive to their LGBTQ activism. Minority candidates want greater freedom to speak independently during an election so they can address the interests of different groups of voters in their riding. To achieve brand authenticity, minority candidates believe their racial/ethnic identities and sexual orientations must be reflected in their campaign communications, but only when appropriate. The need for parties to maintain message control and tout the diversity of their candidates, however, limits minorities' opportunity for individual expression and ability to develop their own political brand.

Still, all types of low-ranking politicians have reservations about the strict message discipline expected by political parties. Those who dare to express dissenting viewpoints can see their political careers stalled or shortened. Nominations are denied, plum committee assignments are withdrawn, and cabinet positions never materialize. Strict message discipline limits what they can say in public and stymies efforts to promote their policy agenda within the party. Low-ranking politicians have no room to maneuver during an election campaign because winning votes requires uniformity. The pervasiveness of brand discipline means that finding another party is rarely a viable solution to these representation tensions.

CONCLUSIONS

Party branding has considerable implications for representative democracy. This extends beyond the competition among party leaders or the number of voters who have a psychological attachment to a party label. We need to look at election candidates and legislators to understand the downmarket effects of the high-level dynamics of party branding.

We have reviewed the benefits and pitfalls of party branding, paying particular attention to the parliamentary system, using Canada as a case study. Among the most potent consequences of party branding for political discourse and representation is stiffening partisanship. The dominance of the party's and leader's brands is particularly acute in the presence of strong party discipline. The party's need to promote a unified brand turns low-ranking politicians into partisan cheerleaders who must enthusiastically support the leader and party policy at every turn. The power of the party leader's inner sanctum increases for reasons that include its vetting of candidates, requiring written statements of agreement with the party, offering and withholding rewards, and encouraging an organizational ethos of deference to those at the top.

When enough parties take this brand orientation to politics, the result is a political arena comprised of a few teams competing for electoral victory and a restriction of policy debate in their own tribe to closed-door sessions. Political parties become gatekeepers over who gets to sit in a legislature that is devoid of representatives willing to challenge the party line. As scripted messengers, candidates and legislators have little wiggle room to espouse views that deviate from party policy, severely constraining political debate. The media characterization of democratic institutions is one of party elites running the show and elected representatives doing their bidding.

Candidates and legislators learn that they are franchisees of a corporate party identity. There is limited opportunity in a brand-centric parliamentary system for politicians who want to have their own public personas and respond to local market conditions. They are welcome to brand themselves as representatives who will listen to their constituents and fight for their interests. But that is as far as most franchisees dare go. In an environment of strict party discipline, a politician takes a risk by publicly challenging the party line. That individual is conditioned to be a brand ambassador.

Party discipline, especially over party policy and campaign messaging, has a dampening effect on political candidacy. Individuals who do not believe they can be successful brand ambassadors either stay behind the scenes as party volunteers or opt not to get involved in partisan politics at all. From the party's perspective, such self-selection is a positive consequence of party branding, because individuals who come forward are more likely to believe in the party brand. This makes them more effective brand ambassadors. The resulting party cohesion makes it easier for the leader to make, and deliver on, election promises to voters. Democracy benefits from fewer bad apples who drag down the party brand because of improper behavior. Candidates and legislators benefit from support materials, and they are better prepared to avoid being drawn into controversy. Voters receive information that improves their ability to make clear choices.

Yet, in terms of representative democracy, there are some downsides to party branding and the pressures to conform. Prospective candidates who want to challenge norms embedded in political institutions, processes and policy will have to do so in private settings. A party machine churning out messages that are repeated by brand ambassadors creates an ominous recruitment barrier for free thinkers. Individuals who vary from institutional norms in terms of gender, racial identity, and sexual orientation can find it harder to be effective party brand ambassadors if the leader and/or party platform does not take seriously the interests of diverse communities. These types of individuals might be particularly frustrated by their inability to adapt the party message to suit their personal and political values. If our

Canadian data are any indication, citizens in democratic systems with strict party discipline who want to be a member of a legislative assembly are increasingly faced with becoming a scripted messenger who does the bidding of those at the top of a brand-oriented party hierarchy.

Over time and space, politicians worldwide navigate the pressures of representing an array of competing interests by leaning on their preferred representational style. In liberal democracies, candidates and elected representatives invariably face a difficult conundrum when national, local, personal and/or party interests collide. For some of them, particularly in parliamentary systems where the party brand is a dominant force, the pressures of representing party interests may prevail. A brand-centric environment has profound implications for representation when lower-ranking politicians are expected to advocate in private and to publicly repeat party messaging. Comparative research is needed to understand the existence of brand ambassadors in other countries and to ascertain to what extent party discipline is emboldened by branding.

ACKNOWLEDGEMENTS

The authors wish to thank the interview participants who made this research possible.

ORCID

Angelia Wagner ⓘ http://orcid.org/0000-0003-0978-1045

REFERENCES

Al-Shuaibi, Ahmad Said Ibrahim, Faridahwati Mohd Shamsudin, and Norzalita Abd Aziz. 2016. "Developing Brand Ambassadors: The Role of Brand-Centred Human Resource Management." *International Review of Management and Marketing* 6 (S7):155–61.

Aucoin, Peter, Mark Jarvis, and Lori Turnbull. 2011. *Democratizing the Constitution: Reforming Responsible Government*. Toronto: Emond Publishing.

Beckwith, Karen. 2007. "Numbers and Newness: The Descriptive and Substantive Representation of Women." *Canadian Journal of Political Science* 40 (1): 27–49. doi: 10.1017/S0008423907070059.

Bernhard, William, and Tracy Sulkin. 2018. *Legislative Style*. Chicago: University of Chicago Press.

Bertilsson, Jon, and Jens Rennstam. 2018. "The Destructive Side of Branding: A Heuristic Model for Analyzing the Value of Branding Practice." *Organization* 25 (2):260–81. doi: 10.1177/1350508417712431.

Bowler, Shaun, and Gail McElroy. 2015. "Political Group Cohesion and 'Hurrah' Voting in the European Parliament." *Journal of European Public Policy* 22 (9): 1355–65. doi: 10.1080/13501763.2015.1048704.

Cain, Bruce, John Frejohn, and Morris Fiorina. 1987. *The Personal Vote: Constituency Service and Electoral Independence*. Cambridge: Harvard University Press.

Carnes, Nicholas. 2018. *The Cash Ceiling: Why Only the Rich Run for Office — and What We Can Do about It*. Princeton, NJ: Princeton University Press.

Carrubba, Clifford, Matthew Gabel, and Simon Hug. 2008. "Legislative Voting Behavior, Seen and Unseen: A Theory of Roll-Call Vote Selection." *Legislative Studies Quarterly* 33 (4):543–72. https://www.jstor.org/stable/40263475 doi: 10.3162/036298008786403079.

Carty, R. Kenneth. 2002. "The Politics of Tecumseh Corners: Canadian Political Parties as Franchise Organizations." *Canadian Journal of Political Science* 35 (4):723–45. doi: 10.1017/S0008423902778402.

Carty, R. Kenneth. 2004. "Parties as Franchise Systems: The Stratarchical Organizational Imperative." *Party Politics* 10 (1):5–24. doi: 10.1177/1354068804039118.

Childs, Sarah, and Mona Lena Krook. 2009. "Analysing Women's Substantive Representation: From Critical Mass to Critical Actors." *Government and Opposition* 44 (2):125–45. doi: 10.1111/j.1477-7053.2009.01279.x.

Crouch, Roberta, Michael Ewer, Pascale Quester, and Michael Proksch. 2016. "Talking with You—Not at You: How Brand Ambassadors Can Spark Consumer Brand Attachment?" In *Marketing Challenges in a Turbulent Business Environment*, edited by Mark D. Groza and Charles B. Ragland, 189–94. New York: Springer.

Downs, Anthony. 1957. *An Economic Theory of Democracy*. New York: Harper & Row.

Eisenhardt, Kathleen M., and Melissa E. Graebner. 2007. "Theory Building from Cases: Opportunities and Challenges." *The Academy of Management Journal* 50 (1):25–32. doi: 10.5465/amj.2007.24160888.

Eshuis, Jasper, and Erik-Hans Klijn. 2012. *Branding in Governance and Public Management*. New York: Routledge.

Eulau, Heinz, John C. Wahlke, William Buchanan, and Leroy C. Ferguson. 1959. "The Role of the Representative: Some Empirical Observations on the Theory of Edmund Burke." *The American Political Science Review* 53 (3):742–56. doi: 10.2307/1951941.

Fenno, Richard F. 1978. *Home Style: House Members in Their Districts*. Boston: Little, Brown.

Fisher-Buttinger, Claudia, and Christine Vallaster. 2008. "Brand Ambassadors: Strategic Diplomats or Tactical Promoters?" In *Marketing Metaphors and Metamorphosis*, edited by Philip J. Kitchen, 132–45. New York: Palgrave Macmillan.

Freelon, Deen. 2017. "Campaigns in Control: Analyzing Controlled Interactivity and Message Discipline on Facebook." *Journal of Information Technology & Politics* 14 (2):168–81. doi: 10.1080/19331681.2017.1309309.

Gulati, Girish J. 2004. "Members of Congress and Presentation of Self on the World Wide Web." Harvard International Journal of Press/Politics 9 (1):22–40. doi: 10.1177/1081180X03259758.

Guzmán, Francisco, and Vicenta Sierra. 2009. "A Political Candidate's Brand Image Scale: Are Political Candidates Brands?" *Journal of Brand Management* 17 (3): 207–17. doi: 10.1057/bm.2009.19.

Haider-Markel, Donald P. 2010. *Out and Running: Gay and Lesbian Candidates, Elections, and Policy Representation.* Washington: Georgetown University Press.

Jackson, Robert J. 1968. *Rebels and Whips: Dissension, Discipline and Cohesion in British Political Parties since 1945.* London: MacMillan and Co.

Jones, Helen. 2016. *How to be a Government Whip.* London, UK: Biteback Publishing.

Kam, Christopher J. 2009. *Party Discipline and Parliamentary Politics.* Cambridge: Cambridge University Press.

Kaneva, Nadia, and Austin Klemmer. 2016. "The Rise of Brandidates? A Cultural Perspective on Political Candidate Brands in Postmodern Consumer Democracies." *Journal of Customer Behaviour* 15 (3):299–313. doi: 10.1362/147539216X14594362874054.

Karlsen, Rune, and Eli Skogerbø. 2015. "Candidate Campaigning in Parliamentary Systems: Individualized vs. Localized Campaigning." *Party Politics* 21 (3): 428–39. doi: 10.1177/1354068813487103.

Karlsson, David. 2013. "Who Do the Local Councillors of Europe Represent?" In *Local Councillors in Europe*, edited by Björn Egner, David Sweeting and Pieter-Jan Klok, 97–119. Berlin: Springer. doi: 10.1007/978-3-658-01857-3_6.

King, Ceridwyn, Debra Grace, and Scott Weaven. 2013. "Developing Brand Champions: A Franchisee Perspective." *Journal of Marketing Management* 29 (11–12):1308–36. doi: 10.1080/0267257X.2013.796322.

Klein, Naomi. 2000. *No Logo.* London: HarperCollins.

Kvale, Steinar. 2007. *Doing Interviews.* Los Angeles: Sage.

Lilleker, Darren. 2015. "Interactivity and Branding: Public Political Communication as a Marketing Tool." *Journal of Political Marketing* 14 (1–2):111–28. doi: 10.1080/15377857.2014.990841.

Loat, Alison, and Michael MacMillan. 2014. *Tragedy in the Commons: Former Members of Parliament Speak out about Canada's Failing Democracy.* Toronto: Vintage Canada.

Löhndorf, Birgit, and Adamantios Diamantopoulos. 2014. "Internal Branding: Social Identity and Social Exchange Perspectives on Turning Employees into Brand Champions." *Journal of Service Research* 17 (3):310–25. doi: 10.1177/1094670514522098.

Malloy, Jonathan. 2006. "High Discipline, Low Cohesion? the Uncertain Patterns of Canadian Parliamentary Party Groups." In *Cohesion and Discipline in Legislatures*, edited by Reuven Y. Hazan, 116–29. New York: Routledge.

Mansbridge, Jane. 1999. "Should Blacks Represent Blacks and Women Represent Women? A Contingent 'Yes." *Journal of Politics* 61 (3):627–57. doi: 10.2307/2647821.

Marland, Alex. 2003. "Marketing Political Soap: A Political Marketing View of Selling Candidates like Soap, of Electioneering as a Ritual, and of Electoral Military Analogies." *Journal of Public Affairs* 3 (2):103–15. doi: 10.1002/pa.139.

Marland, Alex. 2016. *Brand Command: Canadian Politics and Democracy in an Age of Message Control*. Vancouver: UBC Press.

Marsh, David, and Paul Fawcett. 2011. "Branding, Politics and Democracy." *Policy Studies* 32 (5):515–30. doi: 10.1080/01442872.2011.586498.

McGrane, David. 2019. *The New NDP: Moderation, Modernization, and Political Marketing*. Vancouver: University of British Columbia Press.

Men, Linjuan Rita. 2014. "Strategic Internal Communication: Transformational Leadership, Communication Channels, and Employee Satisfaction." *Management Communication Quarterly* 28 (2):264–84. doi: 10.1177/0893318914524536.

Morhart, Felicitas M., Walter Herzog, and Torsten Tomczak. 2009. "Brand-Specific Leadership: Turning Employees into Brand Champions." *Journal of Marketing* 73 (5):122–42. doi: 10.1509/jmkg.73.5.122.

Needham, Catherine. 2005. "Brand Leaders: Clinton, Blair and the Limitations of the Permanent Campaign." *Political Studies* 53 (2):343–61. doi: 10.1111/j.1467-9248.2005.00532.x.

Nimijean, Richard. 2006. "Brand Canada: The Brand State and the Decline of the Liberal Party." *Inroads* 19:84–93.

Och, Malliga and Shauna L. Shames, editors. 2018. *The Right Women: Republican Party Activists, Candidates, and Legislators*. Santa Barbara, CA: Praeger.

Olson, David M. 2003. "Cohesion and Discipline Revisited: Contingent Unity in the Parliamentary Party Group." *The Journal of Legislative Studies* 9 (4):164–78. doi: 10.1080/1357233042000306326.

O'Shaughnessy, Nicholas. 2009. "Selling Hitler: Propaganda and the Nazi Brand." *Journal of Public Affairs* 9 (1):55–76. doi: 10.1002/pa.312.

Pich, Christopher, Dianne Dean, and Khanyapuss Punjaisri. 2016. "Political Brand Identity: An Examination of the Complexities of Conservative Brand and Internal Market Engagement during the 2010 UK General Election Campaign." *Journal of Marketing Communications* 22 (1):100–17. doi: 10.1080/13527266.2013.864321.

Pitkin, Hanna F. 1967. *The Concept of Representation*. Berkeley: University of California Press.

Rehmet, Jonas, and Keith Dinnie. 2013. "Citizen Brand Ambassadors: Motivations and Perceived Effects." *Journal of Destination Marketing & Management* 2 (1):31–8. doi: 10.1016/j.jdmm.2013.02.001.

Scammell, Margaret. 2001. "The Media and Media Management." In *The Blair Effect*, edited by Anthony Seldon, 509–34. London: Little, Brown and Company.

Scammell, Margaret. 2015. "Politics and Image: The Conceptual Value of Branding." *Journal of Political Marketing* 14 (1–2):7–18. doi: 10.1080/15377857.2014.990829.

Shane, Scott A. 1998. "Making New Franchise Systems Work." *Strategic Management Journal* 19 (7):697–707. doi: 10.1002/(SICI)1097-0266(199807)19:7<697::AID-SMJ972>3.0.CO;2-O.

Speed, Richard, Patrick Butler, and Neil Collins. 2015. "Human Branding in Political Marketing: Applying Contemporary Branding Thought to Political Parties and Their Leaders." *Journal of Political Marketing* 14 (1–2):129–51. doi: 10.1080/15377857.2014.990833.

Trimble, Linda. 2008. "Assembling Women, Gendering Assemblies." In *Gendering the Nation-State: Canadian and Comparative Perspectives*, edited by Yasmeen Abu-Laban, 79–96. Vancouver: UBC Press.

Vallaster, Christine, and Leslie de Chernatony. 2005. "Internationalization of Services Brands: The Role of Leadership during the Internal Brand Building Process." *Journal of Marketing Management* 21 (1–2):181–203. doi: 10.1362/0267257053166839.

Xiong, Lina, Ceridwyn King, and Rico Piehler. 2013. "That's Not My Job': Exploring the Employee Perspective in the Development of Brand Ambassadors." *International Journal of Hospitality Management* 35:348–59. doi: 10.1016/j.ijhm.2013.07.009.

Exploring Personal Political Brands of Iceland's Parliamentarians

GUJA ARMANNSDOTTIR, STUART CARNELL AND
CHRISTOPHER PICH

This paper focuses on an under-researched and under-developed typology of political branding and conceptualizes politicians as personal political brands. *Further, this study answers explicit calls for more research devoted to exploring the development of intended brand identity particularly from a brand creator perspective. Members of Parliament from the Republic of Iceland contextualizes this study. This qualitative case-study approach reveals how personal political brands create, construct and communicate their identity. Personal political brand identities were established and managed via a clear brand mantra and offline-online communication tools, which in turn revealed a degree of alignment with their party-political brand. However, this paper also demonstrates the challenges of managing the identities of personal political brands in terms of authenticity and integration particularly with coalition partners. Our paper builds on the six-staged analytical process of personal branding and proposes the* Personal Political Brand Identity Appraisal Framework *as an operational tool to introspectively evaluate personal political brand identity. This framework can be used by political actors across different settings and contexts to assess personal political brands from multiple perspectives.*

INTRODUCTION

In its simplest form, political marketing can be defined as the application of commercial marketing concepts, activities and frameworks to the political setting (Hughes and Dann 2009; Jain *et al.* 2018; Schofield and Reeves 2015). Political parties, politicians, prospective candidates, political institutions such as lobbyists and campaigners utilize commercial marketing techniques and tools to communicate, engage and build long-term relationships with citizens (Billard 2018; Harris and Lock 2010; Kornum and Muhlbacher 2013; Speed *et al.* 2015). Nevertheless, political marketing has evolved significantly as an international niche area of commercial marketing since the seminal work of Lock and Harris (1996). Indeed, political marketing represents a hybrid sub-discipline home to many specialized factions of study (Hughes and Dann 2009; Harris and Lock 2010; Marder *et al.* 2018). However, despite progress made within the political marketing area, more empirical understanding is needed as this will allow the sub-discipline to advance and continue to develop (Harris and Lock 2010; Hughes and Dann 2009; Jain *et al.* 2018; Needham and Smith 2015). Political marketing can only develop if it continues to apply new concepts or reapply advanced theories and frameworks (Nielsen 2016; Scammell 2015; Speed *et al.* 2015).

One well-documented faction of political marketing is the construct of political branding (Marder *et al.* 2018; Speed *et al.* 2015). However, political branding research remains under-researched (Harris and Lock 2010; Lock and Harris 1996; Moufahim *et al.* 2018; Nielsen 2016; Scammell 2015), particularly the internal orientation and intentional, desired positioning otherwise known as *political brand identity*. Existing studies that have tended to focus on the identity of 'party' political brands rather than that of politicians (French and Smith 2010; Lees-Marshment 2001; Lees 2005; Nord and Stromback 2009; O'Cass 2001; Ormrod 2007; Pich and Dean 2015). Further, framing politicians as 'personal brands' allows us to explore the manifestations of intended identities, combined of personal characteristics such as personality traits, experiences feelings, beliefs and personal values (Jain *et al.* 2018; Johnson 2014; Rampersad 2008; Resnick *et al.* 2016), which up until now remained an under-developed research area. This study will not only address the explicit calls for further research in this area, but will also assist political entities to understand their desired identity and make adaptions if required (Baines and Harris 2011; Dann *et al.* 2007; Grimmer and Grube 2017; Ormrod 2011; Ormrod 2007; Panigyrakis and Altinay 2017).

In this paper, we explore the creation and management of personal political brand identity particularly from the perspective of the brand's creators. Further, this will be achieved by bridging two streams of commercial branding theory such as *personal branding* and *brand identity*. More specifically, this study will investigate the creation and management of personal political brand identity by building on the six-staged personal brand auditing framework (Philbrick and Cleveland 2015) to examine the personal political brand identities of politicians from an internal brand-creator perspective. This will address the explicit calls for further research on the internal perspective of political brands, which in turn will extend an under-developed area of political branding (Billard 2018; Harris and Lock 2010; Needham and Smith 2015; Nielsen 2015; Nielsen 2016; O'Cass and Voola 2011; Panigyrakis and Altinay 2017; Scammell 2015; Serazio 2017; Speed *et al.* 2015). First, we discuss the background of political branding research. Then, discussions on internal brand identity, personal branding and personal political brand identity; further research with these concepts in the political context is then highlighted. The findings highlight applicability of the personal brand auditing framework to investigate personal brand identities. Further findings demonstrated that while both personal brands are authentic and clear, there is scope for refinement. This research concludes by identifying further research opportunities in the area of political branding and offers a revised framework to audit-assess personal political brand identity of politician brands.

POLITICAL BRANDS

Political brands are complicated entities (Billard 2018; Lees-Marshment 2009; Lock and Harris 1996; Phipps *et al.* 2010). Further, there are various manifestations of political brands such as political parties, party leaders, pressure groups, politicians, political campaigns and even nations can be conceptualized as brands (Guzmán et al. 2015; Jain *et al.* 2018; Needham and Smith 2015; Peng and Hackley 2009; Smith 2009). Existing research in this specialized area highlights the diversity of political branding research (Bale 2008; Grimmer and Grube 2017; Needham and Smith 2015; Serazio 2017). For example, existing research has focused on party political brands (French and Smith 2010; Grimmer and Grube 2017; Milewicz and Milewicz 2014), human-politician brands (Billard 2018; Davies and Mian 2010; Guzmán et al. 2015; Jain *et al.* 2018), cultural political branding (Smith and Speed 2011), development of new political brands (Panigyrakis and Altinay 2017; Busby and Cronshaw 2015; Nord and Stromback 2009), political brand identity (Pich *et al.* 2018), and political brand image (Guzman and Sierra 2009; Smith 2001). In addition, existing studies have investigated political brand equity (Phipps *et al.* 2010; Smith and Spotswood 2015), political brand personality (Guzmán et al. 2015; Jain *et al.* 2018; Smith 2009), psychological profiling of politicians (de Landtsheer and de Vries 2015) and political brand positioning (Cwalina and Falkowski 2014; Smith 2005) across western (Billard 2018; Marland and Flanagan 2013) and eastern jurisdictions (Grimmer and Grube 2017; Jain *et al.* 2018). However, despite the advancements in political branding research, there are still many areas that continue to be under-researched and under-developed, which makes political branding a *"critical and priority issue"* for further research (Needham and Smith 2015; O'Cass and Voola 2011; Speed *et al.* 2015:130).

One area that seems under-developed is the notion of how to investigate political brands predominantly from the perspective of the brand's creator. More specifically, existing research devoted to an internal brand-creator perspective directs its attention to the political party or politician (Busby and Cronshaw 2015; Cwalina and Falkowski 2014; de Landtsheer and de Vries 2015; Milewicz and Milewicz 2014; Smith and Spotswood 2015). However, very few studies with an internal focus manage to achieve a truly internal perspective. This paucity of research is supported by calls for further exploratory research particularly focused on different typologies of political brands (Billard 2018; Jain *et al.* 2018; Panigyrakis and Altinay 2017; Pich *et al.* 2018; Serazio 2017). Indeed, the majority of these studies practise content or discourse analysis of speeches and published articles rather than 'first-hand insight' from the personal standpoint of the political party or politician (Busby and Cronshaw 2015; Cwalina and Falkowski 2014; de Landtsheer and de Vries 2015; Milewicz and Milewicz 2014; Smith and Spotswood 2015). It is unknown whether this is down to difficulties securing access to political stakeholders or their preferred method. However, Pich *et al.* (2018) is one exception. Pich *et al.* (2018) explored the creation, orientation and demise of a new political 'party' brand from the perspective of the party leader. Their study found new party brands face many challenges particularly barriers from the media and existing political system and difficulties with managing and a national-local campaign. In addition, Pich *et al.* (2018) provided a first-hand account of how difficult it was to build a party brand particularly from self-funding, non-existent ideology, policy and absence of a support base. Pich *et al.* (2018) concluded future political branding research should devote attention to the exploration of the design and management of other typologies of political brands such as politician brands and investigate the relationship with the 'party' political brand from an internal brand-creator perspective. Therefore, the exploration of the development and management of politician political brands from an internal brand-creator standpoint will not only provide deep insight and first-hand accounts but also extend this under-developed area of political branding (Billard 2018; Jain *et al.* 2018; Needham and Smith 2015; O'Cass and Voola 2011; Panigyrakis and Altinay 2017; Pich *et al.* 2018; Scammell 2015; Serazio 2017; Speed *et al.* 2015). However, in order to investigate politician political brands from an internal perspective the concept of *brand identity* will serve as an appropriate theoretical lens to frame the exploration.

POLITICAL BRAND IDENTITY

Brand identity can be conceptualized as the desired perceptions and associations created and communicated by the brand's internal creators and conveys what the brand stands for (Aaker and Joachimsthaler 2002; Aqeel *et al.* 2017; de Chernatony 2007). Further, brand identity signifies an organization's current and envisaged reality (Baumgarth 2018; Nandan 2005). Similarly, Bosch *et al.* (2006) proposed brand identity as the preferred associations and aspired values developed by a brand's creator and focuses on the "*central ideas of a brand and how the brand communicates these ideas to stakeholders*" (de Chernatony 2007:45). In addition, brand identity is all about vision, values and aspiration (Dahlen *et al.* 2010; Gylling and Lindberg-Repo 2006; Ronzoni *et al.* 2018). Indeed, brand identity continues to gain "*worldwide recognition*" and acceptance in academia and industry (Kapferer 2008:171). Thus, brand identity is an internally created manifestation created and developed through *physical properties* such as communication tools and relationships and *intangible properties* such as actual and desired positioning, core beliefs and a brand's heritage. Brand identity has to be consistent and durable yet adaptable and ready to change depending on changes/crises in the internal and external environment (Alsem and Kostelijk 2008; Aqeel *et al.* 2017; Dahlen *et al.* 2010; Gylling and Lindberg-Repo 2006). Therefore, brand identity is a key approach to strengthening and building a brand (Aaker 1996).

Nevertheless, "*the principle task of uncovering identity is exploration*" (Bronn *et al.* 2006:889). This will reveal what the brand stands for and uncovers the brand's aspirations but will also highlight any inconsistencies or challenges with the brand (Baumgarth 2018; Nandan 2005). Once the current-envisaged identity is understood, the brand's creator can adapt or refine the tangible and intangible touchpoints to address any inconsistencies or misalignment. However, there is a paucity of research on the exploration of political brand identity. The few studies that have focused on the internal orientation or identity of political brands [identity] have tended to focus on three broad areas. This includes the investigation of 'party' political brand identity, the business-orientation of 'party' brands or the applicability of brand identity-personality-equity models to the context of 'party' brands (French and Smith 2010; Grimmer and Grube 2017; Jain *et al.* 2018; Lees-Marshment 2001; Lees 2005; Nord and Stromback 2009; O'Cass 2001; Ormrod 2007; Pich and Dean 2015; Pich *et al.* 2018). This suggests there is very little research dedicated to the exploration of the identity of politician political brands particularly from the standpoint of the brand-creator. This would address the explicit calls for further research on the internal perspective of political brands (Billard 2018; Jain *et al.* 2018; Needham and Smith 2015; O'Cass and Voola 2011; Pich *et al.* 2018; Scammell 2015; Serazio 2017; Speed *et al.* 2015). This in turn would allow the discipline of political branding to advance as a specialized area of study (Harris and Lock 2010; Needham and Smith 2015; Nielsen 2015; Nielsen 2016; O'Cass and Voola 2011; Panigyrakis and Altinay 2017; Scammell 2015). However, how can we conceptualize the political brands of politicians and investigate their internal identity? Perhaps the theory of *personal branding* will help conceptualize politician political brands and highlight how we can examine or audit political brands.

PERSONAL POLITICAL BRAND IDENTITY

In its simplest form, personal branding can be defined as the application of traditional branding concepts and frameworks to *people* (Chen 2013). Indeed, personal branding has been described as a '*process by which an individual actively tries to manage others' impressions of their skills, abilities and experiences*' (Johnson 2014:2). In addition, personal branding is strategically employed by celebrities, sports personalities, journalists, business leaders, entrepreneurs, students and politicians as a strategy to project an authentic character, which is distinct from rivals and competitors (Chen 2013; Cortsen 2013; Gehl 2011; Lair *et al.* 2005; Ottovordemgentschenfelde 2017). Further, personal brands are manifestations of intended identities, perceptions combining personal characteristics such as personality traits, experiences, feelings, beliefs and personal values (Johnson 2014; Rampersad 2008; Resnick *et al.* 2016).

Personal brands are structured around *tangible* dimensions such as physical appearance, style, online and offline communications and actions-activities, and also *intangible* dimensions such as lived experiences, life-stories, values, charisma and apparent authenticity and authority (Chen 2013; Gehl 2011; Green 2016). Personal branding can trace its origins to self-identity research developed in the 1940s as a method to express individuality (Philbrick and Cleveland 2015). The practice of personal branding was then 'popularised' by Peters (1997) in his seminal study entitled 'The Brand Called You' which argued the strategy could and should be utilized by everyone beyond the world of business, entertainment and politics (Chen 2013; Lair *et al.* 2005; Marland 2016; Philbrick and Cleveland 2015). Indeed, Shepherd (2005) argued that personal branding is an inside-out process and brands should routinely take stock or audit the current and intended identity. The importance of conducting a personal brand audit or assessment is similar to the work of Philbrick and Cleveland (2015) who

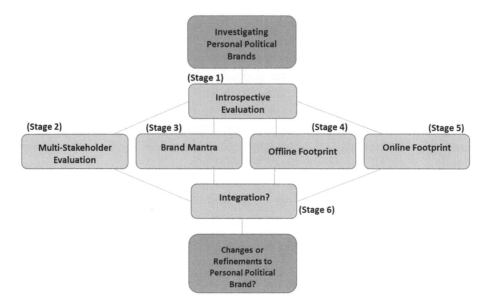

FIGURE 1. Six stages of evaluating personal political brands developed from Philbrick and Cleveland (2015).

outline a six-stage approach to assessing personal brands. This has been developed to consider a 'personal political brand' as outlined in Figure 1.

Stage one focuses on the first stage of the auditing process [introspective evaluation] whereby the personal political brand attempts to understand their current and desired position and ideology. Once this has been uncovered, the second stage where individuals take time to assess the current understanding of their personal brand from the perspective of multiple stakeholders. Stage three involves ascertaining whether the personal political brand has a clear, unique mantra that signifies a consistent vision. If not, this can be created as part of the brand's development. Stage four focuses on investigating the current and desired physical or offline footprint [communicative tools] to develop an intended identity. Stage five focuses on exploring the current digital presence or footprint used by the personal political brand. Finally, stage six involves assessing whether all the stages are integrated or aligned. If not, the politician can develop a strategic plan to refine their brand and ensure closer alignment and consistency with all communicative touch-points and projecting the updated personal brand to the target market (Philbrick and Cleveland 2015). Subsequently, a common theme seems to be present across the personal branding literature namely the significance of conducting periodic audits to assess a personal brand's current identity from an internal standpoint, which will help refine or reconstruct an envisaged identity (Brooks and Anumudu 2016; Philbrick and Cleveland 2015; Shepherd 2005). In addition, the existing literature argues that it is vital for personal brands to monitor their target market, competitors and communicative tactics in order to build long-term relationships with multiple audiences (Shepherd 2005; Ward and Yates 2013).

Nevertheless, personal branding has been extended to various disciplines and subject areas such as self-help management, employability, marketing-communications, entrepreneurship, health sector (Gehl 2011; Green 2016; Harris and Rae 2011; Johnson 2014; Lair *et al.* 2005; Philbrick and Cleveland 2015; Resnick *et al.* 2016; Shepherd 2005; Thompson-Whiteside *et al.* 2017). However, the strategy is challenging and often misunderstood due to the various interpretations of this subject area (Chen 2013; Thompson-Whiteside et al. 2017). For example, personal branding [and personal brands] are often interchangeably referred to as 'self-branding', 'self-marketing', 'self-promotion', 'human-branding', 'self-presentation', 'narrative identity', 'image-management and 'impression management' (Brooks and Anumudu 2016; Chen 2013; Marland 2016; Marwick and Boyd 2011; Resnick *et al.* 2016; Shepherd 2005; Speed *et al.* 2015). Therefore, personal branding remains a contested strategy across academia, thus it is not surprising that there is no universal definition ascribed to personal brands (Marland 2016). Subsequently, this study will build on the work of Philbrick and Cleveland (2015) and utilize the six-staged framework (Figure 1) to assess and audit the personal political brand identities of politicians from an internal brand-creator perspective. The aim of this study is to investigate the personal brand identities of two Icelandic Members of Parliament from an internal perspective. The justification for focusing on the context of Iceland will be discussed in the next section. Nevertheless, the objectives are to explore the personal brand identity of members of the Icelandic Parliament from an internal perspective; compare the personal brand identities of Iceland's political brands and to assess the usability of the Personal brand auditing framework as a tool to understand and manage personal political brands. The first-hand accounts will provide deep insight into how internal brand identity of personal political brands is created and managed, which in turn will address the explicit calls for further research on the internal perspective of political brands (Harris and Lock 2010; Needham and Smith 2015; Nielsen 2015; Nielsen 2016; O'Cass and Voola 2011; Scammell 2015). This will also extend an under-developed area of political branding (Needham and Smith 2015; O'Cass and Voola 2011; Scammell 2015; Speed *et al.* 2015).

METHODOLOGY

This study adopted a qualitative case-study approach to investigate how two politicians create, construct and communicate their political personal brand. Qualitative research was chosen as it aims to build an extensive picture of respondents' background, their feelings and experiences to address the research objectives (Schutt 2004; Warren and Karner 2005). In addition, qualitative research can also be helpful for new or under-researched areas of study (Davies and Chun 2002). A case study approach can be seen as *"an empirical inquiry that investigates a contemporary phenomenon in depth and within its real-life context, especially when the boundaries between phenomenon and context are not clearly evident"* (Yin 2009: 18). Indeed, a case study approach is recognized for its capability to reflect a single or complex research problem and is particularly beneficial when addressing how and why questions (Baxter and Jack, 2008). Further, case studies can focus on an individual, organization, campaign or even location (Lincoln and Guba 1985; Welch *et al.* 2011; Yin 2018). In order to contextualize this study, the *Republic of Iceland* was selected to frame the discussion, which in turn represented an under-researched setting worthy of further research (Nord and Stromback 2009; O'Cass 2001; Ormrod 2007; Pich *et al.* 2018).

Icelandic politics has been rocked by a succession of financial scandals (Henley, 2018), which resulted in Icelandic General Elections contested in 2013, 2016 and 2017 instead of every four years. The sporadic number of General Elections in a short space of time changed the character of the Icelandic Parliament with the appointment of newly elected parliamentarians representing half of the number of seats within parliament (Magnúsdóttir, 2017). Therefore, this paper adopted a purposive sampling approach. Purposive sampling can considered an appropriate sampling technique as this paper had a specific purpose to explore how internal brand identity of personal political brands is created and managed from an internal brand-creator perspective (Alston and Bowles 2007; Zikmund 2003). Iceland is divided into six parliamentary constituencies. Initially, six prospective participants, one from each constituency were emailed via the online parliamentary website with a view to take part in the study. This resulted in two declines, two non-responses and two acceptances. Therefore, as case studies can focus can on individuals (Lincoln and Guba 1985; Welch *et al.* 2011; Yin 2018), two Members of the Icelandic Parliament served as the sample of this study. A profile of each case is set out in Table 1.

The two politicians were both relatively new to the Icelandic Parliament. For example, case one was elected in 2013 for the *Progressive Party*, a centre-right and agrarian party founded in 1916 and currently part of the ruling coalition government (Bergqvist 1999; Wolfram 2017). Case two was elected in 2016 for the *Independence Party*, a liberal-conservative Eurosceptic party founded in 1929, currently the largest party and leading coalition partner in the Icelandic Parliament (Joakim 2006; Wolfram 2017).

TABLE 1. Parliamentary information on the two cases.

Case 1 *Þórunn Egilssdóttir*	Case 2 *Áslaug Arna Sigurbjörnsdóttir*

MP for Progressive Party Member of Althingi for the Northeast Constituency since 2013. In coalition government with the Independence party and Left-Green party since 2017 Deputy Speaker of Althingi since 2015. Chairman of the parliamentary group of the Progressive Party since 2016 and 2015. Member of the Constitutional and Supervisory Committee since 2017. Deputy Chairman of the Icelandic delegation to the West Nordic Council since 2017.	MP for the Independence Party Member of Althingi for the Reykjavík North Constituency since 2016 In coalition government with the Progressive party and Left-Green party since 2017 Deputy Chairman of the parliamentary group of the Independence Party since 2017 Chairman of the Foreign Affairs Committee since 2017. Chairman of the Icelandic delegation to the Inter-Parliamentary Union (IPU) since 2017. Member of the EU-Iceland joint Parliamentary Committee since 2018.

Source: (Althingi 2018a, 2018b).

Therefore, both cases continue to develop their brands in a dynamic, complex market and these first-hand accounts would provide deep insight into the creation and management of intentional identity. This in turn support calls for further research to investigate political brands from an internal perspective (Harris and Lock 2010; Needham and Smith 2015; Nielsen 2015; Nielsen 2016).

This study adopted in-depth elite interviews consistent with an interpretive inductive approach (Alston and Bowles 2007; Zikmund 2003) to explore each political brand identity. Elite interviews can be characterized as comprehensive discussions with a small number of experts or participants with specialist knowledge designed to capture insightful perceptions (Beamer 2002; Lillieker 2003). Interviews were conducted face-to-face in August 2018 and lasted 60 to 120 minutes. In-depth, elite interviews are often seen as a *"special conversation"* (Rubin and Rubin 1995:6) where the role of the interviewer is to build a picture of the feelings, attitudes and views of the interviewee without leading the respondent and creating any bias (Silverman, 2013). The interview guide was developed by the researchers after reviewing the literature on political and personal branding

(Gillham 2005). However, the interview guide represented a broad structure to facilitate the discussion and encourage as natural discussion as possible rather than serve as a strict protocol, which could stifle the *"special
conversation"* (Foddy 2001; Gillham 2005; Rubin and Rubin 1995:6). A
copy of the interview guide can be seen in Appendix 1. The in-depth elite
interviews were enhanced with a number of data collection methods
including non-participant observations such as the review of public websites containing news updates, manifestoes, personal background information and policy related information. In addition, public social media sites
including Twitter, Instagram and Facebook were analyzed to generate
deep insight and a greater understanding of each case (Foddy 2001;
Saunders *et al.* 2012). This in turn allowed methodological triangulation,
which helped strengthen the research findings by comparing and contrasting emerging themes and revealing a holistic view of each political brand
identity (Easterby-Smith, Farmer *et al.* 2006; Saunders *et al.* 2012; Easterby-
Smith, Thorpe, and Jackson 2015).

The elite interviews were conducted in Icelandic and transcribed and
translated into English by the researchers. Transcription was completed
within one week of the interviews. A draft copy of the article was sent to
the participants in a process of participant validation or member checking
to give greater rigor to the research and reduce bias (Warren and Karner
2005). This study adopted a two-staged thematic analytical process to analyze the transcripts and secondary resources-material (Butler-Kisber 2010).
Thematic analysis involves the practice of identifying common themes and
unique codes from the findings in order to interpret and make sense of the
phenomenon (Butler-Kisber 2010; Hofstede *et al.* 2007; Warren and Karner
2005). More specifically, Butler-Kisber (2010) proposed two distinct stages
to manage the analytical process. The first 'coarse grain' stage began at the
interview stage each interview was recorded, transcribed by the researcher
and read and re-read in an iterative process (Braun and Clarke, 2006;
Butler-Kisber 2010). Each interview was reviewed in isolation and initials
codes were generated to review themes and patterns across the interviews
and public material. More precisely, thematic analysis helped with encod-
ing the findings by *"categorizing or the comparing and contrasting of
units and categories of the field texts to produce conceptual understand-
ings of experiences and/or phenomena that are ultimately constructed into
larger themes"* (Butler-Kisber 2010: 47). The fine-grained stage was focused
revisiting themes identified from the coarse-grained stage (Bird *et al.* 2009;
Butler-Kisber 2010; Hofstede *et al.* 2007; Warren and Karner 2005). This
introduced a process of constant comparison, which ensures the researcher
constantly compares the phenomena and the themes and subthemes across
the two cases (Glaser, 2014). The final part of the fine stage analysis considers the secondary data and continues the process of methodological

triangulation reviewing social media sites (Saunders *et al.* 2012). This systematic process revealed several themes and subthemes such as *identity creation, communication tools* and *challenges of brand management*. The following section will present and discuss the uncovered findings.

FINDINGS

This study aims to explore the creation and management of personal political brand identity from a brand creator perspective. The themes which arrived from the thematic analysis were identified as *identity creation, communication tools* and *challenges of brand management* as discussed in the next section.

Identity Creation

When addressing these politicians' identity creation, we explored their political values, their ideology and key issues as well as their personality and personal characteristics as these are all dimensions of a personal brand (Johnson, 2014). Both politicians had a clear, unique brand that signified their vision and values, as identified by the brand identity literature (Bosch *et* al., 2006; Dahlen *et al.* 2010). It was found that case one's values, key issues and ideology were intertwined to give her personal brand credibility. Identity was grounded on personal issues such as a personal passion for representing local rural constituents and a decentralized apporach, yet infastructure for the whole island. For example, case one on three occasions submitted a bill to Parliament which addresses the use of land owned by the government, especally land rented by farmers [she put it forward for the fourth time in September 2018]. This bill has three main objectives; to ensure the possibility of government land being used for farming and that people are given the opportunity to start farming; to define which geographic areas should be rented out and which sold and finally to make sure that nature and tourist consideration are taken into account when all above is addressed (Althingi, 2018c). Another key issue for case one is to keep the whole island habitable. In order do so, the island needs to be connected by optical fiber broadband and transportation needs to be realiable and affordable. For example *"transportation will have to work, it's the foundation [as] the country is large and expansive"* (Interview Case 1). Air travel is not an option for people living farthest away from the services in Reykjavik as it is too expensive.

> *"When I started in parliament then I didn't have a mobile connection where I live [in Vopnafjordur], we had a special solution, so we could watch TV and the internet connection was bad. Nobody believed me when I told them*

that I would be at home over the weekend, but you would need to ring my landline" (Interview Case 1).

When the whole island is all connected then the aim is to start adverting jobs, so you can work from anywhere within Iceland. This is a Progressive party policy and is something the party has been working towards for years. Similarly, case two values reflect her party values and her wish to restrict government intervention within the economy. For example, it was revealed that *"we have so many creative, hard-working people in this country and we trust them to do what's best. We often see that Icelanders can do extraordinary things, not just in football"* (Interview Case 2). She believes the state should focus on providing excellent healthcare and education, take care of transportation, roads, benefit system, the elderly, court of law and police. Her key issues reflect topics important to young people of her generation; education and affordable housing and those are the policies she is working on.

Both politicians claim to portray an authentic personality which consists of positivity and diligence. Both say they are positive and hard-working. Case 2 says she is positive and organized, expressing she wants to have plenty to do. Case 1 says she is positive, realistic and firm. When parliament is operating case 2 is working most days until 7 pm. *"You need to prepare bills you need to address, read for your work in committees and meet people. Over the weekend you can be on TV or radio program, or in meetings around the country"* (Interview Case 2). Case 1 says this is not a family friendly job, you will need a supportive partner, especially if you have some children. She says that everything in the parliament pushes people to live in Reykjavik. However, her view is that it is important to connect with her society and this connection might be lost if she would live all year around in Reykjavik.

Both politicians make sure they were accessible and as a part of this answered all emails and requests from the public. Case 1 says: *"I can't always solve problems or do anything, but it is necessary to show interest in people "*(Interview Case 1). Case 2 says she tries to answer all her correspondences. *"I try to answer them all, can be difficult but I try to be accessible and answer it all, from Twitter, Instagram and Facebook or my email "(*Interview Case 2).

From above it appears that participants strive to be seen as authentic personalities and strong personal brands. Nevertheless, we can only reveal if cases were deemed authentic if we investigate this from an external-voter perspective. This is, however, beyond the scope of this study.

Communications Tools

Brand identity is created and developed through communications and relationship (Gylling and Linderbergrepo, 2006, Shepherd, 2005). In this study the politicians reflected on how they communicated with the people within their constituency both offline and online. Case 1 defines her target market quite broadly as *"hard working people with both feet on the ground, which understands their society"* (Interview Case 1). Case 2 identities 3 different target markets. She says:

> *"It is young females, who believe in right-wing politics. They have not found individuals to follow. This is my biggest target market. Another target market is young males and then I have an older market, to which I try to communicate "*(Interview Case 2).

Indeed, both politicians recognize the importance of communicating their personal brand to voters and both tailor their message to their target market. This is illustrated via both online and offline touchpoints, which create a consistent footprint.

Offline Footprint

Case 1 relies more on offline channels than case 2. Her constituency is geographically large, but this does not stop her from visiting each town/village at least twice a year, during her constituency weeks:

> *"I do more than this. I think I didn't manage to spend a whole weekend here at home over winter. My trip home for Easter was the 6th visit I made since Christmas and New Year. One weekend I flew to Egilsstaðir on Saturday and had a meeting there, came here to Vopnafjordur and had a meeting here on Sunday, drove to Seydisfjordur on the Sunday to have a meeting there before driving back to Egilsstadir to fly back to Reykjavik. I use the trips [back home] for meetings"* (Interview Case 1).

In addition, she mentions that people will ring her up if they need her help. Case 2 writes for the largest subscription newspaper in Iceland which has 17.4% reach in the Reykjavik area for people 18-49 years old (Gallup 2018), but she is aware that her target market is not necessarily reading the paper, but her party members are so it keeps her name and her issues in the spotlight. She does not attend meetings apart from those she does with her party members as young people do not turn up to meetings.

Online Footprint

Both politicians communicate through online media. Firstly, all parliamentary speeches are available on the parliamentary site, Althingi.is. Case 1 uses Facebook and though her profile is not public her posts are. Her posts show her life as an MP, farmer, wife, mother. However, equally as an MP she addresses the key concerns of her electorate in a timely manner.

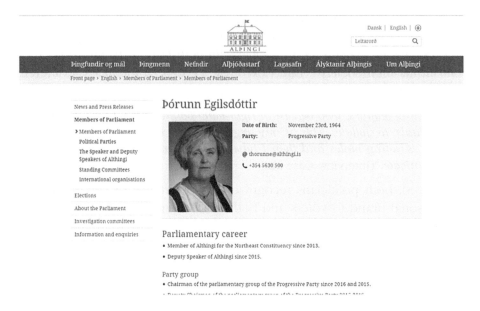

FIGURE 2. Case 1 - Parliamentary page – (Althingi 2018a).

(Facebook case 1). However, she does not use any other online media, see her parliamentary page in figure 2.

Case 2 knows how to use the online media and does so in a strategic manner. Her online footprint is stronger than Case 1's but this could be explained by her target market being young people, who spend time on social media and are interested in following a politician like themselves. Case 2 has thought about how to communicate her identity and how to make the most use of each media. *"I think it is important to try new ways to do so, not because I was trying to distinguish myself from those I was competing with but also because I'm younger than most candidates"* (Interview Case 2). She has public Instagram, Facebook and Twitter and uses all differently. She says she reaches people below 40 years on Twitter and Instagram. She can only write short messages on Twitter and most of her Twitter posts are on politics and current affairs (Twitter Case 2). She posts more about her personal life on Instagram such as holiday pictures and pictures of her with family and friends (Instagram Case 2) but puts all her published material on Facebook. Figure 3 shows the Facebook, Instagram and Twitter pages for case 2.

Both online and offline communications are consistent with the politicians' brand identity and their values. The findings show clearly the opportunities which social media sites gives to politicians, it's easier to promote themselves and show different side to their personality. Case 2 has stratically analyzed how to distinguish herself from other candidates and how

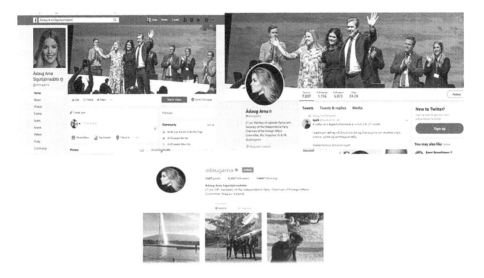

FIGURE 3. Case 2 - Social media pages (Sigurbjörnsdóttir, 2018a, b, c).

she can use the different online platforms to communicate her identity, values and policies. These findings also show that there might be an opportunity for case 1 write more about her views, values and policies, either on social media or in the newspapers to reach a wider audience.

Challenges of Brand Management

The integration stage on the personal brand auditing framework assess whether all the stages are integrated or aligned as communicating a clear, coherent personal brand identity which is vital for success (Pich and Dean, 2015). While the politicians seemed to have developed and communicated strong personal brands, several threats were identified. As both were in coalition government there was a threat of losing their identity and even losing the party identity. Both politicians identified this as a challenge but were aware of this situation as coalition governments are the norm in Icelandic politics. Both politicians identified that working in a coalition government with three different parties as being a challenge even though they also said that it had its benefits as more people would support the government. The main challenge is however to come to agreement and to reach a compromise. Another challenge is to maintain a party identity.

> *"It's easy to lose it when you are part of a coalition government, especially when the parties are different. [...] We regularly remind ourselves why we were elected and how we can achieve our goals with the ministries we have"* (Interview Case 2).

Case 1 said the party was currently doing well at maintaing their identity but this is the second time she has participated in a coalition government. In terms of brand management, both politicians had party activists within their party which they could get feedback from about their brand and brand development. These people offered internal support to help the politicians manage and integrate their brands. Not only did these people give feedback on policies and issues but also on what to wear. Both politicians had thought about adjusting their personal brand. For example case 2 had to think carefully about what she shares with people and how she does this through her social media channels. She has modified her personal brand to show more sides to herself, trying to become more than just a potential candidate to become a fully formed individual who has a place in politics. *"They say Ím just a kid in politics and that Ím undeservedly in parliament. I need to show this is not the case and that I have more to offer than people think* "(Interview Case 2). She says she communicates her personal brand through social media, but she has to be careful: *"I need to hold onto being 27-year-old but at the same time behave as a 40-year-old. I can't party like my peers can do, I can't show everything."* (Interview Case 2). She also says she has to work harder the older MPs as she is *"under the microscope"* [...] *"you can't really be yourself because people will misunderstand you or twist everything. I put some joke on [social media site] and it becomes a front-page news in DV [newspaper]."* (Interview Case 2). Case 2 is likely to have to carefully manage her brand in the future until people accept her as a fully formed MP.

Case 1 says people have all sorts of opinions about her: *"what you should wear, how you look, if you are getting smaller or bigger"* (Interview Case 1). She has also been told she doesn't speak enough during parliamentary meetings. However, case 1 has taken a different approach and not adjusted her personal brand. She worries she will lose her credibility if she starts changing her personal brand, which might be the case as she is an established individual, but some refinement might be done to introduce her to new voters and get her policies across.

These findings show that these politicians' identities are not static, they are dynamic and will continue to evolve and change as politicians get more feedback from their environment. It is likely that there is always going to be tensions or concerns about managing multiple identities to different audiences as it can mean losing your own authentic identity.

Application

This study has applied the six-staged framework (Philbrick and Cleveland, 2015) to assess and audit the personal politician brand identities of Icelandic MPs. However, as the research only addressed the MPs internal perspective

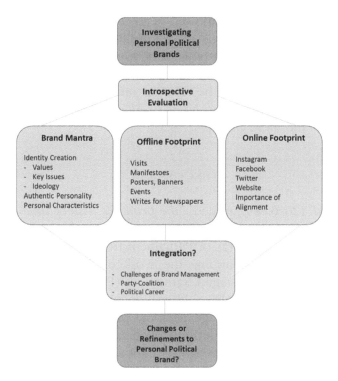

FIGURE 4. The introspective evaluation framework for personal political brands developed from Philbrick and Cleveland (2015).

the multi-stakeholder evaluation stage has been omitted (Figure 4 the introspective evaluation of personal political brands). However, overall the model suggests a refinement and considers the key elements that should be addressed in creating a robust personal political brand identity.

The two politicians demonstrate two very different personal brands, which seem to be tailored to their constituencies. Moreover, both define a strong brand mantra whilst faced with different challenges. Case 1's personal brand is deeply rooted in her life as a farmer, living in a rural part of the island while Case 2's personal brand is young and fresh, she focuses on issues that are important to young people like herself in a process of introspective evaluation. Case 2, as a young politician, is likely to continue to refine, to develop and adjust her personal brand to better fit her target market. While she says that people voted for her, not a 40-year-old woman, she will need to maintain a respected image to suit an MP and on social media she will continue to have challenges with what to communicates and what not to include considering her offline and online footprint. This will be her challenge in the coming years. However, she has reflected more about how to create and maintain her personal brand than case 1.

Case 1 has a clear personal brand but needs to make sure it is still current for her target market and she is not taking advantage of all the different ways she can communicate her policies or who she is. Her view on society and the future of the island is relevant to people but it not necessarily communicated clearly or through the relevant media but investing more time and effort writing either in newspapers or on social media might help communicate the brand more clearly.

DISCUSSION

As Bronn *et al.* (2006:889) argued, *"the principle task of uncovering identity is exploration"*. Indeed, this study explored the personal brand identities of two Icelandic Members of Parliament from an internal perspective. This was achieved by expanding the work of Philbrick and Cleveland (2015) and utilized the six-staged framework (Figure 1) as a broad framework to uncover personal political brand identity and assess its usability as a tool to understand and manage personal political brands. For example, this study highlighted that while both politicians communicated clear and consistent personal brands they had thought about modifying it make it fit better with people's perceptions of them. Further, this study uncovered the preferred associations and aspired values developed by the brand's creator, which in turn highlighted the *"central ideas of a brand and how the brand communicates these ideas to stakeholders"* (Bosch *et al.* 2006; de Chernatony 2007:45). For instance, both politicians' values and ideoloigies seems to be consistent with their lifevalues. Indeed, these internally created manifestations were created and developed through the use of *physical* online and offline communication tools such as Twitter, Facebook and Instagram yet also with traditional tools such as posters, manifestos and attending events (Dahlen *et al.* 2010; Gylling and Lindberg-Repo 2006; Pich *et al.* 2018). In addition, it was found that relationships with various stakeholders such as constituents, businesses and other politicians also helped manage the personal political brand. The personal political brands also utilized *intangible properties* such as expressing current and desired positioning, demonstrating core beliefs and the importance of their heritage to develop their intentional identity. Therefore, our findings concur with the notion that brand identity is all about vision, values and aspiration (Dahlen *et al.* 2010; Gylling and Lindberg-Repo 2006; Pich *et al.* 2018).

These first-hand accounts revealed deep insight into how internal brand identity of personal political brands was created and developed, which in turn addresses the explicit calls for further research on the internal perspective of political brands (Harris and Lock 2010; Needham and Smith 2015; Nielsen 2015; Nielsen 2016; O'Cass and Voola 2011;

Scammell 2015). This also shines some light onto the identities of different typologies of political brands such as politicians, which up until now remains under-developed compared to research on 'party' political brands (French and Smith 2010; Lees-Marshment 2001; Lees 2005; Nord and Stromback 2009; O'Cass 2001; Ormrod 2007; Pich *et al.* 2018; Pich and Dean 2015). Therefore, this research demonstrates the exploration, development and management of politician political brand from an internal brand-creator standpoint supported by the six-staged personal branding framework. This addresses the explicit calls for further research, which in turn enables the discipline of political branding to advance as a specialized area of study (Harris and Lock 2010; Needham and Smith 2015; Nielsen 2015; Nielsen 2016; O'Cass and Voola 2011; Scammell 2015).

The Personal Political Brand Identity Appraisal Framework

This study applied four of the six stages [brand mantra, offline footprint, online footprint and integration] to investigate personal political brand identity outlined in Figure 1. For example, the brand mantra [stage three], offline footprint [stage four], online footprint [stage five] and integration [stage 6] were clearly applicably to assessing the intentional identity. The *brand mantra* included themes related to identity creation such as values, key personal issues and ideology but also personal characteristics of the individual and the importance of an authentic personality. The *Offline and online footprint* captured the tools, techniques and activities used to communicate and project a desired identity. Whereas *integration* revealed the challenges of creating and managing personal political brand identity, the relationships and alignment with the political party and coalition partners but also long-term aspiration of the individual. However, this study also revealed that two of the six stages [introspective evaluation and multi-stakeholder evaluation] were problematic when attempting to evaluate the personal political brands. For example, stage one [introspective evaluation], seemed to be part of the complete evaluative process of all six-stages rather than be considered a standalone stage. Further, by investigating the brand mantra, online and offline footprints and integration would in effect represent an introspective evaluation. Therefore, if stage one was evaluated as a standalone element then that would be merely a replication of the following stages and not reveal new insight. In addition, stage two [multi-stakeholder evaluation] was also difficult in this investigation as this research aimed to explore the personal political brand identity from the brand's creator rather than including additional stakeholders such constituents, supporters, competitors and party members. This in turn will reveal

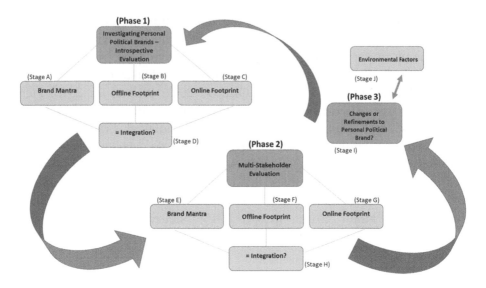

FIGURE 5. The personal political brand identity appraisal framework.

additional insight into integration, alignment and authenticity (Chen 2013; Gehl 2011; Green 2016).

As a result, this study presents a revised framework (Figure 5) designed to evaluate *current* and *desired* personal political brand identity from a multi-stakeholder perspective. The revised and renamed *Personal Political Brand Identity Appraisal Framework* builds on the work of Philbrick and Cleveland (2015) and reflect key themes identified as part of this study (Figure 4). In addition, the Personal Political Brand Identity Appraisal Framework is structured into three systematic phases outlined below.

Phase one would involve four stages exploring the current brand mantra [Stage A], offline footprint [Stage B], online footprint [Stage C], which in turn will reveal an up-to-date reflection of the personal political brand and assess its consistency [Stage D]. Once this introspective evaluation has been conducted, the appraisal would move to phase two and this would involve repeating the exploration of the current brand mantra [Stage A], offline footprint [Stage B], online footprint [Stage C], assess its consistency [Stage D] and overall current evaluation from the perspective of multiple-stakeholders. Multiple stakeholders could include constituents, the media, activists, supporters, party colleagues-officials and competitors. Phase two would be followed by phase three where the current introspective evaluation is compared/contrasted with the multi-stakeholder evaluations [Stage I] and this would highlight changes, refinements or continued development of the personal political brand identity. Phase three would also include an opportunity for politicians to conduct an environmental audit [Stage J] to evaluate factors such as changing political, economic, social and technological trends, monitor the wants and needs of constituents, assess competitor brands, relationships with the political party[s] and coalition partners. This in turn will support the management of the personal political brand and enable the politician to develop a desired identity. The three phased process should be repeated periodically to safeguard the political brand, assess coherency between current and desired positioning and continually develop and manage the identity for a constantly changing environment.

Subsequently, this study also demonstrated how to conceptualize politician political brands with the strategy of personal branding. In addition, this study highlighted that personal political brands were structured around tangible dimensions such as physical appearance, style, online and offline communications and actions-activities, and also intangible dimensions such as lived experiences, life-stories, values, charisma and apparent authenticity and authority (Chen 2013; Gehl 2011; Green 2016). This study presents an updated *Personal Political Brand Identity Appraisal Framework* as a systematic diagnostic tool to assess current and desired identity from a multi-stakeholder perspective and a mechanism to develop and manage political brands periodically. This study concurs with earlier work in that personal branding can be used by celebrities, sports personalities, journalists, business leaders, entrepreneurs, students and also politicians as a strategy to project an authentic character, which is distinct from rivals and competitors (Chen 2013; Cortsen 2013; Gehl 2011; Lair *et al.* 2005; Ottovordemgentschenfelde 2017).

CONCLUSION

This study addressed explicit calls for further research to consider different typologies of political brands moving beyond the extensive research on political 'party' brands (Pich *et al.* 2018). More specifically, this study explored the creation and development of personal political brands and their envisaged identity from the perspective of two Icelandic Members of Parliament. This study demonstrated that the personal brand identities of Members of the Icelandic Parliament represented a clear brand mantra and created-managed via personal values and ideology and based on key issues that were personal to the individual. In addition, this study highlighted that personal brand identities were developed with offline and online touchpoints with the aim of communicating an aligned, clear and authentic political brand in the mind of Icelandic citizens. However, this study also revealed the challenges of managing an integrated personal brand identity given the problematic nature of the party-coalition political system. This study was made possible by bridging two constructs of commercial branding theory such as personal branding and brand identity transferred to the sub-discipline of political branding. In addition, the evaluation political brand identity was supported by building on the six-staged framework (Philbrick and Cleveland 2015) designed to examine the personal brands from an internal brand creator perspective. Nevertheless, this study puts forward an extended and renamed *Personal Political Brand Identity Appraisal Framework* to periodically audit the current and desired identities of politicians from a multi-stakeholder perspective, which will help develop and manage personal political brands.

Nevertheless, like all projects, there were limitations associated with this study and acknowledging the limitations will strengthen the ability to draw conclusions and support calls for further research in this area (Farmer *et al.* 2006; Jack and Raturi 2006; Scandura and Williams 2000). In this study for example, only two Members of Parliament served as participants. However, the elite interviews were longer in duration and this provided a greater opportunity to capture detailed stories of their life experiences and how their identities were created and developed over time (Beamer 2002; Rubin and Rubin 1995). In addition, each elite interview was complemented by reviewing additional public and private material such as manifestos, newspaper articles and other offline communication tools along with accessing their social media platforms and online activity. Reviewing multiple materials and published work is consistent with a qualitative case-study approach as the aim is to build an extensive picture of respondents' background, their feelings and experiences to address the research objectives (Schutt 2004; Warren and Karner 2005). It can also be helpful for new areas of study (Davies and Chun 2002; Yin 2009). In addition, each Member of Parliament represented a single case as case studies are not only restricted to organizations, campaigns or locations but also individuals (Lincoln and Guba 1985; Welch *et al.* 2011; Yin 2018). Further, interpretivist research is grounded in the ability to capture new discoveries and enrich understanding of the phenomenon rather than verify predetermined hypotheses and makes generalizable claims (Gummesson 2005; Riege 2003). Therefore, this study does not make claims of generalisability rather the elite interviews offered the opportunity to reveal deep insight into the phenomenon of personal political brand identities. Future research should build on this study and include a larger sample size across different political parties and across international contexts to compare the intentional identities, which will generate an even greater understanding of personal political brands.

Subsequently, this study contributes to the development of theory and practice. For example, this study contributes to theory by addressing the explicit calls for further research on political brands from an internal perspective (Harris and Lock 2010; Needham and Smith 2015; Nielsen 2015; Nielsen

2016; O'Cass and Voola 2011; Scammell 2015). Indeed, these revealing first-hand accounts into how internal brand identity of personal political brands is created, developed and managed. This study also extends an under-developed area of political branding by conceptualizing politicians as personal political brands (Needham and Smith 2015; O'Cass and Voola 2011; Scammell 2015; Speed *et al.* 2015). In addition, this study makes a second contribution to theory. This research extends the six-stages of personal branding (Philbrick and Cleveland 2015) to the political environment and puts forward the *Personal Political Brand Identity Appraisal Framework;* a systematic three-phased agenda to evaluate current and desired identity from a multi-stakeholder perspective. Practitioners can utilize this research as a guide of how to audit the identities of their own personal political brands and improve their desired positions based on tangible and intangible elements. The *Personal Political Brand Identity Appraisal Framework* will provide practitioners a mechanism to evaluate their identity, assess consistency and investigate alignment with their political party brand.

- Future studies should utilize the *Personal Political Brand Identity Appraisal Framework* to assess the model's applicability, systematic qualities and workability to different settings and contexts from a multi-stakeholder standpoint.
- Future research should investigate personal political brands and their relationship with party political brands and potentially extend the *Personal Political Brand Identity Appraisal Framework* to include a phase to evaluate the identity of party political brands.
- Finally, future studies could operationalize the *Personal Political Brand Identity Appraisal Framework* and measure the identities of personal political brands to develop a scale to quantify the strength of current and desired identity.

REFERENCES

Aaker, D. 1996. *Building Strong Brands*. London: Simon and Schuster UK Ltd.

Aaker, D., and E. Joachimsthaler. 2002. *Brand Leadership*. London: Simon & Schuster UK Ltd.

Alston, M., and W. Bowles. 2007. *Research for Social Workers: An Introduction to Methods*. London: Routledge.

Alsem, K. J., and E. Kostelijk. 2008. "Identity Based Marketing: A New Balanced Marketing Paradigm." *European Journal of Marketing* 42 (9/10):907–14. doi: 10.1108/03090560810891064.

Althingi. 2018a. Members of Parliament; Þórunn Egilsdóttir. Accessed September 15, 2018. https://www.althingi.is/altext/cv/en/?nfaerslunr=164.

Althingi. 2018b. Members of Parliament; Áslaug Arna Sigurbjörnsdóttir. Accessed September 15, 2018. https://www.althingi.is/altext/cv/en/?nfaerslunr=182.

Althingi. 2018c. Tillaga um þingsályktunartillögu um mótun eigendastenfu ríkisins
    með sérstöku tilliti til bújarða. Accessed October 15, 2018. https://www.
    althingi.is/altext/149/s/0020.html?fbclid=IwAR3bLqhxaNmbqNPa0FX-9Td7na
    PmGEk7JvKK5ok6VtP1-UIkCnBb1kmesgo.
Aqeel, Z., M. I. Hanif, and M.S. Malik. 2017. "Impact of co-Branding and Brand
    Personality on Brand Equity: A Study of Telecom Sector in Pakistan." *Journal
    of Business and Retail Management Research* 12 (1):86–93.
Baines, P., and P. Harris. 2011. "Marketing in the 2010 British General Election:
    Perspectives, Prospect, and Practice." *Journal of Marketing Management*
    27 (7–8):647–55. doi: 10.1080/0267257X.2011.591916.
Bale, T. 2008. "A Bit Less Bunny-Hugging and a Bit More Bunny-Boiling?
    Qualifying Conservative Party Change under David Cameron." *British Politics*
    3 (3):270–99.
Baumgarth, C. 2018. "Brand Management and the World of the Arts: Collaboration,
    co-Operation, co-Creation, and Inspiration." *Journal of Product & Brand
    Management* 27 (3):237–48. doi: 10.1108/JPBM-03-2018-1772.
Baxter, P., and S. Jack. 2008. "Qualitative Case Study Methodology: Study Design and
    Implementation for Novice Researchers." *The Qualitative Report* 13 (4):544–59.
Beamer, G. 2002. "Elite Interviews and State Politics Research." *State Politics &
    Policy Quarterly* 2 (1):86–96. doi: 10.1177/153244000200200106.
Bergqvist, C. 1999. *Equal Democracies? Gender and Politics in the Nordic Countries.*
    Copenhagen, Denmark: Nordic Council of Ministers. ISBN 978-82-00-12799-4.
Billard, T. J. 2018. "Citizen Typography and Political Brands in the 2016 US
    Presidential Election Campaign." *Marketing Theory* 18 (3):421–31.
Bird, S., J. L. Wiles, L. Okalik, J. Kilabuk, and G.M. Egeland. 2009. "Methodological
    Consideration of Storytelling in Qualitative Research Involving Indigenous
    Peoples." *Global Health Promotion* 16 (4):16–26. doi: 10.1177/1757975909348111.
Bosch, J., E. Venter, Y. Han, and C. Boshoff. 2006. "The Impact of Brand Identity
    on the Perceived Brand Image of a Merged Higher Education Institution: Part
    One." *Management Dynamics* 15 (2):10–30.
Braun, V., and V. Clarke. 2006. "Using Thematic Analysis in Psychology." *Qualitative
    Research in Psychology* 3 (2):77–101. doi: 10.1191/1478088706qp063oa.
Bronn, P. S., A. Engell, and H. Martinsen. 2006. "A Reflective Approach to
    Uncovering Actual Identity." *European Journal of Marketing* 40 (7/8):886–901.
    doi: 10.1108/03090560610670043.
Brooks, A. K., and C. Anumudu. 2016. "Identity Development in Personal Branding
    Instruction." *Adult Learning* 27 (1):23–9. doi: 10.1177/1045159515616968.
Busby, R., and S. Cronshaw. 2015. "Political Branding: The Tea Party and Its Use
    of Participation Branding." *Journal of Political Marketing* 14 (1–2):96. doi: 10.
    1080/15377857.2014.990850.
Butler-Kisber, L. 2010. *Qualitative Inquiry: Thematic, Narrative and Arts-Informed
    Perspectives.* London, UK: Sage Publications Ltd.
Chen, C. P. 2013. "Exploring Personal Branding on YouTube." *Journal of Internet
    Commerce* 12 (4):332–47. doi: 10.1080/15332861.2013.859041.
Cortsen, K. 2013. "Annika Sorenstam – a Hybrid Personal Sports Brands." Sport,
    Business and Management: An International Journal 3 (1):37–62. doi: 10.1108/
    20426781311316898.

Cwalina, W., and A. Falkowski. 2014. "Political Branding: Political Candidates Positioning Based on Inter-Object Associative Affinity Index." *Journal of Political Marketing* 3 (2):1–5. doi: 10.1080/15377857.2014.990842.

Dahlen, M., F. Lange, and T. Smith. 2010. *Marketing Communications: A Brand Narrative Approach*. West Sussex, UK: John Wiley and Sons Ltd.

Dann, S., P. Harris, G. Sullivan Mort, M. Fry, and W. Binney. 2007. "Reigniting the Fire: A Contemporary Research Agenda for Social, Political and Nonprofit Marketing." *Journal of Public Affairs* 7 (3):291–304. doi: 10.1002/pa.269.

Davies, G., and R. Chun. 2002. "Gaps between the Internal and External Perceptions of the Corporate Brand." *Corporate Reputation Review* 5 (2–3): 144–58. doi: 10.1057/palgrave.crr.1540171.

Davies, G., and T. Mian. 2010. "The Reputation of the Party Leader and the Party Being Led." *European Journal of Marketing* 44 (3/4):331–50.

De Chernatony, L. 2007. *From Brand Vision to Brand Evaluation*. Oxford, UK: Butterworth Heinemann.

De Landtsheer, C., and P. De Vries. 2015. "Branding the Image of a Fox: The Psychological Profile of EU President Herman Van Rompuy." *Journal of Political Marketing* 14 (1–2):200. dio: 10.1080/15377857.2014.990836

Easterby-Smith, M., R. Thorpe, and P. Jackson. 2015. *Management and Business Research*. London: SAGE Publications Ltd.

Farmer, T., K. Robinson, S. J. Elliott, and J. Eyles. 2006. "Developing and Implementing a Triangulation Protocol for Qualitative Health Research." *Qualitative Health Research* 16 (3):377–94. doi: 10.1177/1049732305285708.

Foddy, W. 2001. *Constructing Questions for Interviews and Questionnaires: Theory and Practice in Social Research*. Cambridge, UK: Cambridge University Press.

French, A., and G. Smith. 2010. "Measuring Political Brand Equity: A Consumer-Oriented Approach." *European Journal of Marketing* 44 (3/4):460–77. doi: 10.1108/03090561011020534.

Gallup. 2018. Prentmiðlar Niðurstöður Júlí. Accessed October 15, 2018. https://www.gallup.is/nidurstodur/fjolmidlar/prentmidlar/.

Gehl, R. W. 2011. "Ladders, Samurai, and Clue Collars: Personal Branding in Web 2.0." *First Monday Journal* 16 (9):1–13. doi: 10.5210/fm.v16i9.3579.

Gillham, B. 2005. *Research Interviewing: The Range of Techniques*. Berkshire, England: Open University Press.

Glaser, B. G. 2014. *Memoing: A Vital Grounded Theory Procedure*. Mill Valley, CA: Sociology Press.

Green, M. R. 2016. "The Impact of Social Networks in the Development of a Personal Sports Brand." Sport, Business and Management: An International Journal 6 (3):274–94. doi: 10.1108/SBM-09-2015-0032.

Grimmer, M., and D. C. Grube. 2017. "Political Branding: A Consumer Perspective on Australian Political Parties." Party Politics 25(2):268–281. doi: 10.1177/1354068817710585.

Gummesson, E. 2005. "Qualitative Research in Marketing: Role-Map for a Wilderness of Complexity and Unpredictability." *European Journal of Marketing* 39 (3/4): 309–27. doi: 10.1108/03090560510581791.

Guzmán, F., A. F. Paswan, and E. Van Steenburg. 2015. "Self-Referencing and Political Candidate Brands: A Congruency Perspective." *Journal of Political Marketing* 14 (1–2):175–99. doi: 10.1080/15377857.2014.990837.

Guzman, F., and V. Sierra. 2009. "A Political Candidate's Brand Image Scale: Are Political Candidates Brands?" *Journal of Brand Management* 17 (3):207–17. doi: 10.1057/bm.2009.19.

Gylling, C., and K. Lindberg-Repo. 2006. "Investigating the Links between a Corporate Brand and a Customer Brand." *Journal of Brand Management* 13 (4–5):257–67. doi: 10.1057/palgrave.bm.2540269.

Harris, P., and A. Lock. 2010. "Mind the Gap: The Rise of Political Marketing and a Perspective on Its Future Agenda." *European Journal of Marketing* 44 (3/4): 297–307. doi: 10.1108/03090561011020435.

Harris, L., and A. Rae. 2011. "Building a Personal Brand through Social Networking." *Journal of Business Strategy* 32 (5):14–21. doi: 10.1108/02756661111165435.

Henley, J. 2018. Iceland's New Leader: People don't trust our politicians. *The Guardian* [online], 9 February. Accessed August 15, 2018. https://www.the-guardian.com/world/2018/feb/09/icelands-new-leader-people-dont-trust-ice-landic-politicians.

Hofstede, A., J. Van Hoof, N. Walenberg, and M. De Jong. 2007. "Projective Techniques for Brand Image Research." *Qualitative Market Research: An International Journal* 10 (3):300–9. doi: 10.1108/13522750710754326.

Hughes, A., and S. Dann. 2009. "Political Marketing and Stakeholder Engagement." Marketing Theory 9 (2):243–56. doi: 10.1177/1470593109103070.

Jack, E. P., and A. S. Raturi. 2006. "Lessons Learned from Methodological Triangulation in Management Research." *Management Research News* 29 (6): 345–57. doi: 10.1108/01409170610683833.

Jain, V., M. Chawla, B. E. Ganesh, and C. Pich. 2018. "Exploring and Consolidating the Brand Personality Elements of the Political Leader." *Spanish Journal of Marketing - ESIC* 22 (3):295–318. doi: 10.1108/SJME-03-2018-0010.

Johnson, K. 2014. "The Importance of Personal Branding in Social Media: Education Students to Create and Manage Their Personal Brand." *International Journal of Education and Social Sciences* 4 (1):1–8.

Joakim, N. 2006. *Nordic and Other European Constitutional Traditions*. Leiden: Martinus Njihoff Publisers. p. 34. ISBN 978-978-90-04-15171-0.

Kapferer, J. N. 2008. *The New Strategic Brand Management: Creating and Sustaining Brand Equity Long Term*. London: Kogan Page Ltd.

Kornum, N., and H. Muhlbacher. 2013. "Multi-Stakeholder Virtual Dialogue: Introduction to the Special Issue." *Journal of Business Research* 66 (9):1460–4. doi: 10.1016/j.jbusres.2012.09.008.

Lair, D. J., K. Sullivan, and G. Cheney. 2005. "Marketization and the Recasting of the Professional Self: The Rhetoric and Ethics of Personal Branding." *Management Communication Quarterly* 18 (3):307–43. doi: 10.1177/0893318904270744.

Lees, C. 2005. "Political Marketing in Germany." In *Political Marketing: A Comparative Perspective*, edited by D. Liliker, and J. Lees-Marshment, 2nd ed. Manchester, UK: Manchester University Press.

Lees-Marshment, J. 2009. *Political Marketing: Principles and Applications*. Abingdon, Oxon: Routledge.

Lees-Marshment, J. 2001. "The Product, Sales and Market-Oriented Party: How Labour Learnt to Market the Product, Not Just the Presentation." *European Journal of Marketing* 35 (9/10):1074–84.

Lillieker, D. G. 2003. "Interviewing the Political Elite: Navigating a Potential Minefield." *Politics* 23 (3):207–14.

Lincoln, Y. S., and E. G. Guba. 1985. *Naturalistic Inquiry*. Newbury Park, CA: Sage

Lock, A., and P. Harris. 1996. "Political Marketing – vive la Difference!" *European Journal of Marketing* 30 (10/11):14–31. doi: 10.1108/03090569610149764.

Magnúsdóttir, E. 2017. Óvenjulega mikil endurnýjun. *Morgunblaðið* [online] 7 October. Accessed August 15, 2018. https://www.mbl.is/frettir/kosning/2017/10/07/ovenjulega_mikil_endurnyjun_2/.

Marder, B., C. Marchant, C. Archer-Brown, A. Yau, and J. Colliander. 2018. "Conspicuous Political Brand Interactions on Social Network Sites." *European Journal of Marketing* 52 (3/4):702–24. doi: 10.1108/EJM-01-2017-0059.

Marland, A. 2016. *Brand Command: Canadian Politics and Democracy in the Age of Message Control*. Vancouver: UBC Press.

Marland, A., and T. Flanagan. 2013. "Brand New Party: Political Branding and the Conservative Party of Canada." Canadian Journal of Political Science 46 (4): 951–72. doi: 10.1017/S0008423913001108.

Marwick, A. E., and D. Boyd. 2011. "I Tweet Honestly, I Tweet Passionately: Twitter Users, Context Collapse, and the Imagined Audience." *New Media & Society* 13 (1):114–33. doi: 10.1177/1461444810365313.

Milewicz, C. M., and M. C. Milewicz. 2014. "The Branding of Candidates and Parties: The U.S. news Media and the Legitimization of a New Political Term." *Journal of Political Marketing* 13 (4):233. doi: 10.1080/15377857.2014.990836.

Moufahim, M., V. Wells, and R. Canniford. 2018. "The Consumption, Politics and Transformation of Community." *Journal of Marketing Management* 34 (7–8): 557–68. doi: 10.1080/0267257X.2018.1479506.

Nandan, S. 2005. "An Exploration of the Brand Identity-Brand Image Linkage: A Communications Perspective." *Journal of Brand Management* 12 (4):264–78. doi: 10.1057/palgrave.bm.2540222.

Needham, C., and G. Smith. 2015. "Introduction: Political Branding." *Journal of Political Marketing* 14 (1–2):1–6. doi: 10.1080/15377857.2014.990828.

Nielsen, S.W. 2016. "Measuring Political Brands: An Art and a Science of Mapping the Mind." *Journal of Political Marketing* 15 (1):70–95.

Nielsen, S. W. 2015. "On Political Brands: A Systematic Review of the Literature." *Journal of Political Marketing* 16 (2):118–146. doi: 10.1080/15377857.2014. 959694,.1-29.

Nord, L.W., and J. Stromback. 2009. "Marketing with a Feeling: The Brand New Party Junilistan on the Swedish European Parliamentary Elections 2004." *Journal of Political Marketing* 8 (1):35–45. doi: 10.1080/15377850802605684.

O'Cass, A. 2001. "An Investigation of the Political Marketing Concept and Political Market Orientation in Australian Parties." *European Journal of Marketing* 35 (9/10):1003–25. doi: 10.1108/03090560110401938.

O'Cass, A., and R. Voola. 2011. "Explications of Political Market Orientation and Political Brand Orientation Using the Resource-Based View of the Political Party." *Journal of Marketing Management* 27 (5–6):627–45. doi: 10.1080/0267257X.2010.489831.

Ormrod, R. P. 2011. "Limitations and Implications of Product-Orientated, Sales-Orientated and Market-Orientated Political Parties: Evidence for Public Affairs." *Journal of Public Affairs* 11 (4):395–405. doi: 10.1002/pa.428.

Ormrod, R. P. 2007. "Political Market Orientation and Its Commercial Cousin." *Journal of Political Marketing* 6 (2–3):69–90. doi: 10.1300/J199v06n02_05.

Ottovordemgentschenfelde, S. 2017. "Organizational, Professional, Personal: An Exploratory Study of Political Journalists and Their Hybrid Brand on." *Journalism: Theory, Practice & Criticism* 18 (1):64–80. Vol. doi: 10.1177/1464884916657524.

Panigyrakis, G., and L. Altinay. 2017. "Political Branding in Turbulent Times." *The Service Industries Journal* 37 (9–10):681–3.

Peng, N., and C. Hackley. 2009. "Are Voters, Consumers? a Qualitative Exploration of the Voter-Consumer Analogy in Political Marketing." *Qualitative Market Research: An International Journal* 12 (2):171–86. doi: 10.1108/13522750910948770.

Peters, T. 1997. "The Brand Called You." *Fast Company* 10:83.

Philbrick, J. L., and A. D. Cleveland. 2015. "Personal Branding: Building Your Pathway to Professional Services." *Medical Reference Services Quarterly* 34 (2):181–9. doi: 10.1080/02763869.2015.1019324.

Phipps, M., J. Brace-Govan, and C. Jevons. 2010. "The Duality of Political Brand Equity." *European Journal of Marketing* 44 (3/4):496–514. doi: 10.1108/03090561011020552.

Pich, C., G. Armannsdottir, and L. Spry. 2018. "An Exploratory Case Study Focusing on the Creation, Orientation and Development of a New Political Brand; the Case of the UK Jury Team." *Politics & Policy* 46 (1):141. doi: 10.1111/polp.12243.

Pich, C., and D. Dean. 2015. "Political Branding: Sense of Identity or Identity Crisis? an Investigation of the Transfer Potential of the Brand Identity Prism and the UK Conservative Party." *Journal of Marketing Management* 31 (11–12):1353. doi: 10.1080/0267257X.2015.1018307.

Rampersad, H. K. 2008. "A New Blueprint for Powerful and Authentic Personal Branding." *Performance Improvement* 47 (6):34–7. doi: 10.1002/pfi.20007.

Resnick, S. M., R. Cheng, M. Simpson, and F. Lourenco. 2016. "Marketing in SMEs: A 4Ps Self-Branding Model." *International Journal of Entrepreneurial Behavior & Research* 22 (1):155–74. doi: 10.1108/IJEBR-07-2014-0139.

Riege, A. M. 2003. "Validity and Reliability in Case Study Research: A Literature Review with "Hands-on" Applications for Each Research Phase." *Qualitative Market Research: An International Journal* 6 (2):75–86. doi: 10.1108/13522750310470055.

Ronzoni, G., E. Torres, and J. Kang. 2018. "Dual Branding: A Case Study of Wyndham." *Journal of Hospitality and Tourism Insights* 1 (3):240–57. doi: 10.1108/JHTI-03-2018-0016.

Rubin, H. J., and I. S. Rubin. 1995. *Qualitative Interviewing: The Art of Hearing Data*. London: Sage Publications Ltd.

Saunders, M., P. Lewis, and A. Thornhill. 2012. *Research Methods for Business Students*. Essex: Pearson Professional Ltd.

Scammell, M. 2015. "Politics and Image: The Conceptual Value of Branding." *Journal of Political Marketing* 14 (1–2):7–18. doi: 10.1080/15377857.2014.990829.

Scandura, T. A., and E. A. Williams. 2000. "Research Methodology in Management: Current Practices, Trends and Implications for Future Research." *The Academy of Marketing Journal* 43 (6):1248–64.

Schofield, P., and P. Reeves. 2015. "Does the Factor Theory of Satisfaction Explain Political Voting Behaviour?" *European Journal of Marketing* 49 (5/6):968–92. doi: 10.1108/EJM-08-2014-0524.

Schutt, R. K. 2004. *Investigating the Social World: The Process and Practice of Research*. London: Sage Publications Ltd.

Serazio, M. 2017. "Branding Politics: Emotion, Authenticity, and the Marketing Culture of American Political Communication." *Journal of Consumer Culture* 17 (2):225–41. doi: 10.1177/1469540515586868.

Shepherd, I. D. H. 2005. "From Cattle and Coke to Charlie: Meeting the Challenge of Self-Marketing and Personal Branding." *Journal of Marketing Management* 21 (5–6):589–606. doi: 10.1362/0267257054307381.

Sigurbjörnsdóttir, Á. A. 2018a. Twitter page. Accessed September 15, 2018. https://twitter.com/aslaugarna?ref_src=twsrc%5Egoogle%7Ctwcamp%5Eserp%7Ctwgr%5Eauthor.

Sigurbjörnsdóttir, Á. A. 2018b. Facebook page. Accessed September 15, 2018. https://www.facebook.com/aslaugarna/.

Sigurbjörnsdóttir, Á. A. 2018c. Instagram page. Accessed September 15, 2018. https://www.instagram.com/aslaugarna/?hl=en.

Silverman, D. 2013. *Doing Qualitative Research, a Practical Handbook*. 4th ed. London: Sage.

Smith, G. 2009. "Conceptualising and Testing Brand Personality in British Politics." *Journal of Political Marketing* 8 (3):209–32. doi: 10.1080/15377850903044858.

Smith, G. 2005. "Positioning Political Parties: The 2005 UK General Election." *Journal of Marketing Management* 21 (9–10):1135–49. doi: 10.1362/026725705775194184.

Smith, G. 2001. "The 2001 General Election: Factors Influencing the Brand Image of Political Parties and Their Leaders." *Journal of Marketing Management* 17 (9–10):989–1006. doi: 10.1362/026725701323366719.

Smith, G., and R. Speed. 2011. "Cultural Branding and Political Marketing: An Exploratory Analysis." *Journal of Marketing Management* 27 (13–14):1304–21. doi: 10.1080/0267257X.2011.628449.

Smith, G., and F. Spotswood. 2015. "The Brand Equity of the Liberal Democrats in the 2010 General Election: A National and Local Perspective." *Journal of Political Marketing* 12 (2–3):182–196. doi: 10.1080/15377857.2013.781478.

Speed, R., P. Butler, and N. Collins. 2015. "Human Branding in Political Marketing: Applying Contemporary Branding Thoughts to Political Parties and Their Leaders." *Journal of Political Marketing* 14 (1–2):129–151. doi: 10.1275/15333457.2013.781278.

Thompson-Whiteside, H., S. Turnbull, and L. Howe-Walsh. 2017. "Developing an Authentic Personal Brand Using Impression Management Behaviours: Exploring Female Entrepreneurs' Experiences." *Qualitative Market Research: An International Journal* 21 (2):166–181. doi: 10.1108/QMR-01-2017-0007.

Ward, C., and D. Yates. 2013. "Personal Branding and e-Professionalism." *Journal of Service Science (JSS)* 6 (1):101–4. doi: 10.19030/jss.v6i1.8240.

Warren, C. A. B., and T. X. Karner. 2005. *Discovering Qualitative Methods: Field Research, Interviews and Analysis*. Los Angeles, CA: Roxbury Publishing Company.

Welch, C., R. Piekkari, E. Plakoyiannaki, and E. Paavilainen-Mantymaki. 2011. "Theorising from Case Studies: Towards a Pluralist Future for International Business Research." *Journal of International Business Studies* 42 (5):740–62. doi: 10.1057/jibs.2010.55.

Wolfram, N. 2017. *"Iceland". Parties and Elections in Europe*. http://www.parties-and-elections.eu/iceland.html.

Yin, R.K. 2018. *Case Study Research and Applications, Design and Methods*. 6th ed. Thousand Oaks, CA: Sage.

Yin, R. K. 2009. *Case Study Research*. 4th ed. Thousand Oaks, CA: Sage.

Zikmund, W. G. 2003. *Business Research Methods*. USA: Thomson Learning South-Western.

APPENDIX 1. INTERVIEW GUIDE – PERSONAL BRAND IDENTITIES – ICELAND

Opening – Introduction

- Research outline-objectives
- Outline confidentiality, informed consent - audio tape – contact details for participant

Biographical Information

- How long in politics?
- How/why did you get into politics?
- Political background?
- Party politics?
- Other roles/jobs?
- Current role?

Icelandic Political Brand Identity

- What does it mean to be a Member of Parliament?
- How does the political system in Iceland work?
- Day in the life of an Icelandic Member of Parliament?
- Core values? Heritage?
- Key issues of concern?
- Personality?
- Ideology?
- What makes you different from your political competitors?
- How do you communicate your identity?
- What does it mean to be an MP?
- How do you feel about party politics? Political parties?
- Political allies? Political rivals?
- Relationships?
- Target Market?
- Overall self-image

Coalition Politics

- How does it work?
- Positives/negatives?
- Party identity?
- Coalition identity?
- Personal identity-party-coalition?

Policies

- Key policies of interest? Why?
- Party policies?
- Coalition policies?
- Policy most proud of and least proud of?
- One thing you would change tomorrow?

Personal Perceptions

- Party politics or nonparty politics
- Approachable? Engaging?
- Communication with voters-citizens?
- Your personal political 'brand' in three words?
- How do your constituents see you?
- Political heroes inside-outside Iceland
- If you were PM tomorrow, what would you do?

Closure

- Questions for me
- Summarize Findings
- Reinforce Ethical Procedures
- Contact Information

Why Cryptocurrencies Want Privacy: A Review of Political Motivations and Branding Expressed in "Privacy Coin" Whitepapers

JOHN HARVEY (iD)

INES BRANCO-ILLODO

New currencies designed for user anonymity and privacy – widely referred to as "privacy coins" – have forced governments to listen and legislate, but the political motivations of these currencies are not well understood. Following the growing interest of political brands in different contexts, we provide the first systematic review of political motivations expressed in cryptocurrency whitepapers whose explicit goal is "privacy." Many privacy coins deliberately position themselves as alternative political brands. Although cryptocurrencies are often closely associated with political philosophies that aim to diminish or subvert the power of governments and banks, advocates of privacy occupy much broader ideological ground. We present thematic trends within the privacy coin literature and identify epistemic and ethical tensions present within the communities of people calling for the adoption of entirely private currencies.

WORKERS OF THE WORLD, UNITE! YOU HAVE NOTHING TO LOSE BUT YOUR BLOCKCHAINS!

Cryptocurrencies have their political roots in anarchist, hacker, hippy, and cypherpunk cultures (Maurer, Nelms, and Swartz 2013). Many designers, activists, and advocates of cryptocurrency want to dismantle the nation state and its associated corporations (Karlstrøm 2014). Subversion of government and the removal of commercial influence over money is a widespread theme in cryptocurrency canonical literature (e.g. Nakamoto 2008), but this trope is no longer universal. Indeed, increasingly, those cryptocurrencies that succeed in creating value for their users are often explicitly branded and positioned to aid hegemonic political interests.

Recent work on political branding highlights the diverse nature of political brands (Smith and French 2009) and draws attention to the need to understand political branding in different contexts (Needham and Smith 2015). This article contributes to the understanding of political branding by uncovering different types of motivation underpinning privacy coins. We show how notions of politics emerge in cryptocurrencies which are explicitly positioned as political brands.

Through the notion of *privacy as politics*, we submit that cryptocurrencies, although often branded and positioned as apolitical or anti-political (Herian 2018), are always a form of "alternative" political movement. The desire to be a-political represents a political position itself (Kostakis and Giotitsas 2014) and it is important to understand the political underpinnings behind the blockchain technology as it is driving social change (Filippi and Loveluck 2016). The identification of political dimensions and ideologies in cryptocurrency challenges the idea that digital currency is removed from the influence of politicians (Dierksmeier and Seele 2018) and unveils a new context to research political branding. This is important because political ideology drives consumer decisions (Crockett and Pendarvis 2017) and in the context of cryptocurrency those decisions are likely to be significantly different if digital currencies are associated with particular political ideologies.

In the following sections of this article, we briefly review extant literature around (1) cryptocurrency and the recent emergence of "privacy coins"; (2) The relation of privacy to politics, including nuanced definitions of anonymity and privacy; and (3) the integration of cryptocurrencies, privacy and alternative political brands that will inform the subsequent discussion. Afterwards, we outline the methods used to generate a corpus of whitepapers and conduct a systematic review. In following section, we present an exposition of the findings and discussion. Focus is directed toward emergent themes within the literature and ethical and epistemic conflicts present in the positioning of privacy cryptocurrencies. In the final section, we conclude the article and put forward an agenda for future research to help broaden the academic study of privacy coins and their social impact.

CRYPTOCURRENCIES AND THE POST-BITCOIN EMERGENCE OF "PRIVACY COINS"

In the wake of the 2008 financial crash, a pseudonymous author named Satoshi Nakamoto outlined a vision for an alternative monetary future using Bitcoin and the blockchain protocol (Nakamoto 2008). Nakamoto drew attention to the failings of modern banking institutions and sought to challenge their dominance by enabling decentralized peer-to-peer transactions. People, Nakamoto argued, should be free and able to control their personal wealth anonymously without relying on a centralized third party (Dodd 2017).

Anonymity is a central issue for many Bitcoin users. No fixed identity is explicitly linked to a Bitcoin wallet address and "privacy" is a key concern in Nakamoto's initial Bitcoin whitepaper (Nakamoto 2008). However, the idea that underpins Bitcoin (a public distributed ledger) raises some tricky challenges for maintaining user privacy. While it is easy to protect the identity of the owner of a Bitcoin wallet, it is harder to protect users from inferred conclusions about their identity that can be reached by analyzing wallet transfers. If Account A sends a specific amount at a specific time to Account B it is sometimes possible to triangulate and determine the offline identities of the people associated with the transaction. Indeed, in reviewing the privacy of Bitcoin, Nakamoto noted that:

> The traditional banking model achieves a level of privacy by limiting access to information to the parties involved and the trusted third party. The necessity to announce all transactions [in the Bitcoin protocol] publicly precludes this method, but privacy can still be maintained by breaking the flow of information in another place: by keeping public keys anonymous. The public can see that someone is sending an amount to someone else, but without information linking the transaction to anyone. This is similar to the level of information released by stock exchanges, where the time and size of individual trades, the 'tape', is made public, but without telling who the parties were. As an additional firewall, a new key pair should be used for each transaction to keep them from being linked to a common owner. Some linking is still unavoidable with multi-input transactions, which necessarily reveal that their inputs were owned by the same owner. The risk is that if the owner of a key is revealed, linking could reveal other transactions that belonged to the same owner. (Nakamoto 2008, 6)

Various authors have shown that blockchain analysis can reveal connections between users and their transactions, and that further data can be inferred because of these connections which might jeopardize privacy

(Ober, Katzenbeisser, and Hamacher 2013, Reid and Harrigan 2013, Ron and Shamir 2013). Cookies have been shown to jeopardize the privacy of cryptocurrency payments (Goldfeder et al. 2018) and similarly IP addresses have been associated with Bitcoin account use, which can provide a basis for identity inference (Bohannon 2016). Despite the clear value Nakamoto placed on "privacy," the metadata that Bitcoin usage generates makes it a less than optimal solution for maintaining true privacy of users. Consequently, a wide variety of cryptocurrency designers and advocates have criticized the architecture of Bitcoin and proposed alternative overlays to the existing design or entirely new solutions (Meiklejohn and Orlandi 2015). These alternative cryptocurrencies typically try to hide or obfuscate user metadata and are thus widely referred to as "privacy coins" (Nakamoto 2008).

Privacy coins vary in technological sophistication, but they have gained widespread notoriety from their increasing use in nefarious transactions, particularly on the so-called "Dark-web" (Recorded Future 2018). Reports illustrate that privacy coins are being used by rogue states (Hurlburt 2017), drug dealers (Van Hout and Bingham 2013), illicit traders; and that they help hide sexual exploitation (Zulkarnine et al. 2016), terrorism, weapons trafficking (Weimann 2016), and money laundering (Dostov and Shust 2014). These activities have caught the eye of governments around the world. But governments are not simply interested in illicit behavior, some have legislated against, and even banned cryptocurrencies because absolute privacy of transactions threaten the possibility of audited ownership and taxation (Dierksmeier and Seele 2018). "Know your customer" regulations, which associate passport details with exchange users, are now widely adopted worldwide to surveil fiat-crypto conversions and provide the possibility of audit trails (Berentsen and Schar 2018).

Despite the negative press cryptocurrencies receive, they also present an opportunity to positively transform the economic lives of people. Whether in banking the unbanked billions of people around the world (Larios-Hernández 2017), eliminating the fees imposed on remittances sent by the poorest workers in the world to their families (Scott 2016), or providing novel means for people to share, donate, or tip, many new cryptocurrencies have an obviously prosocial aim (Pittman 2016). Indeed, many crypto initiatives clearly fall within the category of *prosocial interaction design* (Harvey, Golightly, and Smith 2014), echoing the old Marxist adage that good philosophy aims not merely to describe or interpret the world, instead the point is to change it. The imagination, development, and adoption of a new currency is always a potentially transformative political act.

Cryptocurrencies have been championed by advocates of a range of political philosophies. Nakamoto originally argued that Bitcoin was "very attractive to the libertarian viewpoint if we can explain it properly," but also added "I'm better with code than with words though." But as Maurer, Nelms, and Swartz (2013, 262) note "in the world of Bitcoin, there are gold-bugs, hippies, anarchists, cyberpunks, cryptographers, payment systems experts, currency activists, commodity traders, and the curious" Although arguments made in favor of cryptocurrency are justifications for shrinking or eradicating the influence of government or banks over money, there are nonetheless at the time of writing numerous movements by national governments towards adopting cryptocurrency in place of or alongside fiat currency. For example, the Marshall Islands have been heavily criticized by the International Monetary Fund over their plans to introduce a digital currency in 2019, and Venezuela have reportedly raised over 5 billion USD in an initial coin offering in early 2018 (Petro 2018). This tension illustrates that cryptocurrency is no longer the preserve of those seeking to subvert the dominant monetary systems, it is also being co-opted by those national banks and governments it was created to counteract. We might ask the question then, what political purpose do privacy coins serve, and for whom?

PRIVACY AS POLITICS

Every society "sets a distinctive balance between the private sphere and public order based on the society's political philosophy" around two alternative societal models, namely Authoritarian (i.e. rejecting legally or socially protected privacy) and Democratic societies (i.e. having a strong commitment to individualism and freedom) (Westin 2003, 3). A long history of privacy research exists within the computing and politics academic literatures, respectively. Recent research draws attention to how metadata associated with ubiquitous forms of computing can inadvertently reveal identity or behavior of people without them giving informed consent (Luger and Rodden 2013). Although no single definition of privacy is accepted, the concept is obviously nuanced and has a meaning which cannot be universally understood outside of the particular contexts in which it is a concern (Smith, Dinev, and Xu 2011). Privacy becomes a more ambiguous concept when human-computer interaction is enabled by data managed or processed centrally by commercial or governmental third parties. Privacy online is treated variously as either an inalienable right to which individuals and groups are entitled, or as a commodity best thought of as something which has an economic value that can be evaluated and traded as part of a cost-benefit analysis (Walsh, Parisi, and Passerini 2017).

   In this article, we subscribe to Westin's (1967, 7) classic definition of privacy as "the claim of individuals, groups, or institutions to determine for themselves when, how, and to what extent information about them is communicated to others." Westin's (1967) account introduces subtlety into the understanding of privacy, by making a distinction between privacy "states" and privacy "functions." Four privacy states that individuals are said to experience can be paraphrased as: (1) Solitude: the most complete state of privacy, here the individual is separated from the group and the observations of other people; (2) Intimacy: here the individual is acting as part of a small group that can exercise corporate seclusion to achieve a close, relaxed or frank relationship between individuals; (3) Anonymity: here privacy relates to the individual that when in public spaces is able to find freedom from surveillance and identification; and (4) Reserve: this occurs when an individual's need to limit communication about their self is protected by the willing discretion of those surrounding them.

Westin contrasted states of privacy with functions, suggesting that in democratic societies privacy can "perform" different instrumental roles for individuals according to their own personal lives. Functions are said to include: (1) Personal autonomy: the need to maintain social processes that safeguard a person's sense of individuality and avoid being manipulated or dominated wholly by others; (2) Emotional release: the recognition that people "perform" many different roles in their lives e.g. father, son, husband, friend, lover, colleague, boss, student, teacher, and that privacy affords at least temporary respite from these roles to relax from the pressure of playing social roles; (3) Self-Evaluation: privacy serves not only a processing but a planning need by providing time to anticipate, to recast, and to originate. Every individual integrates their experiences into a meaningful pattern through self-evaluation and this activity requires privacy; and (4) Limited and Protected Communication: among mature adults all communication is partial and limited, based on the complementary relation between reserve and discretion.

We also note that where money and surveillance technology are concerned what is private today may not be private tomorrow. Consequently, privacy can be conceptualized either as a static, unchanging and universal value maintained by social rules or more pragmatically as something dynamic, which requires constant vigilance to revise and update protective measures according to changing socio-cultural and technological contexts. The relation between digital money and privacy has been an ongoing source of concern for computing academics for over three decades. In 1985, Chaum (1985) argued that new forms of transaction systems would work to ensure user privacy and make "Big Brother obsolete." Okamoto and Ohta (1991) similarly suggested that any future Universal Electronic Cash would ideally ensure that "the privacy of the user should be protected. That is, the relationship between the user and his purchases must be untraceable by anyone." But in practice this is has proven a difficult challenge to implement. It requires a system that can guarantee the untraceability of money and the unlinkability of people to said money, but it also requires a system which can publicly record transactions to ensure decentralized trust, while also preventing the "double spend" problem i.e. the risk of fraud through a currency being spent twice.

The possibility of trust within Bitcoin and most other cryptocurrencies comes from a massively distributed ledger that serves as an immutable historical record of transactions. Money, as Hart (2000) argues, always serves as a form of social memory. Whether as a special-purpose money used in a limited domain, or as a general-purpose money meant to operate across all spheres of human life, money functions as memory to establish ongoing social relations. Distributed memory is fundamental to the operation of Bitcoin. But the immutable transaction history which enables trust between strangers is also a potential source of identifying the behavior of individual accounts, even when identity is pseudonymized. This raises not just a technical problem, but also a political one: given that monetary transactions and the externalities which are associated with trade affect people beyond those transacting, should money ever be entirely private to the two individuals that transact? One criticism of Bitcoin raised by Dodd (2018) is that many advocates frame the political economy of the cryptocurrency as if it exists as a "thing" outside of human control, a natural, or in other words, nonsocial process.

> *If Bitcoin succeeds in its own terms as an ideology, it will fail in practical terms as a form of money. The main reason for this is that the new currency is premised on the idea of money as a 'thing' that must be abstracted from social life in order for it to be protected from manipulation by bank intermediaries and political authorities. The image is of a fully mechanized currency that operates over and above social life. In practice, however, the currency has generated a thriving community around its political ideals, relies on a high degree of social organization in order to be produced, has a discernible social structure, and is characterized by asymmetries of wealth and power that are not dissimilar from the mainstream financial system.* (Dodd 2018)

Economic transactions and the money that accompany them do not exist in a void free of social consequences, and as Seele (2018) notes, "let us not forget: crypto means secret." Secrecy and currency are not common bedfellows, and the social implications of secret transactions echo far beyond the dyad of sender and recipient. If humanity widely adopts privacy coins for the practical purposes of paying wages and buying goods and services, the political ramifications will be gargantuan for existing social institutions. Considering the neglect of privacy issues in branding (Ohm 2012) and the political underpinnings of privacy (Westin 2003), now is an opportune moment to assess how privacy coin designers conceptualize, justify and implement privacy protective technologies to attain different political ends.

CRYPTOCURRENCIES, PRIVACY AND POLITICAL BRANDS

A minimal definition of political branding is "political representations that are located in a pattern, which can be identified and differentiated from other political representations" (Nielsen 2017). According to Nielsen, "identification" and "differentiation" are the two simple attributes that need to be emphasized in the definition of political brands (Nielsen 2016, 71; Nielsen 2017, 126), meaning the concept can be applied widely to numerous research objects. Although most political branding research to date has focused on policies, parties and politicians (Speed, Butler, and Collins 2015), recent studies suggest the importance of exploring how political brands are positioned in different contexts and settings (Needham and Smith 2015). Among new contexts of inquiry researchers have investigated "nations, parties, nongovernmental organizations, interest organizations, leaders, candidates, policies, communication, or rhetoric" (Nielsen 2017, 120) and the symbolism in the construction of selected Islamist audio-visual propaganda made available on the internet (O'Shaughnessy and Baines 2009). These approaches illustrate the diverse nature of political brands as a concept (Smith and French 2009) researched from multiple perspectives (Nielsen 2016). The need to understand alternative political brands becomes more relevant in a climate where political parties show an image of crisis and the traditional dominant modes of political organization are being challenged (Husted et al. 2018).

Cryptocurrencies such as Bitcoin are designed to eradicate the influence of politicians and bankers over the productive control of money, such that top-down coercion is removed from the system. Political and commercial institutions are thus to be avoided by design, and their influence is therefore reduced (Dierksmeier and Seele 2018). Although government influence on cryptocurrencies is limited, some authors suggest that many advocates of Bitcoin use it for political reasons (Ron and Shamir 2013), while others suggest that the blockchain system (underpinned by a "neoliberal political economy" that enables cryptocurrency transactions) is trying to hide the politics involved (Herian 2018). The politics of cryptocurrencies are made visible where designers identify and differentiate varied approaches to privacy. In the following section, we outline a method for studying cryptocurrencies through the descriptions that designers give of privacy, to reveal the varied ways these systems are positioned as political brands.

METHODOLOGY

Research Method

We conducted a systematic review of cryptocurrency whitepapers using a method inspired by the PRISMA protocol (Preferred Reporting Items

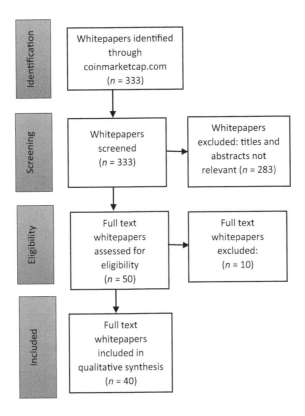

FIGURE 1. Systematic review method for generating a corpus of privacy coin whitepapers.

for Systematic Review and Meta-Analysis) (Shamseer et al. 2015), a "well-respected evidence-based approach from medical science" recently used in management research (Kranzbühler et al. 2018, 434). Review protocols are used to help protect against arbitrary decision making during the review, and also to enable the reader to assess the presence of selective reporting, by documenting a clear and replicable process. Although systematic reviews have been used before in the area of political branding (Nielsen 2017) they are a relatively novel approach within the field. An overview of the method can be seen in Figure 1 which was used as follows.

IDENTIFICATION

First, an initial corpus of cryptocurrency whitepapers was selected by using the market cap tracking website coinmarketcap.com (Coinmarketcap.com, 2018). This service follows the live price fluctuations of cryptocurrency exchanges and publish the details on their websites. Aggregated statistics are used to rank the total volume and market value of each currency/token such that potential investors can broadly analyze the market. It is important to note that it is practically impossible to review all privacy coin whitepapers, due to the enormous growth in coins which have created hardforks of existing privacy coins. Many of these coins are referred to as "altcoins" and others more disparagingly as "shitcoins" due to their low market capitalization, lack of innovation and user engagement. On the day the corpus of whitepapers was generated 1981 coins/tokens were listed on coinmarketcap.com with a known total market capitalization of $193,560,063,184. We observed that 98% of the USD value of this market was shared between the top 333 coins and we decided to focus on those coins as the limit of our corpus because they are demonstrably successful compared with the innumerable copycats. Those included have persuaded the imagination, and perhaps more importantly the wallets, of users across the globe.

SCREENING

Using these ranked lists the top 333 cryptocurrencies (as of 11/09/2018) were identified and the associated whitepaper of each coin/token was specifically analyzed for the presence of "privacy" claims where the designers sought to create a financial instrument that masks user behavior and metadata which could be inferred to reveal identity.

Whitepapers occupy an unusual genre of writing, straddling technical report and manifesto simultaneously. Most papers not only describe their innovation but also aim to persuade the audience to use the currency as a solution to particular political economy problems. Although many are written by practicing cryptographers and economists, most are styled in a pseudo-academic fashion to ensure rigor and accessibility. They are thus as much a stylistic heir to the tradition of pamphleteering as to academic journals. To our knowledge most of the whitepapers selected in the corpus were not subjected to the traditional academic double-blind peer review process, other than a few notable exceptions (e.g. Zerocoin and Zerocash – Sasson et al. 2014). But those currencies that receive popular attention do nonetheless receive whitepaper scrutiny and discussion by users and investors on public Web forums such as Bitcointalk, Reddit, and Telegram.

ELIGIBILITY

After the corpus was assembled, the research team read the abstracts and/or introductions of each paper to look for claims of privacy. If an abstract used privacy or an obvious synonym for obfuscation (e.g. "anonymous," "pseudonymous," "cloaking," "hiding," "obscuring," "dark"), the full paper was included in the corpus. The papers were then assessed for full eligibility by examining the design described in each paper for evidence of technological innovation explicitly regarding privacy. Those papers that described privacy as an aim but did not describe a particular privacy innovation were excluded at this stage.

INCLUDED

The inclusion criteria used to assess whitepaper suitability for the corpus were twofold. To be included in the corpus a coin/or token must: (1) advertise its purpose as defending and/or improving privacy of its users; and (2) Develop technology to create untraceability or unlinkability in the specific domain in which the currency is used. As a result of this stage, we removed 10 whitepapers that did not meet these criteria and we obtained a sample of 40 whitepapers (over 1000 pages of text) for scrutiny.

Data Analysis

After completing the stages of identification, screening, eligibility, and inclusion, we focused on data analysis. Drawing on Westin's (1967) definition of privacy around the states (i.e. solitude, intimacy, anonymity, reserve) and functions of privacy (i.e. personal autonomy, emotional release, self-evaluation and limited and protected communication), we developed a series of questions to ask of each paper to compare the practical, political and technical aspects of privacy described by each whitepaper. The questions included: (1) is privacy described as an end in itself or is privacy instrumental to some other moral aim? (e.g. happiness, safety); (2) is privacy described as a right or a commodity?; (3) what technologies are deployed to protect privacy?; (4) what states of privacy if any are said to be protected by the technology?; (5) What function of privacy is served by the technology?; (6) Is there an obvious allegiance to a political philosophy?; (7) Does the solution propose a general or special purpose money?; (8) Is privacy seen as a static or one-off solution to a problem or is it a dynamic/processual phenomenon worthy of ongoing consideration and revisionist development?

The selected whitepapers were scrutinized in two ways. First, we used the aforementioned questions to analyze each whitepaper and use *a priori* coding to generate preliminary answers in a spreadsheet (see Table 1). The results were then used to guide the identification of emergent themes in relation to the broader privacy as politics literature. Second, we carefully examined the selected whitepapers to gather in-depth inductive insights into the political motivations expressed in the whitepaper authors' own terms. These results provided the basis for examining the corpus across (1) privacy as politics themes within the whitepapers, which indicated convergent/divergent motivations for developing and fostering

TABLE 1 Privacy coins and associated whitepapers included within the corpus for further analysis

Currency name	Ranking (#1–#500)	Market capitalization	General or special purpose money?	An end or a means?	A right or a commodity?	Is privacy protection static or dynamic?	States of privacy protected	Function of privacy	Allegiance to political philosophy?
Monero (Noether 2018 – though multiple papers written)	10th	$1,773,363,977	General	End	Right	Dynamic	Yes – Anonymity	Protect users in a court of law	No
Dash (Duffield and Diaz 2018)	11th	$1,652,700,450	General	End	Commodity	Static	Yes – Anonymity	Protected communication	No
Zcash (Sasson et al. 2014)	21st	$561,792,867	General	End	Commodity	Static	Yes – Anonymity	Protected communication	No
Bytecoin (Van Saberhagen 2013)	24th	$375,452,075	General	End	Commodity	Static	Yes – Anonymity	Protected communication	Egalitarian
Verge (Verge 2018)	41st	$195,109,417	General	End	Commodity	Static	Yes – Anonymity	Protected communication	Libertarian
Basic Attention Token (Basic Attention Token 2018)	46th	$155,687,403	Special	End	Commodity	Static	Yes – Anonymity	Protected communication	Libertarian
Komodo (Komodo 2018)	53rd	$116,249,238	General	End	Commodity	Dynamic	Yes – Anonymity, Reserve	To protect freedom	Libertarian
Cryptonex (Cryptonex 2017)	54th	$113,665,784	General	End	Commodity	Static	Yes – Anonymity	Protected communication	No
Wanchain (Wanchain 2017)	62nd	$93,891,052	Special	End	Commodity	Dynamic	Yes – Anonymity	Protected communication	No
Aion (Spoke and Nuco Engineering Team 2017)	64th	$90,866,325	General	End	Commodity	Static	Yes – Anonymity	Protected communication	No
Bitcoin Dark (Lee 2014)	72nd	$78,689,089	General	End	Commodity	Static	Yes – Reserve	Protected communication	No
Horizen (Viglione, Versluis, and Lippencott 2017)	76th	$72,210,878	General	End	Commodity	Static	Yes – Anonymity	Protected communication	Libertarian
Ark (Ark 2018)	82nd	$65,281,755	General	End	Commodity	Dynamic	Yes – Anonymity	Protected communication	No
Bitcoin Private (Brutman et al 2018)	87th	$61,856,082	General	End	Commodity	Static	Yes – Anonymity	Protected communication	No
ZCoin (Miers et al. 2018)	92nd	$57,576,857	General	End	Commodity	Static	Not Explicit	Protected communication	No
PIVX (Pivx 2018)	97th	$53,540,561	General	End	Right	Static	Yes – Anonymity	Protected communication	Libertarian
Enigma (Zyskind, Nathan, and Pentland 2018)	108th	$43,749,692	General	End	Commodity	Static	Yes – Anonymity	Protected communication	No
Aurora (Aurora Labs 2018)	112th	$41,548,918	General	End	Commodity	Static	Yes – Anonymity	Protected communication	Libertarian
Civic (Civic Technologies 2017)	119th	$37,923,916	General	End	Commodity	Static	Not explicit	Protected communication	No

Skycoin (Skycoin 2017)	131st	$32,744,135	General	Means	Commodity	Dynamic	Yes Anonymity	Protected communication	No
Storj (Wilkinson et al. 2016; Storj Labs, 2018)	133rd	$32,500,268	General	End	Commodity	Static	Yes – Reserve	Protected communication	No
Particl (Kaiser 2017)	179th	$22,874,281	General	End	Commodity	Dynamic	Yes – Anonymity	Protected communication Personal autonomy Consumer protection	No
Digital Note (DigitalNote 2018)	194th	$20,677,499	General	End	Commodity	Static	Yes – Anonymity	Protected communication	Libertarian
ZClassic (Creighton 2018)	196th	$20,061,237	General	End	Commodity	Dynamic	Yes-Anonymity	Protected communication	Democracy
NIX (NIX 2018)	230th	$16,005,206	General	Means	Right	Dynamic	Yes – Anonymity	Protected communication Personal security	'Empowering'
Quantum Resistance (Waterland 2016)	233rd	$15,927,975	General	End	Commodity	Static	Yes – Anonymity	Protected communication Business protection	No
Pura (Pura 2018)	242th	$14,907,661	General	Means	Right	Static	Not explicit	Protected communication	Democracy
Mainframe (Clarke et al., 2018)	247th	$14,647,533	Special	End	Right	Static	Yes – Anonymity	Protected communication Compliance	Sovereignty
IOTeX (IoTex Team 2018)	248th	$14,488,970	General	End	Commodity	Dynamic	Yes – Anonymity	Protected communication Safe acquisition	No
ION (Matlack, Pfeiffer, and Nelson 2016)	255th	$14,111,834	General	End	Commodity	Static	Yes – Anonymity	Protected communication Consumer protection	No
NavCoin (Navcoin 2018)	257th	$13,959,244	General	End	Commodity	Static	Yes – Anonymity	Protected communication Business Protection	Democracy
CPChain (CPChain Team 2018)	266th	$12,864,672	General	End	Commodity	Static	Yes – Anonymity	Personal autonomy, Safe acquisition	No
TokenPay (Capo et al. 2017)	269th	$12,723,732	General	End	Commodity	Static	Yes-Anonymity	Protected communication Business Protection	No
PACcoin (PAC coin 2018)	276th	$12,012,093	General	End	Commodity	Dynamic	Yes – Anonymity	Protected communication	No
Aeon (Aeon 2014)	284th	$11,528,314	General	End	Commodity	Dynamic	Yes – Anonymity	Not explicit	Join the revolution

(Continued)

TABLE 1 (*Continued*).

Currency name	Ranking (#1–#500)	Market capitalization	General or special purpose money?	An end or a means?	A right or a commodity?	Is privacy protection static or dynamic?	States of privacy protected	Function of privacy	Allegiance to political philosophy?
Stakenet (Stakenet 2018)	285th	$11,484,925	General	End	Commodity	Dynamic	Yes – Anonymity	Personal autonomy, Safe transaction	No
Bulwark (Bulwalk 2018)	310th	$9,970,454	General	End	Commodity	Dynamic	Yes – Anonymity	Personal autonomy	Libertarian
BitNewChain (Bitnew-Chain 2018)	318th	$9,761,978	General	End	Commodity	Dynamic	Yes – Anonymity	Protected comms/ trans. Consumer protection	No
CloakCoin (Cloakcoin 2018)	320th	$9,671,115	General	End	Commodity	Dynamic	Yes – Anonymity	Protected communication	Libertarian
WABnetwork (Wab 2018)	331st	$9,089,798	General	End	Commodity	Static	Yes – Anonymity	Safe transactions	No

privacy; (2) identify tensions in the way privacy is framed epistemically and ethically in relation to politics; and (3) develop an agenda for future research based on issues that emerged from the analysis that indicate worthiness of further inquiry.

PRIVACY COINS AS POLITICAL BRANDS

Following the questions outlined in the data analysis section, we identified a number of political themes around privacy. These are shown explicitly for the cryptocurrency whitepapers examined in Table 1. The table shows that allegiance to distinct political ideologies is present in many of the whitepapers and can be seen in the championing of ideals such as "*Economic Liberalism*" (DigitalNote 2018), "*Libertarianism*" (e.g. Horizen – Viglione, Versluis, and Lippencott 2017; CloakCoin 2018) "*Egalitarian*" (Bytecoin – Van Saberhagen 2013), "*Democracy*" (e.g. Aion – Spoke and Nuco Engineering Team 2017; Stakenet 2018), "*Sovereignty*" (Mainframe – Clarke et al. 2018), "*Empowerment*" (Pura 2018), and "*Revolution*" (Aeon 2014).

Despite the variety of political positions expressed, privacy coin whitepapers are almost always ambitious too, as the vast majority aim to become a general-purpose money rather than special purpose within a limited domain. Privacy is overwhelmingly seen as an end in itself, but there is some variation in the corpus over whether privacy should be seen as a right or commodity, and whether privacy requires a static or dynamic evaluation. Although the political justifications for privacy coins are varied, the *state* of privacy which privacy coins aim to protect according to Westin's definitions is, almost always, *anonymity*. Indeed a keyword search across all documents reveals that 31 of the 40 whitepapers included even use the same terminology explicitly as "anonymous" or "anonymity" in order to justify their existence.

Cryptocurrency designers have a wide range of political beliefs, but perhaps the common feature mentioned in the majority of whitepapers are variants of freedom. Freedom, however, is a multi-faceted concept, and one can find references to freedom from governments, freedom from banks, freedom from multi-national companies, freedom from financial enslavement, freedom from exploitative charges, and freedom from surveillance. These claims for freedom are spread with inconsistent application throughout the corpus and depend largely on the domain specific aims of the designers.

Although the *functions* of privacy described in the whitepapers are primarily to protect communication and personal autonomy, we find reasons that go beyond Westin's (1967) categories. The politics of "privacy" claims are, generally speaking, less explicit than the broader and more common political aim of seizing the productive capacity of money from existing institutions. That said, there are a number of obvious convergent themes within privacy coin whitepapers that identify shared motivations for a range of societal stakeholders. Different motivations for privacy emerged from our review of cryptocurrency whitepapers. Although existing research indicates the need for brands to think about ways to protect and compete on privacy, scholars have neglected this approach (Ohm 2012), which is salient when approaching cryptocurrencies as political brands as their motivations manifest in different ways. We now discuss each of them in turn:

Privacy as a Guarantor of Fungibility

> *Fungibility is an attribute of money that dictates that all units of a currency should remain equal. When you receive money within a currency, it should not come with any history from the previous users of the currency or the users should have an easy way to disassociate themselves from that history, thus keeping all coins equal. At the same time, any user should be able to act as an auditor to guarantee the financial integrity of the public ledger without compromising others privacy.* Dash (Duffield and Diaz 2018)

> *Fungibility is a core component of money, it requires that all the pieces of a currency remain equal. For example, when you get coins via Private$PAC, these coins should not have any fingerprints from their previous transactions or users.* (PAC Coin 2018)

Money is used for all sorts of purposes, some of which are deemed illegitimate or criminal by governments. As money passes between people it can become tainted by the actions of previous owners, for example through illicit transactions involving drugs, weapons, stolen goods, money laundering, or perhaps more worryingly as a consequence of the subjective whims of a dictatorial regime. "Dirty" money is therefore potentially at risk of being expropriated or seized by the state. By obfuscating the history of coin transactions some privacy coins (e.g. Dash – Duffield and Diaz 2018; PAC Coin 2018; Komodo 2018; Stakenet 2018) pursue the goal of a truly fungible money, wherein all coins are equally valued regardless of their historical trajectories and associated owners. In this respect, privacy coins try to attain the quality of fungibility already possessed by offline cash in the form of physical coins and banknotes. A further consequence of expropriated money is price instability for the rest of the market. As expropriation may become increasingly commonplace as governments resist the integration of cryptocurrency into wider society, designers have recognized that these instances do not happen in isolation from the rest of the financial system, and that fungibility can help to support financial resilience for the broader currency implementation.

Privacy as Personal Security

To protect their privacy, users thus need an instant, risk-free, and, most importantly, automatic guarantee that data revealing their spending habits and account balances is not publicly accessible by their neighbors, co-workers, and merchants. (Zerocash – Sasson et al. 2014)

If a malicious agent does not know how much money you own, it becomes harder to target potential victims. Privacy thus provides a safeguard through hiding resources. But the broader claims made by coins like Zerocash (Sasson et al. 2014), Particl (Kassier 2017), and CPChain Team (2018) is that personal security is also the responsibility of the network. This is particularly a problem when consumers are not in a position to be sufficiently aware of potential privacy leaks or threats and thus are unable to provide informed consent. Personal security then is not just a matter of individuals ensuring they have the resources to defend and protect themselves, it is a much broader claim about the incomplete knowledge users possess and a political motivation to ensure maintenance of fiscal standards regardless. This judgment about user knowledge is not just a claim about the present moment, it is also extended into the future in recognition that all people are in a process of developmental learning, as can be seen in the quote below:

Many of humanity's most meaningful advancements in art, technology, and other human endeavors began in situations where the creator had the security of privacy in which to explore, to discover, to make mistakes, and to learn thereby. (Komodo 2018)

Although issues relating to Westin's privacy state of *reserve* are only rarely discussed in the whitepapers, there is nonetheless evidence that some designers see privacy as a safeguard for ensuring the future personal growth of their users. This is a more sophisticated account of privacy than a static understanding permits, instead recognizing that the acquiescence of others is a necessary precondition for the maturation of any person, and as such should be defended.

Privacy as Consumer Protection

Consumers expect a certain level of convenience when it comes to transferring value in exchange for goods and services, and this is why payment processing on the web has become commonplace. Along with this expectation of convenience, there is an assumed level of privacy that comes with such a transaction. Unfortunately, over the past two decades there have been entities who profit off of creating an online 'profile' of a consumer by tracking online credit card transactions. This is incredibly invasive and serves as a large supporting premise for why a consumer would want to transact online with cryptocurrency. (Bitcoin Private – Brutman et al. 2018).

Commercial intrusion into consumers' lives is widely cited in the privacy coin literature as something to be resisted, for example:

> *The online services we use are increasingly demanding more of our personal data, a disturbing trend that threatens the privacy of users on a global scale. Entities such as Google, Facebook and Yahoo have grown into colossal, seemingly unaccountable corporations by monetizing their users' personal data.* Particl (Kaiser 2017)

Multiple privacy coins (e.g. Aurora Labs 2018; Bitcoin Private – Brutman et al. 2018; Particl (Kaiser 2017); TokenPay – Capo et al. 2017; Enigma – Zyskind, Nathan, and Pentland 2018) explicitly comment on the use of privacy measures to protect consumers now and in imagined future scenarios. These arguments rely heavily on protecting the privacy state of *anonymity* (i.e. freedom from surveillance in public places) and the function of *protected communications*. For instance, if an account balance and behavior is unknown it is impossible to serve targeted advertisements based on behavioral segmentation. Behavioral advertising is now the norm across the Web, but it hinges on measuring, monitoring and updating a record of identity. Similarly, if an account balance is closely followed by companies it becomes possible to use that information for dynamic or differential pricing i.e. charging you more because of who you are or based on the increased likelihood that you will pay more at particular moments. This thread in the privacy literature is thus an attempt to develop consumer sovereignty in the marketplace.

Privacy as Business Protection

> *Meet Randal. As an entrepreneur, he is very aware of the importance of protecting the identities and finances of his clients safe. This is especially true as he provides anonymous genetic screening for diseases such as Parkinson's disease and Dementia. A breach of client data could ruin the lives of his clients, not only his business. After realizing that typical financial solutions provided no actual guarantee that leaks and breaches would not affect his business or his client, he began to use Verge to transact business.* (Verge 2018)

Privacy aims are widely extended to focus on businesses in many of the whitepapers in the corpus (e.g. Bitnew-Chain 2018; CPChain Team 2018; Verge 2018; Skycoin 2017; Ark 2018; Bitcoin Dark – Lee 2014; Wanchain 2017; Iotex Team 2018). Concealed transactions can help mask the relations between buyer and seller. Transactions up and downstream in supply chains can therefore be concealed from prying eyes. This is particularly important where a breach of privacy may jeopardize the lives of vulnerable clients, but it is also a means of maintaining competitive advantage. Third party financial intermediaries such as banks and credit providers have unprecedented access to transaction information of businesses across the globe. Although many consumers are increasingly vigilant with their privacy in the post-Snowden world we now inhabit, there is perhaps far less scrutiny given to the surveillance of corporate entities who are often seen as those adversaries being fought against. Organizations are especially vulnerable to privacy invasion. The obfuscation of supply chain relations is a defensive mechanism against competitors, but it is also potentially a means to deliberately hide information from consumers who may boycott a product when an organization fails to deliver on supply chain moral expectations.

Privacy as Safe Acquisition/Transaction

The majority of discussion around privacy in relation to cryptocurrencies focuses on maintaining privacy before, during and after currency has been spent. But the acquisition process is similarly important for maintaining user privacy. The way that people acquire cryptocurrencies varies widely depending on their circumstance. Some people earn currencies as networks reward miners or "masternodes" for validating transactions, while others directly exchange their fiat money for cryptocurrencies on third party websites, and some are also the beneficiaries of direct payments, gifts, donations or anonymous tips. In each of these use cases, people acquire cryptocurrencies through different means and each carry their own respective privacy risks. A range of whitepapers (e.g. CPCChain Team 2018; Bulwalk 2018; Verge 2018; Basic Attention Token 2018; Komodo 2018; DigitalNote 2018) draw attention to maintaining privacy during acquisition *and* transactions for a variety of reasons. For example, as discussed earlier, if a user is linked to a wallet address or ID then it becomes potentially fruitful for attackers to direct unwanted attention at that same address for malicious reasons. During the mining process for instance, miners can group together and censor transactions by actively not adding transactions to the proposed block. As more people become involved in hosting nodes for remuneration within these networks' privacy may evolve to become more focused on guaranteed earnings than maintaining discretion when spending. If cryptocurrency is ever to become widely used for paying wages, it is likely that privacy measures that manage coin acquisition would also need to be widely adopted.

Privacy as Compliance

The General Data Protection Regulation (GDPR) passed by the EU in 2016 requires enterprise IT practices to comply with strict privacy measures. Granting IT Admins a platform focused on user sovereignty, corporations can design streamlined systems without the risk of leaking information in transit. Liability is reduced when sensitive data is isolated within a secure system. (Clarke et al. 2018, Mainframe)

The media commentary around privacy coins has almost invariably drawn attention to what society loses when financial transactions become hidden. But this position loses sight of the already well-established legal frameworks surrounding interpersonal computing. A range of privacy coin whitepapers also draw attention to the need to act in accordance with preexisting standards and comply where necessary (Sasson et al. 2014; Zerocoin – Miers et al. 2018; TokenPay – Capo et al. 2017; Mainframe – Clarke et al. 2018). Privacy as compliance is likely to become increasingly important for those limited-domain projects which utilize blockchain, cryptocurrencies or tokens as a special-purpose money which can inadvertently reveal metadata about their users. Here, privacy is less to do with a crusading moral purpose. Instead, it is *de jure* privacy, an adherence to a state of affairs in accordance with the law.

EPISTEMIC AND ETHICAL TENSIONS IN THE POLITICS OF PRIVACY COINS

Three clear political tensions emerged from the inductive analysis, these relate to: (1) an inherent conflict of political ideologies in maintaining privacy, (2) disagreement in the practical implementation of privacy, and (3) the ethical implications of conflicting privacy conceptualizations due to technical limitations in design.

Tension One: "We the People" without the "We"

> *I don't believe we shall ever have a good money again before we take the thing out of the hands of government. That is, we can't take it violently out of the hands of government. All we can do is by some sly roundabout way introduce something they can't stop.* [Hayek quoted in Ammous (2018)].

Nakamoto recognized Bitcoin's sensibility to libertarian political philosophy and this remains a clear thread running through many privacy coins. The relation to libertarian ideas is clearest when privacy coin whitepaper authors cite the work of "Austrian School" economists such as Friedrich Hayek. Indeed, in the prophetic statement shown above, Hayek recognized the practical issue of creating an ideal currency well before the advent of cryptocurrency or even the Internet. A good money in the eyes of this philosophy is a money not controlled by any one individual, and yet even if the money is not violently created, it nonetheless requires at worst coercion or at best a gentler form of persuasion. This echoes the work of Dodd (2017) cited earlier that draws attention to the implicit social structure involved in maintaining a trustless, decentralized currency. A typical argument made in favor of privacy coins can be seen below:

> I care about more than cryptocurrencies. In fact they are a means to an end, the end being political empowerment of individuals… Our goal is to create a backdrop that allows pioneers to forge a method of societal organization that politically empowers individuals to become their own bank and, eventually, their own government. (Pura 2018).

Empowerment is a central theme in the literature, but this creates a tension when the political goal is also privacy. Pura (2018) cited above also discuss an aim to improve the "common good" through enabling individuals rather than allowing central authorities to make decisions about intervening through capital projects. One evident tension here is that without the knowledge of how money flows between different actors it is difficult to properly understand financial inequity through empirical means. Many of the rights granted to marginalized groups over the past hundred years were only guaranteed by a state after collective efforts drew attention and scrutiny to the mistreatment or corrosive power relations than exist between individuals. If all transactions between individuals become private, then it becomes impossible to trace the flows of capital and the associated structures of domination that potentially disempower marginalized groups.

Tension Two: Decisional Privacy vs Universal Privacy

> The superior privacy layer that NIX offers solves many concerns in the cryptocurrency ecosystem. Because NIX believes that users should have the power of privacy, it is not a required feature, simply an optional one. (NIX 2018)

How should privacy be practically embedded in privacy coins? All transactions by their nature include two parties. If both parties wish to reveal their interaction to other people should they be allowed to do so if they do not jeopardize the privacy of others? Some currencies are designed with modular privacy features that enable users to reveal details publicly when acting (e.g. NIX, Zcash). This has been criticized by privacy universalists such as Monero, who argue that the revelation of details by one user threatens the broader integrity of privacy for the rest of the network (sometimes called *networked privacy* – Boyd 2012). The cherry-picked approach to privacy, is referred to as *decisional privacy*, and is criticized because it is seen as impinging on the rights of third parties.

Decisional privacy is a well-established concept within the literature (e.g. Wacks 2015) and in this instance it refers to the right of an individual to choose what information is revealed during an interaction. The consequence of privacy coins that wish to facilitate decisional privacy is that the currencies will thus become special-purpose monies of limited domain, rather than a generally acceptable protocol, regardless of the privacy interest being defended. The likely outcome of this tension is that decisional and universal privacy coins are likely to coexist in the future and consequently eat the market share of each other, potentially precluding the positive network effects that could emerge if users privileged one design over the other.

Tension Three: Unlinkability or Taint Resistance?

Should designers aim to make technology which can make transactions unintelligible *or* invisible? This is the technical challenge, which privacy coin designers face and attempt to provide a solution to. Complete invisibility may be technically impossible as new technology continues to emerge and make robust protections become obsolete. This has important implications for user literacy too. If a user adopts a currency they are often confronted with a whitepaper or marketing material which promises anonymity, but this anonymity could come from invisibility of transactions or a technical intervention which makes behavioral traces become unintelligible. Both positions are seldom articulated as being distinct within the whitepaper corpus. Yet the anonymity claimed by so many privacy coins has been criticized as a kind of pseudonymity by many technical papers, and this is not well-reflected in whitepapers. Meiklejohn and Orlandi (2015) introduce the sophisticated notion of *taint resistance* when analyzing the claims made by privacy overlays. Existing notions of unlinkability for electronic cash require that a valid coin belonging to one user is indistinguishable from a valid coin belonging to another.

> *In Bitcoin, it is impossible to satisfy this definition: a bitcoin essentially is its spending history, and it is thus trivial to distinguish two valid bitcoins. Any notion of anonymity that is useful for Bitcoin must therefore focus less on the coins themselves and more on ownership.*

Specifically, the concept "attempts to capture how well an adversary can discern the ownership of a bitcoin based on its previous spending history. Our definition has the advantage that we can not only provide proofs of security (i.e., prove that a protocol achieves optimal taint resistance), but that it also provides a concrete measurement of the degree to which a proposed solution is effective in improving anonymity." Although many of the coins make outlandish claims about the quality of privacy protection, and some speak as though their solution to privacy is static, there is nonetheless recognition within other papers that privacy requires vigilance. Taint resistance is clearly a different ethical standpoint on privacy to unlinkability (regardless of its potential future design possibility). The notion neatly captures the frailty of many existing uses of privacy when used in whitepapers to attract a broad audience. Expressing this ethic clearly is perhaps the single most important step to ensuring the possibility of informed consent. The failure to seek such consent will invariably lead to differences in understanding emerging between designers and users.

FUTURE DIRECTIONS FOR RESEARCH

Several issues became apparent when conducting the literature review, which warrant further attention. Although we can be confident in our assertions about designers' intentions of privacy coins, we can be less sure about the motivations that are associated with user adoption. Most privacy coins treat privacy as an end in itself, which therefore means users may adopt the coins according to shared, different or even conflicting ultimate motivations. We suggest that further empirical scrutiny should be given to the following research questions:

1. Is this the domain of a truly decentralized and egalitarian social project, or does cryptocurrency – with its arsenal of jargon and technical barriers – actually preclude adoption from those marginalized or disenfranchised people who would benefit most from privacy features?
2. Why do people use privacy coins? Scaremongering abounds in the media portrayal of privacy coins and yet this is often based on unsubstantiated claims about the actual use of the currencies. Although this is a tricky environment to conduct research in given that privacy coin users obviously want privacy, there is nonetheless a burgeoning community of users in online forums (e.g. Reddit, Bitcointalk, and Telegram) who have willingly expressed their views in public and on record. There are literally hundreds of thousands of people involved in these communities and many of them may be willing to disclose their views in person or in large-scale questionnaires.
3. How does the relative prevalence of privacy coin adoption vary in relation to the broader political landscapes that people inhabit? Cryptocurrencies are a potentially subversive force for the existing monetary system in democratic countries, but they are potentially an emancipatory force for people living under the shadow of totalitarian regimes. Greater empirical scrutiny on the country-specific adoption rates of privacy coins would help to theorize the dynamics involved in their uptake as well as their revolutionary potential.

CONCLUSION

This article contributes to the understanding of political branding by shedding light on how notions of politics emerge in privacy coins and uncovering different ways in which cryptocurrencies underpin political brands.

The identification of political dimensions and ideologies in cryptocurrency challenges the idea that digital currency is removed from the influence of politicians (Dierksmeier and Seele 2018) and unveils a new context to research political branding.

Privacy often seems to be a secondary consideration in the world of cryptocurrency. Indeed, although Nakamoto paid lip service to the value of privacy their initial political aims seem more concerned with building a decentralized and resilient system that seizes the production of money from the state rather than guaranteeing the privacy of every individual user. As a consequence, the design of other cryptocurrencies since have largely echoed the ordering of these political points, the former being more urgent than the latter. One can readily find evidence of this in the claims made by cryptocurrency evangelists online that preventing governments from printing money will prevent war, genocide, poverty or other catastrophic events that blight human lives.

Privacy, although politically important, has historically been an add-on to the primary aim of decentralization. This has meant designers are now wrestling with the double-headed technical challenge of untraceability and unlinkability. We believe that many of these currencies already offer features that make tracking financial payments extremely difficult. How scrupulous those payments are is perhaps politically less important than what will happen to existing institutions. No amount of legislation is likely to prevent the growth of privacy coins in all areas of the economy in the next decade. Although many privacy coin designers would have us believe that transactions that do not involve us do not affect us, this clearly is not the case. As commerce becomes private, debate must become public.

ORCID

John Harvey (iD) http://orcid.org/0000-0003-4188-1900

REFERENCES

Aeon. 2014. "AEON Coin is the Next Generation of Anonymous Cryptocurrency." Accessed September 21, 2018. https://docs.google.com/document/d/11GxjLV8uszoCTRcPYmpXGYH7cUmHvriODD9lggu_gW8/edit.

Ammous, S. 2018. *The Bitcoin Standard: The Decentralized Alternative to Central Banking.* Hoboken, NJ: Wiley.

Ark. 2018. "A Platform for Consumer Adoption." Accessed September 21, 2018. https://ark.io/Whitepaper.pdf.

Aurora Labs. 2018. "Aurora: A Decentralized Financial Institution Utilizing Distributed Computing and the Ethereum Network." Accessed September 21, 2018. https://auroradao.com/assets/Aurora-Labs-Whitepaper-V0.9.5.pdf.

Basic Attention Token. 2018. "Basic Attention Token (BAT) Blockchain Based Digital Advertising." Accessed September 21, 2018. https://basicattentiontoken.org/BasicAttentionTokenWhitePaper-4.pdf.

Berentsen, A., and F. Schar. 2018. "The Case for Central Bank Electronic Money and the Non-Case for Central Bank Cryptocurrencies." *Federal Reserve Bank of St. Louis* Review 100 (2):97–106. doi: 10.20955/r.2018.97-106.

Bitnew-Chain. 2018. "Next-Generation Decentralized Application Platform for Commercial Applications." Accessed September 21, 2018. https://www.btn.org/download/BTN-Tec-white_paper_finalV1.1.pdf.

Bohannon, J. 2016. "The Bitcoin Busts." *Science* (New York, N.Y.) 351 (6278):1144–6. doi: 10.1126/science.351.6278.1144.

Boyd, D. 2012. "Networked Privacy." *Surveillance & Society* 10 (3/4):348. doi: 10.24908/ss.v10i3/4.4529.

Brutman, J., J. Layton, C. Sulmone, G. Stuto, G. Hopkins, and R. Creighton. 2018. "The Revolution of Privacy Fulfilling Satoshi's Vision for 2018 and Beyond." Accessed September 21, 2018. https://btcprivate.org/whitepaper.pdf.

Bulwalk. 2018. "Bulwark Cryptocurrency Whitepaper." Accessed September 21, 2018. https://bulwarkcrypto.com/docs/EN_-_Bulwark_Cryptocurrency_Whitepaper.pdf.

Capo, D., C. Salazar, J. Pacetti, and Y. Kalfoglou. 2017. "TokenPay The World's' Most Secure Coin." Accessed September 21, 2018. https://www.tokenpay.com/whitepaper.pdf.

Chaum, D. 1985. "Security without Identification: Transaction Systems to Make Big Brother Obsolete." *Communications of the ACM* 28 (10):1030–44.

Civic Technologies. 2017. "Civic White Paper." Accessed September 21, 2018. https://tokensale.civic.com/CivicTokenSaleWhitePaper.pdf.

Clarke, A., A. Craig, B. Hagen, C. Youngblood, C. Jaquier, D. Perillo, L. Tavazzani, M. Larson, M. Hagen, M. Mosic., et al. 2018. "Mainframe: The web3 Communications Layer." Accessed September 21, 2018. https://mainframe.docsend.com/view/j39qpui.

CloakCoin. 2018. "Enigma A Private Secure and Untraceable Transaction System for Cloakcoin." Accessed September 21, 2018. https://www.cloakcoin.com/user/themes/g5_cloak/resources/CloakCoin_Whitepaper_v2.1.pdf.

Coinmarketcap.com. 2018. "All Cryptocurrencies." Accessed September 11, 2018. https://coinmarketcap.com/all/views/all/.

CPChain Team. 2018. "Decentralized Infrastructure for Next Generation Internet of Things." Accessed September 21, 2018. https://www.cpchain.io/CPChain_Whitepaper_English.pdf.

Creighton, R. 2018. "ZClassic." Accessed September 12, 2018. https://zclassic.org/pdfs/whitepaper.pdf.

Crockett, D., and N. Pendarvis. 2017. "A Research Agenda on Political Ideology in Consumer Research: A Commentary on Jung et al.'s 'Blue and Red Voices." *Journal of Consumer Research* 44 (3):500–2.

Cryptonex. 2017. "Privacy Policy." Accessed September 21, 2018. https://cryptonex.org/privacypolicy.pdf.

Dierksmeier, C., and P. Seele. 2018. "Cryptocurrencies and Business Ethics." *Journal of Business Ethics* 152 (1):1–14. doi: 10.1007/s10551-016-3298-0.

DigitalNote. 2018. "DigitalNote XDN-project." Accessed September 21, 2018. https://digitalnote.biz/whitepaper_stake_award.pdf.

Dodd, N. 2017. "The Politics of Bitcoin." In *Money in a Human Economy*, edited by K. Hart, vol. 5. London: Berghahn Books.

Dodd, N. 2018. "The Social Life of Bitcoin." *Theory, Culture & Society* 35 (3):35–56.

Dostov, V., and P. Shust. 2014. "Cryptocurrencies: An Unconventional Challenge to the AML/CFT Regulators?" *Journal of Financial Crime* 21 (3):249–63.

Duffield, E., and D. Diaz. 2018. "Dash: A Payments-Focused Cryptocurrency [White paper]." Accessed September 21, 2018. https://github.com/dashpay/dash/wiki/Whitepaper.

Filippi, P. and B. Loveluck. 2016. "The Invisible Politics of Bitcoin: Governance Crisis of a Decentralised Infrastructure." *Internet Policy Review*, 5 (3).

Goldfeder, S., H. Kalodner, D. Reisman, and A. Narayanan. 2018. "When the Cookie Meets the Blockchain: Privacy Risks of Web Payments via Cryptocurrencies." *Proceedings on Privacy Enhancing Technologies* 4:179–99.

Hart, K. 2000. *The Memory Bank: Money in an Unequal World*. London: Profile Books.

Harvey, J., D. Golightly, and A. Smith. 2014. "HCI as a Means to Prosociality in the Economy." Paper presented at Proceedings of the SIGCHI Conference on Human Factors in Computing Systems, 2955–64, ACM, New York, April 26–May 1.

Herian, R. 2018. "The Politics of Blockchain." *Law and Critique* 29 (2):129–131.

Hurlburt, G. 2017. "Shining Light on the Dark Web." *IEEE Computer* 50 (4):100–5.

Husted, E., M. Fredriksson, M. Moufahim, and P. J. Gronbaek. 2019. "Political Parties: Exploring the Inner Life of Party Organisations." *Theory and Politics in Organisation*. http://www.ephemerajournal.org/sites/default/files/pdfs/papers/CfP%20Political%20parties.pdf

IoTex Team. 2018. "Disclaimer for White Paper." Accessed September 21. 2018. https://iotex.io/white-paper.

Kaiser, I. 2017. "A Decentralised Private Marketplace: DRAFT 0.1 [Particle]." Accessed September 21, 2018. https://github.com/particl/whitepaper/blob/master/decentralized-private-marketplace-draft-0.1.pdf.

Karlstrøm, H. 2014. "Do Libertarians Dream of Electric Coins? the Material Embeddedness of Bitcoin." *Distinktion: Scandinavian Journal of Social Theory* 15 (1):23–36.

Komodo. 2018. "An Advanced Blockchain Technology, Focused on Freedom." Accessed September 21, 2018. https://komodoplatform.com/wp-content/uploads/2018/05/2018-05-09-Komodo-White-Paper-Full.pdf.

Kostakis, V., and C. Giotitsas. 2014. "The (A) Political Economy of Bitcoin. TripleC: Communication, Capitalism & Critique." *Open Access Journal for a Global Sustainable Information Society*, 12 (2):431–440.

Kranzbühler, A. M., M. H. Kleijnen, R. E. Morgan, and M. Teerling. 2018. "The Multilevel Nature of Customer Experience Research: An Integrative Review and Research Agenda." *International Journal of Management Reviews* 20 (2): 433–56.

Larios-Hernández, G. J. 2017. "Blockchain Entrepreneurship Opportunity in the Practices of the Unbanked." *Business Horizons* 60 (6):865–74.

Lee, J. 2014. "Teleport: Anonymity through off-blockchain transaction information transfer – A Dark Paper for BTCD." Accessed September 21, 2018. https://whitepaperdatabase.com/bitcoindark-btcd-whitepaper/.

Luger, E., and T. Rodden. 2013. "An Informed View on Consent for UbiComp." Paper presented at Proceedings of the 2013 ACM International Joint Conference on Pervasive and Ubiquitous Computing, 529–38.

Matlack, A., M. Pfeiffer, and R. Nelson. 2016. "ION White Paper v. 0.1." Accessed September 21, 2018. https://github.com/ionomy/ion/wiki/ION-Technical-Whitepaper.

Maurer, B., T.C. Nelms, and L. Swartz. 2013. "When Perhaps the Real Problem Is Money Itself!': The Practical Materiality of Bitcoin." *Social Semiotics* 23 (2): 261–77.

Meiklejohn, S., and C. Orlandi. 2015. "Privacy-Enhancing Overlays in Bitcoin." Paper presented at International Conference on Financial Cryptography and Data Security, 127–41, Springer, Berlin, Heidelberg.

Miers, I., C. Garman, M. Green, and A. D. Rubin. 2018. "Zerocoin: Anonymous Distributed E-Cash from Bitcoin." Accessed September 21, 2018. http://zero-coin.org/media/pdf/ZerocoinOakland.pdf.

Nakamoto, S. 2008. "Bitcoin: A peer-to-peer electronic cash system [White paper]." Accessed September 21, 2018. https://bitcoin.org/bitcoin.pdf.

Navcoin. 2018. "The Unbreakable Code Navtech Decentralisation Whitepaper." Accessed September 21, 2018. https://cryptorating.eu/whitepapers/NavCoin/NAV-Coin-Whitepaper.pdf.

Needham, C., and G. Smith. 2015. "Introduction: Political Branding." *Journal of Political Marketing* 14 (1–2):1–6.

Nielsen, S. W. 2016. "Measuring Political Brands: An Art and a Science of Mapping the Mind." *Journal of Political Marketing* 15 (1):70–95.

Nielsen, S. W. 2017. "On Political Brands: A Systematic Review of the Literature." *Journal of Political Marketing* 16 (2):118–46.

NIX. 2018. "NIX Platform Whitepaper 2.0." Accessed September 21, 2018. https://nixplatform.io/docs/NIX-Platform-Whitepaper.pdf.

Noether, S. 2018. "Review of cryptonote white paper [Monero]." Accessed September 21, 2018. https://downloads.getmonero.org/whitepaper_review.pdf.

O'Shaughnessy, N. J., and P. R. Baines. 2009. "Selling Terror: The Symbolization and Positioning of Jihad." *Marketing Theory* 9 (2):227–41.

Ober, M., S. Katzenbeisser, and K. Hamacher. 2013. "Structure and Anonymity of the Bitcoin Transaction Graph." *Future Internet* 5 (2):237–50.

Ohm, P. 2012. "Branding Privacy." *Minnesota Law Review* 97:907–89.

Okamoto, T., and K. Ohta. 1991. "Universal Electronic Cash." Paper presented at Annual International Cryptology Conference, 324–37, Springer, Berlin, Heidelberg.

PAC Coin. 2018. "A 3rd Generation Peer to Peer Cryptocurrency. Built for the People, Lead by Social Governance." Accessed September 21, 2018. https://download.paccoin.net/PAC_White_Paper_2018_Final.pdf.

Petro. 2018. "White Paper 1.0 Financial Proposal." Accessed September 21, 2018. https://whitepaperdatabase.com/venezuela-petro-cryptocurrency-ptr-english-whitepaper/.

Pittman, A. 2016. "The Evolution of Giving: Considerations for Regulation of Cryptocurrency Donation Deductions." *Duke Law & Technology Review* 14:48.

Pivx. 2018. "PIVX Zerocoin Privacy." Accessed September 21, 2018. https://pivx. org/white-papers/.

Pura. 2018. "A Digital Cash Movement for the Common Good." Accessed September 21, 2018. https://mypura.io/wp-content/uploads/2018/08/Whitepaper_0.3.pdf.

Recorded Future. 2018. "Litecoin Emerges as the Next Dominant Dark Web Currency." Accessed September 12, 2018. https://go.recordedfuture.com/hubfs/reports/cta-2018-0208.pdf.

Reid, F., and M. Harrigan. 2013. "An Analysis of Anonymity in the Bitcoin System." In *Security and Privacy in Social Networks*, edited by Y. Altshuler, Y. Elovici, A. B. Cremers, N. Aharony, and A. Pentland, 197–223. New York, NY: Springer.

Ron, D., and A. Shamir. 2013. "Quantitative Analysis of the Full Bitcoin Transaction Graph." Paper presented at International Conference on Financial Cryptography and Data Security, 6–24, Springer, Berlin, Heidelberg.

Sasson, E. B., A. Chiesa, C. Garman, M. Green, I. Miers, E. Tromer, and M. Virza. 2014. "Zerocash: Decentralized Anonymous Payments from Bitcoin." Paper 2014 IEEE Symposium on Security and Privacy (SP), 459–74, San Jose, CA. doi: 10.1109/SP.2014.36.

Scott, B. 2016. "How Can Cryptocurrency and Blockchain Technology Play a Role in Building Social and Solidarity Finance?" UNRISD Working Paper No. No. 2016-1.

Seele, P. 2018. "Let us Not Forget: Crypto Means Secret. Cryptocurrencies as Enabler of Unethical and Illegal Business and the Question of Regulation." *Humanistic Management Journal* 3 (1):133–9.

Shamseer, L., D. Moher, M. Clarke, D. Ghersi, A. Liberati, M. Petticrew, P. Shekelle, and L.A. Stewart. 2015. "Preferred Reporting Items for Systematic Review and Meta-Analysis Protocols (PRISMA-P) 2015: Elaboration and Explanation." *BMJ* 349:g7647.

Skycoin. 2017. "Skycoin Business Whitepaper." Accessed September 18, 2018. https://downloads.skycoin.net/whitepapers/Skycoin-Whitepaper-v1.0.pdf.

Smith, G., and A. French. 2009. "The Political Brand: A Consumer Perspective." *Marketing Theory* 9 (2):209–26.

Smith, H. J., T. Dinev, and H. Xu. 2011. "Information Privacy Research: An Interdisciplinary Review." *MIS Quarterly* 35 (4):989–1016.

Speed, R., P. Butler, and N. Collins. 2015. "Human Branding in Political Marketing: Applying Contemporary Branding Thought to Political Parties and Their Leaders." *Journal of Political Marketing* 14 (1-2):129–51.

Spoke, M., and Nuco Engineering Team. 2017. "Aion: Enabling the decentralized Internet." Accessed September 18, 2018. https://aion.network/media/en-aion-network-technical-introduction.pdf.

Stakenet. 2018. "Whitepaper Version: 3.0." Accessed September 21. 2018. https://stakenet.io/Whitepaper_Stakenet_V3.0_EN.pdf.

Storj Labs. 2018. "Storj: A Decentralized Cloud Storage Network Framework." Accessed September 18, 2018. https://storj.io/storj.pdf.

Van Hout, M. C., and T. Bingham. 2013. "Silk Road', the Virtual Drug Marketplace: A Single Case Study of User Experiences." *International Journal of Drug Policy* 24 (5):385–91.

Van Saberhagen, N. 2013. "CryptoNote V2.0 [Bytecoin]." Accessed September 17, 2018. https://bytecoin.org/old/whitepaper.pdf.

Verge. 2018. "Verge: The Most Private Crytocurrency [white paper]." Accessed December 5, 2018. https://vergecurrency.com/static/blackpaper/Verge-Anonymity-Centric-CryptoCurrency.pdf.

Viglione, R., R. Versluis, and J. Lippencott. 2017. "Zen White Paper." Accessed September 21, 2018. https://www.horizen.global/assets/files/Zen-White-Paper.pdf.

Wab. 2018. "WAB Whitepaper." Accessed September 19, 2018. https://wab.net-work/Whitepaper-en.pdf.

Wacks, R. 2015. *Privacy: A Very Short Introduction*. Oxford: Oxford University Press.

Walsh, D., J. M. Parisi, and K. Passerini. 2017. "Privacy as a Right or as a Commodity in the Online World: The Limits of Regulatory Reform and Self-Regulation." *Electronic Commerce Research* 17 (2):185–203.

Wanchain. 2017. "Wanchain: Building Super Financial Markets for the New Digital Economy." Accessed September 18, 2018. https://wanchain.org/files/Wanchain-Whitepaper-EN-version.pdf.

Waterland, P. 2016. "Quantum Resistant Ledger (QRL)." Accessed September 17, 2018. https://github.com/theQRL/Whitepaper/blob/master/QRL_whitepaper.pdf.

Weimann, G. 2016. "Going Dark: Terrorism on the Dark Web." *Studies in Conflict and Terrorism* 39 (3):195–206.

Westin, A. F. 1967. *Privacy and Freedom*, vol. 1. New York, NY: Atheneum. doi: 10.1093/sw/13.4.114-a.

Westin, A.F. 2003. "Social and Political Dimensions of Privacy." *Journal of Social Issues* 59 (2):431–53.

Wilkinson, S., T. Boshevski, J. Brandoff, J. Prestwich, G. Hall, P. Gerbes, P. Hutchins, and C. Pollard. 2016. "Storj A Peer-to-Peer Cloud Storage Network." Accessed September 21, 2018. https://storj.io/storj.pdf.

Zulkarnine, A.T., R. Frank, B. Monk, J. Mitchell, and G. Davies. 2016. "Surfacing Collaborated Networks in Dark Web to Find Illicit and Criminal Content." In IEEE Conference on Intelligence and Security Informatics (ISI), 109–14, Tucson, AZ.

Zyskind, G., O. Nathan, and A. Pentland. 2018. "Enigma: Decentralized Computation Platform with Guaranteed Privacy." Accessed September 21, 2018. https://enigma.co/enigma_full.pdf.

The Emergence of Science as a Political Brand

TODD P. NEWMAN

This article seeks to explain how science has emerged as political brand. While science and politics have intersected for centuries, more recent social, cultural, and political events led to increased attention to the role of science in everyday life and how science is used in policy decision-making. This led to a tipping point in 2017 when the March for Science was formed, following what many in the U.S. and countries around the world viewed as anti-science stances by political leaders. The political spectacle of the March for Science not only brought increased attention to the scientific community, but also emerged to define the brand of science in society. Drawing on research from the role of brands in consumer culture – including political marketing, brand resonance, and brand community – I describe the implications of the science brand for the scientific enterprise, and the ways in which the scientific community consider the strategic communication of their brand within the political marketplace.

INTRODUCTION

The relationship between science and politics is complex. Often times it is difficult to separate science from politics given the fact that scientific knowledge constitutes the interests of various social actors and institutions. While the overlapping boundaries of science and politics existed for centuries, this relationship experienced a considerable shift since the mid-twentieth century. For instance, science issues such as climate change remain a politicized issue across developed countries. This example is most pronounced in the U.S., as conservatives are more likely than liberals to reject the scientific evidence on human's impact on the climate system (Dunlap and McCright 2015). Similarly, polarization over the safety of genetically modified organisms (GMOs) gained prominence in the UK leading to restrictive policies on the technology. More recently, skepticism surrounding the safety of vaccinations emerged in communities across a number of countries.

While there are a number of factors that contribute to the challenges that science faces in contemporary society, the politicization around science issues is rooted in more fundamental conceptions about the way in which the public views the impact of scientific advances and technological innovations on the various social, cultural, economic, and political values that shape their worldviews (Kahan 2012). Science and its "cultural authority" continues to be viewed through one's ideological worldview, and as a result, scientific issues have become key aspects of identity used in political contexts across the world.

Within the last several years, individuals who share these common worldviews have emerged as a prominent community in matters of public debate across a number of countries. Noticing the growing anti-scientific sentiment among policy decision-makers, the March for Science – an international group calling for political leaders and politicians to enact evidence-based policies within the public interest – emerged following the election of Donald J. Trump in the U.S. and in reaction to his administration's anti-science policies. Similarly, a number of other countries that were experiencing strong anti-science sentiment from political leaders organized similar marches (Wessel, 2017). In the UK, "Scientists for EU" emerged following "Brexit" to advocate the importance of the European Union to the scientific enterprise. It is estimated that over 1 million individuals attended rallies and marches in the U.S. as well as countries around the world.

As these examples illustrate, science and science-based issues have emerged as a positioning tactic in the political marketplace. This is not only as a way to engage voters, but also to differentiate from other political candidates, political parties, and interests. More distinctly, science has emerged as a political brand – an issue that provides meaning, identity, and symbolic value to a group of individuals (Scammell 2007). While the growing field of the "science of science communication" continues to assess the social, cultural, and psychological factors that influence the relationship between science and society (Hall-Jamieson, Kahan, and Scheufele 2017), there is less attention to how science is used strategically by political actors to differentiate themselves within the political marketplace. As a marketing tactic, various entities use positioning and differentiation to strategically position their brand in the consumer and political marketplace, influencing perceptions among customers (Newman and Newman 2018). Yet, there is little known about how science as a brand is used strategically.

This article therefore seeks to identify how scientific issues fit into branding and political marketing frameworks. The article focuses specifically on the growth of science as a political brand within the U.S. political system, and discusses the implications of this trend for politics more broadly. In so doing, this article will use the 2017 March for Science as a case study to assess the brand community that has evolved around this issue and how it serves as an important alternative political brand that must be taken into consideration.

THE POLITICIZATION OF SCIENCE IN THE U.S

In order to understand the evolution of science as a politicized issue in the U.S., and why the 2017 March for Science was a critical turning point, it is important to look back at the factors that contributed to the breakdown of trust in science along socio-political lines. Up until the 1970s, conservatives in the U.S. actually had more trust in science, relative to liberals and moderates, and overall public trust for science was fairly constant before declining in the 1970s (Gauchat 2012). The legitimacy and credibility of science can be traced to the notion of the "cultural authority of science", which states that scientific knowledge is tied to perceptions about the extent to which science is politically neutral and objective, as well as the extent to which the scientific community can leverage its credibility and expertise to assess and certify various policy and practices (Jasanoff 2004).

Beginning with the emergence of the New Right in the 1960s and 1970s in the U.S., conservatives grew skeptical of organized science and the intellectual establishment because of the way they viewed modern science as conflicting with their positions on religion and limited government, among others (Mooney, 2005). More specifically, science conflicted with two key constituencies of the New Right: corporations and the religious right. For instance, the growth of regulatory science in the U.S., such as the Environmental Protection Agency – which was passed by Republican President Richard Nixon – was perceived as negatively impacting corporate profit margins. Likewise, topics such as evolution and embryonic stem cell research were at odds with the moral standing of the religious right. These viewpoints – and the symbolic construction among conservatives of the scientific community – grew more widespread within the expanding conservative media enterprise of radio, books, television, and eventually social media and the deliberate attempt to discredit the scientific enterprise (Oreskes and Conway 2011).

A number of recent events have also contributed to the politicization of science as a salient issue to the U.S. public. For instance, the George W. Bush Administration was viewed as increasingly hostile to the scientific community, most notably on the topic of embryonic stem cell research. Likewise, climate change continues to be highly politicized and significant attention is brought to the contention of this issue despite the fact that strong scientific consensus on human's impact on the climate. Politicians often use climate change as a context to gain attention to broader issues. For instance, in 2008, a year after the U.S. Supreme Court ruled that the Environmental Protection Agency could regulate greenhouse gases as a form of pollution, Americans for Prosperity – a conservative non-profit group – devised the "No Climate Tax" pledge that over four hundred members of Congress signed as way to prevent lawmakers from addressing climate change (Davenport and Lipton 2017).

Most recently, the Trump Administration's budget cuts to science funding were viewed by many in the scientific community to be a tipping point. In the Trump Administration's first budget to Congress in 2017, it called for reducing the budget of the National Institutes of Health by 20% and reducing the budget of the Department of Energy by nearly 20% as well. In addition, the budget contained deep cuts to the Environmental Protection Agency, National Oceanic and Atmospheric Administration (NOAA), as well as NASA (Science News Staff 2017). As these cuts were seen as one of the starkest rebukes of science, it prompted the March for Science in 2017 as a response to what many in the scientific community and their supporters saw as a need to support and safeguard the scientific community. Yet as one of the most significant cultural displays of support for science, studies found that only 2% of marchers identified as Republican, thus highlighting the extent to which being "pro-science" has developed into a cultural phenomena among liberals, and ultimately leading to the alienation of any opportunity of mending political divisions (Mervis 2017).

POLITICAL BRANDING AND SCIENCE ISSUES

While one can trace the social and cultural drivers of the decline in trust of the cultural authority of science, it is within this context that researchers have uncovered that when science challenges deeply held beliefs, and ultimately threatens ones perceived "tribe", they are likely to engage in motivated reasoning, thus contributing to increased levels of politicization on scientific issues (Kunda 1990; Kahan et al. 2012). As party identity and ideology are salient cues to partisans, rather than offering assessment of scientific issues, they defend how their community responds to these issues regardless of what the scientific evidence might represent (Blank and Shaw 2015). Interestingly, despite the numerous articles and books documenting "anti-science" tendencies of conservatives, recent research within this context has uncovered that liberals and self-identified Democrats are just as likely to reject science when it goes against issues that are important to their community (Berezow and Campbell 2012; Nisbet, Cooper, and Garrett 2015). Most notably we see this highlighted in the context of vaccinations, biotechnology, and nuclear power, among others. So how is it that "pro-science" attitudes emerged to be a brand identity among a select segment of the public?

It is within this context that it is important to consider how political parties and political actors, both in the U.S. and around the world, use science issues as a positioning strategy to their competitive advantage. For example, how can insights from research on political branding begin to provide a framework to assess how science has evolved as a brand in its own right? What are the meanings associated with science as a brand and how do they fit into political discourse? In the consumer product marketplace, branding has significant implications for how corporations seek to differentiate their products and services from their competition, and thus increase their market share. The art of positioning – emphasizing attributes of your product that stand out from competitors – is a tactic that is increasingly relied upon. In the political marketplace, we see that branding serves this same purpose (Park, Jaworski, and MacInnis 1986).

The field of political marketing has long followed the use of marketing strategies by politicians and political parties as a way to differentiate the unique image of a party or politician from another (Newman 1999; Newman and Newman 2018), as well as in the area of environmental policy (Falkowski and Cwalina, 2000). As such, political marketing has acknowledged the importance of branding in the marketplace of voters, relying on numerous conceptions about the way that branding operates from more macro-based frameworks – such as brand community, brand management, and brand culture – which focus on the social construction of the brand by various actors (O'Guinn, Muñiz, and Paulson 2019), to micro-based frameworks – such as brand relationship, brand perspective, and brand personality – which focuses on how the public views the brand of specific entities and the influence this has on behavior (Winther Nielson 2016). As Smith and Speed (2011) argue, political branding seeks to address the interplay between brand identity – the managerial attention for the brand – and brand image – consumer perceptions of the brand. So, how has science evolved to be a brand in its own right, and what is its strategic use by political actors?

According to Scammell (2015) there are three core brand dimensions: the brand provides symbolic value, it impacts consumer choice, and it results from producer-consumer interaction. Political branding builds on this conception by emphasizing political representation of the brand both as a way of differentiation and identification. Taken together, the cultural authority of science is a political brand that politicians, political parties, and the public have attached to. Research on Consumer Culture Theory (CCT) provides an insightful framework for understanding how consumers, the marketplace, and cultural meanings unify to develop a brand meaning (Arnould and Thompson 2005, 2007). Within this context, a number of related frameworks emerged that consider the role of brands in consumer culture. The area of brand resonance, for instance, identifies the "nature of the relationship that customers have with the brand and the extent to which they feel that they are 'in synch' with the brand" (Keller 2001, 15). Keller defines brand resonance using four different categories:

1. *Behavioral loyalty*: How often and how much do consumers purchase of a particular brand?
2. *Attitudinal attachment*: To what extent do consumers have a strong personal attachment to the brand beyond necessity?
3. *Sense of community*: To what extent does the brand foster a sense of community with other individuals, including users, customers, or employees?
4. *Active engagement*: To what extent are consumers willing to invest time, energy, money, or other resources into the brand beyond just consumption.

Relatedly, Suarez and Belk (2017) focused on the cultural resonance of brands. In other words, in what way do brands position themselves with the cultural transformations that take place in society? However, as brands attach themselves to particular transformations in society, this may lead to rejection or resistance to certain brands due to its perceived association with a particular ideology to which the consumer is opposed (O'Guinn and Muñiz 2004; Varman and Belk 2009; Izberk-Bilgin 2010).

As previously discussed in this article, there are a number of factors and cultural events that led to the decline of trust in science among conservatives in the U.S., as well as the creation of science as a brand identity among liberals. However, ideological positioning on science issues and the cultural authority of science reached a tipping point in 2017 with the emergence of the March for Science, helping to solidify science as a brand community as well as establishing a platform for this brand to evolve. In the next section, the March for Science is used as a case study to illustrate how a strong brand for science evolved among the scientific community, and thus the implications for how science is "marketed" to the public. While the March for Science consisted of a number of marches and rallies across the world, I focus specifically on the U.S. context due to this being the context where this group evolved, as well as the unique cultural dynamics within the U.S. that shape how meanings associated with science fit with political discourse. Relying on a number of studies focused on those who participated in the March for Science, I discuss how these findings relate to several branding frameworks.

THE MARCH FOR SCIENCE

Following the election of Donald J. Trump in 2016 and the subsequent control by Republicans of the White House and U.S. Congress, a number of key positions in government agencies were filled with science skeptics and non-scientists, ultimately fueling concerns about the administration's anti-science stance. Moreover, the administration revealed plans to significantly cut funding for science (Science News Staff 2017). Criticism to this policy first developed traction on social media following the release of the budget, leading to a Facebook community of over half a million users organizing the need to set up a March for Science in Washington DC (Guarino 2017). The social media presence for this movement evolved into a Twitter account and website which helped to organize these developments around the world. This growing sense of urgency culminated on April 22, 2017 when approximately 1 million people in 600 cities around the world participated in the March for Science to increase attention to the role of science in everyday life. The marchers largely consisted of scientists and their supporters, who for the first time abandoned a long tradition of keeping science out of politics and calling on members of the public to support the scientific enterprise (St. Fleur 2017).

While the March was intended to bring attention to science in a non-partisan, non-political way, several commentators cautioned about the unintended consequences of the March for Science if it was positioned as a march against Trump and strayed into partisan messaging (e.g. Wessel 2017). For instance, some science communication scholars argued that the blurring between science and activism might only deepen partisan differences as well as jeopardize the credibility of scientists (e.g. Nisbet 2017). Yet, other researchers found that scientists who do engage in certain forms of advocacy do not risk harm to their credibility or the scientific community (Kotcher et al. 2017).

Field surveys taken at the March for Science in Washington, DC revealed that the marchers overwhelmingly supported Hillary Clinton in the 2016 election, and by one account only 2% of the marchers identified as Republican (Mervis 2017; Ross et al. 2018). Moreover, participants in the March for Science in Washington were over 85% White, and close to 80% were between the ages of 25 and 64. The March for

Science acted as a significant media event, with the major news net-works around the world reporting on the March, and in so doing echo-ing the negative sentiment of the Trump administration's policies towards the scientific community and the role of science in society more generally (Yong 2017).

While the March for Science elevated the concerns of science, research following the march suggests that it did little to mend the ideo-logical divisions within the U.S. For example, when asked about whether they support or oppose the goals of the March for Science, 47% of self-identified Republicans oppose the goals while only 25% approve. Conversely, 68% of self-identified Democrats support the goals, while only 14% oppose (Funk and Rainie 2017).

Following Atkin's (2004) description of branding as an exercise of facilitating "consumer tribes", the foundation of the "pro-science" stance among liberals during this event acts as a central foundation of community, providing a sense of belonging to support their "pro-science" identity. In much the same way that brand communities develop around specific prod-ucts and loyalty to them, the same principles applied to the emergence of the pro-science position at this time. These issues and the communities that have developed around them with shared values, represent a vibrant brand community that is growing within society (Muniz and O'Guinn 2001).

Moreover, within the context of CCT, the March for Science defined the identity and design of the science brand within the political market-place. The political context that prompted the formation of the March for Science also provided other political actors, including politicians and non-governmental organizations, to use this opportunity to negotiate how to define the brand identity of science. This includes using the brand for their political purposes as well as through supporting the scientific community. In addition, the March for Science cultivated a greater intensity and depth with this community's relationship to science as well as the level of activity with this engagement. Looking at Keller's (2001) framework for brand res-onance, the March for Science aligned with each of the four categories. The March for Science created a representation of science in terms of the who, what, and why for science. In turn, this representation fostered greater support, and most importantly according to Keller's framework, an active engagement now among consumers of this brand.

The CCT framework, as well as other frameworks examining the role brands in consumer culture, is useful for understanding how the science brand continues to be negotiated among different actors, as well as the mean-ing that different political actors attach to it. To understand this, it is also important to emphasize the many social-processes that surround brands, including the role of media in its symbolic construction (Muñiz and Schau

2007; Etgar 2008). For instance the decline of trust in the cultural authority of science among conservatives was fueled by the reach of a coordinated ideological media ecosystem of books, magazines, and news outlets that helped to reinforce the symbolic construction of questioning the objectivity, neutrality, and legitimacy of scientific knowledge. The same affordances of a fragmented media ecosystem – which provides the ability for consumers to selectively consume or avoid different perspectives – contributes to how dialog and engagement, particularly on social and digital media, become integral to this process of brand co-creation (Hatch and Schultz 2010).

Likewise, as cultural resonance makes the science brand healthier in many aspects, it also made it more fragile in the sense of cultivating resistance. Looking back at the origins of the March for Science, the group emerged out a need to highlight a greater appreciation for the use of science as well as calling for evidence-based public policy. "Post-normal" science, however, suggests that even when there is scientific consensus on an issue, policy-decision making on these issues is contentious (Funtowicz and Ravetz 2018); debates about science are less about the "science" and more about how society views different policy alternatives (Kahan 2012). As the March for Science conveys greater meaning to the brand of science in society, it in turn allows greater avoidance to the brand as well. For example, Varman and Belk (2009) and Izberk-Bilgin (2010) demonstrate how resistance to brands is linked to their perceived association with particular ideologies to which the consumer is opposed. As the March for Science symbolically constructed a brand for science within society, it in turn communicated to others the ideological homogeneity of this brand, thus making it more distinct for those who feel this group stands for issues that they disagree with.

STRATEGIC IMPLICATIONS FOR THE BRANDING OF SCIENCE

For science and evidence-based decision making to be effective, the science brand needs to attract a diverse group of stakeholders on the merits of its ideological argument or platform. The way in which this brand has developed in the political marketplace raises issues of concern. Part of this has to do with the partisan messaging of the March for Science supporters fueled by the angst of the Trump Administration's science policy and appointments, and the continued emphasis of "us" versus "them" tactics.

On one hand, the symbolic value of the cultural authority of science as a significant brand within the political marketplace is effective to the extent that it serves as a brand community. For example, support for the Green Party surged in recent elections across the European Union (Henley 2019). For many Democratic politicians, and increasingly more so given the start of the presidential primary season in the U.S., science issues are seen as central to candidate platforms as well. For example, Jay Inslee – the Democratic governor of Washington – is running on climate change as the central issue of his campaign. Moreover, the Green New Deal, introduced in February 2019 by Democratic Senator Ed Markey and Democratic Representative Alexandria Ocasio-Cortez cite the imbalance of power which has contributed to climate change as a leading factor in their call for transitioning the U.S. to nationalize involvement in the labor and energy markets, and in so doing call for zeroing out greenhouse gas emissions within a decade (Wolf, 2019).

The centrality of these issues among liberals, and the salience of pro-science movements such as the March for Science, suggest the need to reflect on how this issue has emerged as a political brand in its own right, and the way that it continues to be used in the political marketplace to secure votes and engagement. However, this type of positioning is unlikely to help grow the science brand outside of its already fervent supporters. While the cultural authority of science has complex historic roots that led to skepticism by conservatives, it is important now to reflect on what the brand of science represents in the political marketplace and what strategies those who want the best available science to be used in society need to consider.

Cross culturally, it is also important to consider how the science brand may differ and the way in which a worldwide group, such as the March for Science, can balance these different meanings. In the other words, the perceived association of science with a particular ideology is not universal. While the ideological divide is more clear in the U.S. and other Western countries, the emotional and ideological connections in other countries and the historical context differ. Thus, just as global brands have to be attentive to the different social, cultural, and political contexts that they sell their product, so to must science.

Developing a branding strategy for science is a complex endeavor. While commercial marketing and branding goes back over 100 years following dramatic shifts and changes in technology, manufacturing, advertising, and consumer preferences, there has been less attention paid to how these same principles apply to science and its role in society. For example as Larry Page – the co-founder of Google – stated in a talk to the American Academy of the Advancement of Science, the world's largest general science organization: "Science has a really serious marketing problem and nobody pays attention to that since none of the marketers work for science."

Thus, one of the foremost issues to consider in assessing the cultural authority of science as an influential political brand is the association and meaning that the public assigns to it (John et al. 2006). For instance, the premise of marketing is to understand the needs, wants, and desires of consumers, and use that information to develop promotional activities to motivate consumers to purchase a product or service. Yet, as numerous leaders from the scientific community have acknowledged, there has been a failure of communication between scientific institutions, scientists, and the public about how science affects their everyday life, and the importance of federal funding to the scientific endeavor (e.g. Leshner 2003). Most troubling, recent evidence suggests that within the U.S., only one in four Americans believe that federal funding for science research is irreplaceable, and believe that reducing science funding should be one of the key priorities for congress to reduce the deficit (ScienceCounts 2015). In reality, the federal government accounts for close to 50% of all scientific research funding (Sargent 2018). The need therefore for the scientific community to understand how science fits into the public's life, and what role science plays in fulfilling their needs, wants, and desires is critical.

Recent research into this topic by ScienceCounts – a non-profit organization that seeks to promote public awareness and support for science – finds that the majority of the U.S. public think of science in terms of hope, in other words as a source of optimism, forward looking, and a path to a better tomorrow (ScienceCounts 2015). As a tactic, March for Science marchers may have been more successful if they emphasized hopeful outcomes of science as opposed to their use of "us" versus "them" tactics. Likewise, we know from numerous studies on message framing that when issues are communicated in a way that aligns with values and beliefs that a specific group holds strongly, they are much more likely to embrace that issue (Nisbet and Mooney 2007; Nisbet and Newman 2015). For instance, biomedical research and public health as a theme for science held strongly across the ideological spectrum. In addition, conservatives and Republicans are much more likely to support federal funding for scientific research when it is in the context of national security and defense.

CONCLUSION

The emergence of alternative political brands is of increasing importance to both scholars and practitioners seeking to understand the contemporary political environment. As this article suggests, the need to look at science as a brand is increasingly important given that it has evolved into a strong brand community as well as brand identity among a target audience in the U.S. as well as around the world. However, unlike other political brands, science is unique in that at its core it is about the nature of knowledge and how we collectively use that knowledge to inform public policy. To that end, it is important to understand the multiple meanings that the science brand carries among different segments of the public and how it resonates with them.

This includes further empirical research on those who are part of the March for Science community and the extent to which and in what way they see themselves as a brand community and their own connection to the community. Likewise, while the March for Science served to develop a brand identity among a specific community, it is also critical examine ways in which this community can be expanded to other publics so that the brand of science is perceived to resonate not along political lines, but rather the fundamental value and role of science in our everyday lives.

There are a number of different branding frameworks that researchers and practitioners in science communication can draw from to better understand the use of and application of the science brand to achieving various goals. This includes understanding the socio-cultural context that led to science emerging as a politicized issue, but also the way in which different communities symbolically construct science and the meanings attached to it. Moreover, for researchers in political marketing and branding, science serves as an important contemporary issue to look at within the political marketplace. Comparative research looking at the socio-cultural context of the relationship between science and society in other countries, and the extent to which brand communities have emerged to give meaning and context to this issue, is necessary to understand how to increase public support and engagement for science, but also work to mend the social, cultural, and political factors that affect the use of science in society.

DISCLOSURE STATEMENT

No potential conflict of interest was reported by the author(s).

REFERENCES

Atkin, D. 2004. *The Culting of Brands*. London: Portfolio.

Arnould, E. J., and C. J. Thompson. 2005. "Consumer Culture Theory (CCT): Twenty Years of Research." *Journal of Consumer Research* 31 (4):868–882. doi: 10.1086/426626.

Arnould, E. J., and C. J. Thompson. 2007. "Consumer Culture Theory (and We Really Mean Theoretics): Dilemmas and Opportunities Posed by an Academic Branding Strategy." In *Research in Consumer Behavior. Vol. 11: Consumer Culture Theory*, p. 3–22, edited by R. W. Belk and J. F. Sherry Jr. Oxford: Elsevier.

Berezow, A., and H. Campbell. 2012. *Science Left Behind: Feel-Good Fallacies and the Rise of the Anti- Scientific Left*. New York, NY: Public Affairs.

Blank, J. M., and D. Shaw. 2015. "Does Partisanship Shape Attitudes toward Science and Public Policy? The Case for Ideology and Religion." *The ANNALS of the American Academy of Political and Social Science* 658 (1):18–35. doi: 10.1177/0002716214554756.

Davenport, C., and E. Lipton. 2017. (June 3). How GOP leaders came to view climate change as fake science. *The New York Times.* Accessed https://www. nytimes.com/2017/06/03/us/politics/republican-leaders-climate-change.html

Dunlap, R. E., and A. M. McCright. 2015. "Challenging Climate Change: The Denial Countermovement." In *Sociological Perspectives on Global Climate Change,* edited by R. E. Dunlap and R. J. Brulle, 300–332. New York, NY: Oxford University Press.

Etgar, M. 2008. "A Descriptive Model of the Consumer Co-Production Process." *Journal of the Academy of Marketing Science* 36 (1):97–108. doi: 10.1007/ s11747-007-0061-1.

Falkowski, A., and W. Cwalina. 2000. Political marketing of environmental policy. *Journal of Mental Changes,* 6 (2), 67–87.

Funk, C., and L. Rainie. 2017. (May 11). Americans divided on whether recent science protests will benefit scientists causes. *Pew Research Center.* Accessed www.pewinternet.org/2017/05/11/americans-divided-on-whether-recent-science-protests-will-benefit-scientists-causes/.

Funtowicz, S., and J. K. Ravetz. 2018. "Post-Normal Science." In *Companion to Environmental Studies.* Vol. 443, No. 447, p. 443–447. Routledge in Association with GSE Research.

Gauchat, G. 2012. "Politicization of Science in the Public Sphere: A Study of Public Trust in the United States, 1974 to 2010."*American Sociological Review* 77 (2): 167–187. doi: 10.1177/0003122412438225.

Guarino, B. 2017. (April 21). The March for Science began with this person's throwaway line on reddit. The Washington Post. Accessed www.washington-post.com/news/speaking-of-science/wp/2017/04/21/the-march-for-science-began-with-this-persons-throwaway-line-on-reddit/?utm_ term=.6968f7cdd3a7

Hall-Jamieson, K., D. Kahan, and D. A. Scheufele (Eds.). 2017. *The Oxford Handbook of the Science of Science Communication.* New York: Oxford University Press.

Hatch, M. J., and M. Schultz. 2010. "Toward a Theory of Brand co-Creation with Implications for Brand Governance." *Journal of Brand Management* 17 (8): 590–604. doi: 10.1057/bm.2010.14.

Henley, J. 2019. (May 26). Greens surge as parties make greatest ever showing across Europe. Accessed https://www.theguardian.com/politics/2019/may/26/ greens-surge-as-parties-make-strongest-ever-showing-across-europe

Izberk-Bilgin. E. 2010. "An Interdisciplinary Review of Resistance to Consumption, Some Marketing Interpretations, and Future Research Suggestions." Consumption, *Markets & Culture* 13 (3):299–323. doi: 10.1080/ 10253861003787031.

Jasanoff, S. 2004. *States of Knowledge: The Knowledge and Co-Production of Science and Social Order.* London: Routledge.

John, D. R., B. Loken, K. Kim, and A. B. Monga. 2006. "Brand Concept Maps: A Methodology for Identifying Brand Association Networks." *Journal of Marketing Research* 43 (4):549–563. doi: 10.1509/jmkr.43.4.549.

Kahan, D. M. 2012. "Cultural Cognition as a Conception of the Cultural Theory of Risk." In *Handbook of Risk Theory: Epistemology, Decision Theory, Ethics, and Social Implications of Risk*, 725–759. Amsterdam, Netherlands: Springer.

Kahan, D. M., E. Peters, M. Wittlin, P. Slovic, L. L. Ouellette, D. Braman, and G. Mandel. 2012. "The Polarizing Impact of Science Literacy and Numeracy on Perceived Climate Change Risks." *Nature Climate Change* 2 (10):732–735. doi: 10.1038/nclimate1547.

Keller, K. L. 2001. *Building Customer-Based Brand Equity: A Blueprint for Creating Strong Brands*, 3–27. Cambridge, MA: Marketing Science Institute.

Kotcher, J. E., T. A. Myers, E. K. Vraga, N. Stenhouse, and E. W. Maibach. 2017. "Does Engagement in Advocacy Hurt the Credibility of Scientists? Results from a Randomized National Survey Experiment." *Environmental Communication* 11 (3):415–429. doi: 10.1080/17524032.2016.1275736.

Kunda, Z. 1990. "The Case for Motivated Reasoning." *Psychological Bulletin* 108 (3):480–498. doi: 10.1037/0033-2909.108.3.480.

Leshner, AI. 2003. "Public Engagement with Science." *Science* (*New York*, N.Y.) 299 (5609):977. doi: 10.1126/science.299.5609.977.

Mervis, J. 2017. Rain Doesn't Stop Researchers from Doing Science at the March. *Science.* Accessed http://www.sciencemag.org/news/2017/04/rain-doesn-t-stop-researchers-doing-science-march

Mooney, C. 2005. *The Republican War on Science*. New York: Basic Books.

Muniz, A. M., and T. C. O'Guinn. 2001. "Brand Community." *Journal of Consumer Research* 27 (4):412–432. doi: 10.1086/319618.

Muñiz, A. M., Jr., and H. Jensen Schau. 2007. "Vigilante Marketing and Consumer Created Communications." *Journal of Advertising* 36 (3):35–50. doi: 10.2753/JOA0091-3367360303.

Newman, B. I. (Ed.). 1999. *Handbook of Political Marketing*. Thousand Oaks, CA: Sage Publications, Inc.

Newman, B I., and T. P. Newman. 2018. *Brand*. Dubuque, IA: Kendall Hunt.

Nisbet, E. C., K. E. Cooper, and R. K. Garrett. 2015. "The Partisan Brain: How Dissonant Science Messages Lead Conservatives and Liberals to (Dis) Trust Science." *The ANNALS of the American Academy of Political and Social Science* 658 (1): 36–66. doi: 10.1177/0002716214555474.

Nisbet, M. 2017. "The March for Science: Partisan Protests Put Public Trust in Scientists at Risk." *Quality* 41 (4):18–20.

Nisbet, M. C., and T. P. Newman. 2015. "Framing, the Media, and Environmental Communication." In *The Routledge Handbook of Environment and Communication*, edited by A. Hansen and R. Cox, 325–338. New York: Routledge.

Nisbet, M. C., and C. Mooney. 2007. "Science and Society. Framing Science." *Science* (*New York*, N.Y.*)* 316 (5821):56–56. doi: 10.1126/science.1142030.

O'Guinn, T. C., and A. M. Muniz. Jr. 2004. "The Polit- Brand and Blows Against the Empire: The Collectively Approved Brands of the New-New Left." In

Advances in Consumer Research, edited by Barbara Kahn and Mary Frances Luce, Vol. 31. Provo, UT: Association for Consumer Research, 100.

O'Guinn, T. C., A. M. Muñiz, Jr, &, and E. Paulson. 2019. "A Sociological Critique and Reformulation of Brands." In *The Oxford Handbook of Consumption*, edited by F. F. Wherry and I. Woodward. New York, NY: Oxford University Press, p.127-150.

Oreskes, N., and E. M. Conway. 2011. *Merchants of Doubt: How a Handful of Scientists Obscured the Truth on Issues from Tobacco Smoke to Global Warming*. New York: Bloomsbury Publishing USA.

Park, C. W., B. J. Jaworski, and D. J. MacInnis. 1986. "Strategic Brand Concept-Image Management." *Journal of Marketing* 50 (4):135–145. doi: 10.1177/002224298605000401.

Ross, A. D., R. Struminger, J. Winking, and K. R. Wedemeyer-Strombel. 2018. "Science as a Public Good: Findings from a Survey of March for Science Participants." *Science Communication* 40 (2):228–245. doi: 10.1177/1075547018758076.

Sargent, J.F. Jr., 2018. U.S. Research and Development Funding and Performance: Fact Sheet. Accessed Congressional Research Service Website: https://fas.org/sgp/crs/misc/R44307.pdf

Scammell, M. 2007. "Political Brands and Consumer Citizens: The Rebranding of Tony Blair." *The Annals of the American Academy of Political and Social Science* 611 (1):176–192. doi: 10.1177/0002716206299149.

Scammell, M. 2015. "Politics and Image: The Conceptual Value of Branding." *Journal of Political Marketing* 14 (1–2):7–18. doi: 10.1080/15377857.2014.990829.

ScienceCounts. 2015. "Unpublished Data from "Raising Voices for Science: Exploratory and Benchmarking Survey" (Survey Conducted October 2015.").

Science News Staff. 2017. NIH, DOE office of science face deep cuts in trumps first budget. *Science*. Accessed http://www.sciencemag.org/news/2017/03/nih-doe-office-science-face-deep-cuts-trumps-first-budget

Smith, G., and R. Speed. 2011. "Cultural Branding and Political Marketing: An Exploratory Analysis." *Journal of Marketing Management* 27 (13–14): 1304–1321. doi: 10.1080/0267257X.2011.628449.

St. Fleur, N. 2017. (April 22). Scientists, Feeling Under Siege, March Against Trump Policies. The New York Times. Accessed https://www.nytimes.com/2017/04/22/science/march-for-science.html

Suarez, M., and R. Belk. 2017. "Cultural Resonance of Global Brands in Brazilian Social Movements." *International Marketing Review* 34 (4):480–497. doi: 10.1108/IMR-07-2014-0252.

Varman, R., and R. W. Belk. 2009. "Nationalism and Ideology in an Anticonsumption Movement." *Journal of Consumer Research* 36 (4):686–700. doi: 10.1086/600486.

Wessel, L. 2017. (February 8). The marches for science, on one global interactive map. *Science*. Accessed http://www.sciencemag.org/news/2017/02/marches-science-one-global-interactive-map

Winther Nielsen, S. 2016. "Measuring Political Brands: An Art and a Science of Mapping the Mind." *Journal of Political Marketing* 15 (1):70–95. doi: 10.1080/15377857.2014.959682.

Wolf, Z. A. 2019. (February 14). Here's what the Green New Deal actually says. *CNN*. Retrieved from: https://www.cnn.com/2019/02/14/politics/green-new-deal-proposal-breakdown/index.html

Yong, E. 2017. (March 27). What exactly are people marching for when they March for Science? The Atlantic. Accessed www.theatlantic.com/science/archive/2017/03/what-exactly-are-people-marching-for-when-they-march-for-science/518763/

Symbolic Political Communication, and Trust: A Young Voters' Perspective of the Indonesian Presidential Election

IHWAN SUSILA

DIANNE DEAN

RAJA NERINA RAJA YUSOF

ANTON AGUS SETYAWAN AND FARID WAJDI

Communication in political marketing plays an important role in political mobilization, building trust both in political actors and the government. Politicians construct their messages through careful branding as the power of the cultural symbols and signs conveyed through the brand are potent heuristic devices. This is particularly important in emerging democracies, where there is limited political knowledge and understanding. Therefore, this research explores how young voters understand the symbolic communication fashioned by political actors in Indonesia and how it relates to their brand. Indonesia is an interesting area for study; it is both secular and the world's largest Muslim democracy. Using a phenomenological approach, a total of 19 in-depth interviews with young voters were conducted to gain rich insight into perceptions of the complexity of political symbolism, and trust among young voters. This study conceptualized political communication as a dual approach. The political brand promise is intrinsically linked to cultural references and conveyed through symbolic communication combined with a distinctive brand message. This builds trust, which then affects political participation. This conceptual framework provides insights into the importance of culture in branding which has implications for policy makers and actors in emerging and established democracies.

INTRODUCTION

In political marketing, information and trust are two important characteristics that influence voting behavior (Duch 2001). Political information is crucial to enable voters within a democracy to engage in the electoral decision making process, and political parties and governments use a range of persuasion mechanisms to achieve their goals (Cialdini 2007; Dillard and Shen 2012). However, in newly established democracies the level of political information and education is lower, compared to countries with more established democracies (Morduchowicz et al. 1996). This has implications for engagement and trust in political communications which will in turn affect the quality of the emerging democratic system. Therefore, more accessible and transparent communication tools and channels need to be developed to reach the electorate given the expansion of social media and the continued influence of mass media. The tools and channels are only part of the picture, as the message, and how it is conveyed is crucial. For political parties/candidates and the incumbent government, modern political marketing communication strategies emphasize the importance of reaching their target audience with a coherent message that is designed to appeal to their needs and wants. Given the lack of political literacy in emerging democracies, politicians need to construct their message, conveyed through a recognizable symbolic narrative, that is easily understood by their prospective voters. For McAdams (1997, 28) "stories are less about facts and more about meanings" but these stories or myths, constructed over time, must be coherent, and consistent in order to ensure they are believable. Leaders have always been aware of the power of symbolism, rhetoric, and image when they communicate to voters (Edelman 1964), and understand how this symbolism can reinforce or even change voters' decisions. Increasingly, branding has been used in politics to bundle symbolism, ideology, values, and policy promises into a political party/candidate brand, one that encapsulates national myths and stories within the culture. Brands as heuristic devices or information shortcuts are helpful for citizens with limited education and political knowledge so they are able to engage in the electoral process. For Indonesia, this is a crucial issue, as the largest Muslim democracy in the world and a secular government, there are varying levels of education and political knowledge. Moreover, there are tensions regarding the relationship between democracy and Islam (Goddard 2002; Tessler 2002; Potrafke 2012; Sarmazdeh 2012); issues relating to corruption (Henderson and Kuncoro 2011), combined with the complex electoral system (Sebastian 2004), and increasingly, the concerns about fake news which tap into the same myth creating narrative (Tapsell 2018). All of which impact on trust. Therefore, the first aim of this study focuses on how young voters in Indonesia perceive the political candidates' messages and imagery during the election campaign. Second, to understand how they relate to them and finally to evaluate if or how they build trust and thus influence their electoral behavior. This research has implications for not only Indonesia as an emerging democracy but also other emerging and established democracies.

POLITICAL LITERACY, KNOWLEDGE, AND POLITICAL BRANDING

Political literacy has been conceptualized as "the potential for informed participation … and central to empirical theories of democracy" (Cassel and Lo 1997). For Converse (1964), education and experience are core components of political literacy; the better educated have a more sophisticated understanding of political issues; and as people age they gain more experience of the political system and issues. This is more nuanced than political knowledge, which focuses on knowledge of political facts (Delli Carpini and Keeter 1993). Moreover, political literacy is only one aspect that informs people of politics, as there are also factors such as family, milieu including exposure to different cultures and lifestyles (Dean 2008). Thus, lack of political literacy or knowledge does not exclude people from electoral participation rather they may use other stimuli to build an understanding of how their world will be affected and thus inform their decision. Symbolic interactionism theory argues that reality is constructed through social meaning and places emphasis on symbols and metaphors that represent movement, signs, language, facial expressions, and how observers make sense of these symbols (Blumer 1969; Lakoff and Johnson 1980/ 2003). Indeed, we frequently make sense of our world and make decisions through what Marcus, Neuman, and MacKuen (2000) characterize as our affective intelligence. In Indonesia, citizens regularly rely on symbolic communication and during election campaigns stories, cultural myths and rituals are embedded in the political messages and political symbols to provide information to voters while simultaneously providing entertainment (Alakali, Sambe, and Tondo 2014). For some citizens, this is a low level engagement with politics, using heuristics to make electoral decisions and brands are heuristic devices imbued with symbolism. Therefore, the party or candidate seeks to brand themselves through a series of values, beliefs, and promises. These are underpinned by ideology and bundled under the signature of the brand, which is culturally embedded in familiarity and tradition (Jevons 2005; Peng and Hackley 2009). For Kapferer (2008), he identified a series of brand internal dimensions including personality, culture, and self-image that are presented to the receiver and then reflected back to the brand creator through the external dimensions of physique, relationship, and reflection. This reinforces the view that brands are multidimensional constructs (White and de Chernatony 2002; Veloutsou 2008) and more importantly they are social objects (Muniz and O'Guinn (2001), co-created by the brand creator and their user emerging from the cultural conditions of the time. Indeed, for Holt (2010, 2) cultural branding theory suggests that brands materialize from "an emergent kind of opportunity that is specific to a historical moment and a particular group of people." Thus, a brand narrative is developed through the cultural myths, stories, collective memories, and in the case of politics, ideology. Extant research on Indonesian elections has shown that young citizens build their understanding of politics and political parties through "stories and symbolic representations of political candidates" (Susila, Dean, and Harness 2015).

Therefore, a brand is more than just its logo, it includes a range of stories and myths that fit into the lives of citizens and it provides "added value based on factors over and above its functional performance" (Knox 2004). For Grynaviski (2010), symbols are commodities that provide politicians with a cost-efficient mechanism to signify their value to voters. This is why so many political candidates and parties are preoccupied with building their brands and personalizing their candidature, with imagery of capability, character, and trustworthiness, to win elections (Pich and Dean 2015). Moreover, the resilience of the individual or party brand has a direct impact upon reputation and trust (Dermody and Hanmer-Lloyd 2004) which in turn, has an enduring effect on voting intentions and helps to shield candidate or party brands from any negative campaign strategies designed to undermine their reputation during an election campaign.

Political marketing can make an important contribution when trust in political organizations begins to decline (Harris and Lock 2010). Democracy requires trustworthy candidates and institutions (Newton 2001; Offe 2001) to produce good governance and manage the corruption that is inherent in Indonesian politics (Henderson and Kuncoro 2011). Therefore, designing a relational strategy to build trust is critical for political parties and candidates in empowering voters to be involved in the electoral process (Dean and Croft 2001). For Dermody and Hanmer-Lloyd (2004), governments can only govern through the agreement of people within the structure of democracy. Mayer, Davis, and Schoorman (1995) defined trust as a positive assessment of the performance of government and party leaders. Trust can also be defined as the desire to accept vulnerabilities based on positive expectations about the intentions or behavior of others (Mayer, Davis, and Schoorman 1995). Vulnerability triggers risk and many experts claim that trust is linked to risk (Das and Teng 2004; Luhmann 2000; Mayer, Davis, and Schoorman 1995; Rousseau et al. 1998), so risk factors are important to be identified, because they will affect the decision making process. The issue of trust has been a concern in discussions of politics and public life (Newton 2001; Hardin 2002; Dermody, Hanmer-Lloyd, and Scullion 2010; Schiffman, Thelen, and Sherman 2010). Several specific studies have been conducted on how and why the public trust or distrust public officials and its consequences (Burns, Kinder, and Rahn 2003; Schiffman, Thelen, and Sherman 2010). Orr and Bennett (2017) recognize "that political organizations have been a rich fund of colorful stories and powerful visions" but there is scant research that explores the power of stories, myths, and rituals that may build trust in a political brand. Therefore, the primary aim of this research is to understand how young voters access the rich fund of political stories and how it affects their engagement and also their electoral participation.

CONTEXT

As the largest Muslim democracy in the world, Indonesia has experienced an evolutionary approach to democracy through three distinct periods including Parliamentary Democracy, Guided Democracy, and *Pancasila* (pronounced: pahn-cha-see-lah) Democracy. Indonesia held the first free and fair general elections to the national parliament in 1955 (Liddle 2000). However, the period of parliamentary democracy did not last long and was replaced by the authoritarian Guided Democracy, followed by the New Order which continued the authoritarian regime by applying the *Pancasila* Democracy (Thompson 2001; Eklof 1999).

   After the fall of the New Order regime, Indonesia entered a transitional democratic period and has since had five democratically elected presidents. This system of Presidential elections marked a new era of democracy in Indonesia with a rather unpredictable party system, a wide range of political parties and troubled with a series of innate flaws (Tan 2006). Those presidents were Burhanudin Jusuf Habibie, Golkar Party (21 May 1998–20 October 1999), Abdurrahman Wahid, National Awaking Party (20 October 1999–23 July 2001), Megawati Sukarnoputri, Indonesia Democratic Party of Struggle (23 July 2001–20 October 2004), and Susilo Bambang

Yudoyono, Democratic Party (20 October 2004–20 October 2009 and continued from 20 October 2009 to 20 October 2014), and currently Joko Widodo, Indonesia Democratic Party of Struggle (20 October 2014–20 October 2019).

Indonesia's Presidential election preparation began in September 2017 when the General Election Commission (KPU) opened registration for political parties to participate in the election. This was followed by the second stage which began in August 2018 opening registration for Presidential candidates (KPU 2019). Presidential candidates who participated in the 2019 election were the incumbent Joko Widodo and Prabowo Subianto. Rivalry between these two candidates is a continuation of the previous Presidential election in 2014.

In the 2014 Presidential election, Joko Widodo (Jokowi) was a low profile candidate, former mayor of Surakarta and characterized as outside the political and military elite, with a focus anticorruption and a man of the people. He stood against Prabowo Subianto, a former Lieutenant General in the Army and former Chief Commander of KOSTRAD (Komando Cadangan Strategis Angkatan Darat) an elite Indonesian Army corps. Prabowo Subianto represented the traditional political elites and was closely associated with the three decade long New Order era under President Suharto, who was widely regarded as a dictator. Prabowo, accused of human rights violations under Suharto, married to former President Suharto's daughter (since divorced) and ran for the 2009 vice Presidential election and 2014 Presidential election with an antipoverty platform with a promise of a new job creation campaign (Mietzner 2014).

However, the image of both candidates was refined during the 2019 Presidential election. Jokowi presented himself as the peoples' leader who has working hard for Indonesia's development and prosperity, while Prabowo Subianto emerged as a nationalist leader collaborating with Muslim groups and Islamic political parties (Suryadinata 2019) with an anti-foreign rhetoric (Maulia 2019).

METHODOLOGY

This research was developed in accordance with the principles of phenomenology (Easterby-Smith, Thorpe, and Jackson 2008; Krauss 2005). The design of this study was interpretive to gain insight into the language of politics and symbolic communication. Using a phenomenological approach, this research sought to build a rich understanding of social interactions and relationships between an individual's lifeworld and political engagement (Berger and Luckman, 1966/1991; Cunliffe 2008; Edvardsson, Tronvoll, and Gruber 2011). Phenomenology builds an understanding how people make sense of the world through stories as "stories are less about facts and more about meaning" (McAdams 1997, 28). It elucidates the interpersonal interactions and collective experiences through which meaning can be constructed (Moran 2000; Kvale 1996; Lowrie 2007). Further, it takes into consideration the perspectives and experiences of young citizens and the researcher so meaning is constructed "prior to, during and after the actual exchange and use(s) takes place" (Peñaloza and Venkatesh 2006). The researcher and the young citizen build an understanding of their engagement with politics, which is both intersubjective and dialogic, thus the researcher and the citizen co-create and produce a collective understanding of how politics fits into the citizens' lifeworld (Cunliffe and Coupland 2012). The discussions of political experiences and their lifeworld were a valuable data resource, which could explain how trust is built among young citizens in the Indonesian political environment.

Participants were selected through purposive sampling. Purposive sampling is a form of judgmental sampling where the researcher selects their participants according to their personal judgement and is classified as nonprobability sampling (Goulding 2002). A total of 19 in-depth interviews were conducted in September/October 2018 among young voters or Millenials who are characterized as between the ages of 18–30. This group is seen as "change seeking, better informed, mobile savvy and connected" but in contrast, they are also politically apathetic, less nationalistic, and 53% claim they will not vote (Chen and Syailendra 2014). Half the population is under the age of 28.5 (Indonesia Investments 2017) which is significant and therefore an interesting group to study. They share similar values to young people globally who are seen as cynical, apathetic, and disengaged from their electoral system. They "don't know, don't care, don't vote" (Heath and Park 1997) and are inclined less to vote than the older generations (Clarke et al. 2004). Due to cultural constraints in Indonesia, it was very difficult to interview women therefore the majority of the participants were men (see Table 1). The participants were students, entrepreneurs, civil servants, and employees in private companies.

Participants were sought through snowball sampling until theoretical saturation was reached (Kvale 1996). The interviews were conducted at the participants' homes at a time convenient for them and the interviews were conducted in Indonesian. Interviews were recorded digitally, notes were taken during the interview and memos were constructed after each interview identifying any emergent themes to explore these in more depth in later interviews (Glaser 2014). Participants' discussions were varied and lasted from 1 hour to 2 hours. Each interview was recorded digitally and then transcribed verbatim in Indonesian, then translated and then the data were analyzed ordered into themes. The data, including notes memos and transcripts, were read and reread to identify the connections between emergent themes

TABLE 1 Sample.

No.	Male participants	No.	Female participants
1	Male/30/Private Employee	1	Female/19/Student
2	Male/28/Entrepreneur	2	Female/25/Private Employee
3	Male/27/Private Employee	3	Female/20/Student
4	Male/21/Student	4	Female/22/Student
5	Male/20/Student	5	Female/22/Private Employee
6	Male/19/Student	6	Female/27/Civil Servant
7	Male/25/Private Employee	7	Female/20/Private Employee
8	Male/29/Private Employee	8	Female/19/Private Employee
9	Male/26/Civil Servant		
10	Male/21/Entrepreneur		
11	Male/21/Private Employee		

identified during the fieldwork. The transcripts were then read again using what Kvale (1996, 235) describe as the "theoretical reading." All personal information in the transcript has been deleted to ensure confidentiality of the participants according to the ethical procedures of the researcher's institution.

FINDINGS AND DISCUSSION

The findings of this study are based on young Indonesian voters' perceptions of the symbolic communications used by Presidential candidates as part of their brand during the 2019 Presidential election campaign. Findings indicate that for many participants political marketing communication does indeed increase young peoples' trust of political participation. However, this is dependent upon the cultural values and stories embedded in the communications and presented in a format that relates to the citizens' own cultural norms. The form of communication consists of two synergistically interlinked components, which are symbolic communication and brand message and these build political trust, which leads to political participation. Key aspects of symbolic communications are how the message is conveyed through speech, including: the candidate's accent, tempo of message delivery, their vocabulary used, their presentational style, and storytelling. These are all embedded within Indonesian or more specifically, Javanese cultural references. However, these elements are an intrinsic part of the candidate's personal characteristics, which are integral to building the brand. Their brand is developed through the articulation of political issues within the campaign promises that resonate with young voters; how these personal characteristics fit with those promises – are they believable? Other factors that contribute to the brand promise is the significance of their choice of clothing, traditional Javanese or Western business suits; how media friendly they are – how they present themselves and their brand promise to the electorate, plus the persuasiveness of their campaign promises. These all epitomize the brand's vision and mission leading to the brand promise. Thus a successful brand promise cannot be separated from the cultural references within the context in which it operates.

Symbolic Communication

The role of symbolic communication in politics has been considered by Edelman (1964, 116) in his seminal text and argued that "Language becomes a sequence of Pavlovian cues rather than an instrument of reasoning." The symbolic nature of how the candidate delivers his message has meaning for the receiver. For instance, participants recognized the accent of politician and this indicated a number of cultural values. Moreover, Joko Widodo's story began, as Mayor of Solo, who built a reputation as a politician who uses "dialogue, negotiation and persuasion" (Bunnell et al. 2013) rather than "force" to manage a local street vendor conflict, which reflects his "gentle" Javanese qualities. He was elected on a platform of anticorruption and was seen as a "clean able, populist leader" (Hamayotsu 2015). As President of the Republic of Indonesia, he contested the 2019 Presidential election and for some participants it appears that his reputation has not been tarnished by his time in office.

> We know Jokowi, he has strong Javanese accent. Especially from the way he talks, his language clearly shows that Joko Widodo is Javanese People. (Male/30/Private employee)

The Javanese accent not only illustrates that Jokowi is from Java, but for the participant, this indicates that he holds the Javanese cultural values of softness, service, and loyalty:

> Let's say, I think Pak Jokowi keeps his Javanese accent. Intentionally or not, Pak Jokowi as if tries to emphasize his service to the people, and that he is from Java (*Wong Jowo*), which is actually a symbol: From a cultural and historical perspective, it is common that Javanese is equal to gentleness, to serve, loyalty, protection, or it is more closely related to "offer" or "invite" instead of commanding. Implicitly, it builds people's perception that he is a figure with strong Javanese values. Of course this will help his image building for more people. (Male/28/Entrepreneur)

In line with the accent that builds a picture of the character of the candidate, voice tempo was also identified by participants as a core component of message delivery as it increases clarity, which enables citizens to build a richer understanding of the message. A private employee who was a participant in this study stated:

Let's say Pak Jokowi is as far as we know, that is, Pak Jokowi who is broadcasted on TV for example, was a kind of figure who conveyed something with a slow tempo. (Female/19/Student)

In addition, the vocabulary used complements the accent and tempo of voice so that participants can also grasp the political message through the use of a frequently used vocabulary. The use of limited ranges of words, that are familiar but articulate, focused, and resonate with the target audience, allow the prospective voters to understand and appreciate how the promises delivered in the message will benefit them.

... with vocabulary that might be limited, it might be targeted for people with basic-secondary education so that they will understand better. (Male/27/Private Employee)

For another student, the clarity and candid style of delivery is helpful for Prabowo, to emphasize his own military background. The army continues to be the most trusted institution in Indonesia due historically to their influence during the transition from dictatorship to democracy (Fossati, Yew-Foong, and Negara 2017). A retired General so maintains an association with the trustworthiness and power of the army which for some participants implies strength, power, and straightforwardness, and builds a clear differentiation from Jokowi. A firm and straightforward delivery style is more easily attached to his memory:

But, once again that style is quite helpful as when ... I remember at that time, how Prabowo, in his vision and mission, emphasizes his disagreement with foreign ownership by saying "not even a tiny bit ... I will not give blah blah to foreigners," again it proves his straightforward style, the remnant of his military background in the past, it describes the mission Prabowo will bring. (Male/20/Student)

For some young voters who tend to be more critical of politicians, repetition of words, phrases, and messages, fail to add clarity to the action articulated rather, it makes the message meaningless. A student stated:

We can remember from Pak Jokowi that when he addressed an issue, when he is confronted, or given questions about an urgent problem, he will sort of give clue, one word and repeat it for three times. For example, after a natural disaster occurred, when a reporter asked him, he will conclude by saying "evacuation, evacuation, evacuation," or for example when there is a problem of product scarcity, he will emphasize "distribution, distribution, distribution!" It somehow becomes an abstract idea, the essence of his action. (Male/21/Student)

Therefore, a simple message that resonates with the target audience through language, tone, and tempo is key to clear communication. The mode of delivery and how candidates present their message is also crucial, a critique of Jokowi highlighted how annoying and meaningless it was for some to repeat the same word over.

In developing political communication, candidates or political parties need to create distinctive characteristics so that they are easily recognized, and citizens can differentiate between one candidate to another. These help to build the brand providing a synergy between the candidates' values, their history, and their policy promises which are immediately recognizable. Special characteristics can arise from the speech style, body posture, and background of the candidate.

> Of course (there is a special characteristic), especially on this modern era ... Special characteristic will extremely help the prospective voters to remember the candidates. (Female/20/Private Employee)

> Let's say we compare it with Pak Prabowo. Prabowo Subianto is a military person huh? For prospective voters who are interested in straightforward figures, of course, Prabowo's style is what they need. Good emphasis, straightforward delivery, excellent language skills, doesn't that describe Pak Prabowo? (Male/21/Private Employee)

Specific features brought by candidates or political parties can help the potential voters remember which candidates they will vote for in general elections and these characteristics can even improve their airtime on mass media.

One distinction that has emerged from these discussions is that these candidates did indeed have a different persona. Jokowi with his relaxed, nonconfrontational "Javanese" style was in direct contrast to the "military, strong, straightforward" presentational style of Prabowo. However, for one participant, Prabowo was considered to be a familiar figure but in a new political environment so the characteristics and values from his earlier incarnation are difficult to separate while creating his new image.

> As for Pak Prabowo, so far, most people know him better as a New Order figure, the term Pak Prabowo is indeed an old product, or an old stock, although he was a new figure in political world, but if we judge from the figure's side, from what we remember, that is Pak Prabowo. (Male/29/Private Employee)

This links directly to the personal stories developed over time that help to differentiate them from competitors. For McAdams (1997, 102), "To create a personal myth is to fashion a history of the self" but Prabowo's dilemma is how much does he want to retain and how much does he want to remove.

The manner of communication used has shown the inter relationship between the candidates background and their political, civilian, and societal role and how that contributes to the development of the political self. One participant stated:

The point is that by employing such method, they will have their respective targets. There are segments here, and the language of speech, accent, automatically represent history, about how they are formed, and it automatically forms the segments for them. (Male/25/Private Employee)

Thus, their accent, manner of speaking, and mode of delivery are developed over time and help to illustrate who they are, where they are from and how their background contributed toward their values and beliefs. This was how this participant saw how these factors are interlinked:

The style of language and accent convey the historical side of who they are, well the history itself indirectly represents their vision and mission. (Female/ 22/Students)

Furthermore, this builds the story of the candidate which is told through the cultural references that citizens are familiar with, Moreover, whether they agree or disagree with them, they have an image of this person that is imbued with the qualities derived from their family background, their career history, and their values and beliefs.

These symbolic communication factors are clearly related to the personal characteristics of the candidate and thus linked to their vision and mission or their brand promise. However, there are other components that are closely related to the delivery of party platforms and ideas of political candidates. The clothing worn, how media friendly the candidates are, what issues resonate with citizens, and what campaign promises are promoted.

Brand Message

A number of participants were aware of how campaigns had been marketized, leading to a complex picture of the personal brand and which is inseparable from the vision and mission of political brand. There was some frustration for some participants who hoped that marketing may engender innovative new programs:

Maybe the marketing style will shift. I hope there will be more unique and new programs and vision-mission they will present. (Female/25/ Private Employee)

As discussed earlier, meaning is created through movement, signs, language, facial expressions, and also posture. The findings of this study revealed that colors and clothing chosen was also of strategic importance to building the brand. The participants of this study understood that the color and design of clothes often worn by political candidates have the intention to express specific messages to the potential voters.

For clothes and apparel, the last electoral campaign was quite interesting. But I am not sure from this year. There is nothing iconic from both of them. (Female/22/Private employee)

The reliance on clothing and color to emphasize tradition, values, or culture was a strong indicator of the political brand and was used to differentiate between the candidates. The clothing style and symbolic colors were understood by prospective voters as a leadership style that is clean from corruption and modest for instance with the use of the white shirt. A participant stated:

Yes, I know that it (white shirt) as if to market clean governance that focuses on people. (Male/26/Civil Servant)

We said that white symbolizes clean governance, we see good intention from Jokowi to abolish corruption, stop nepotism. At least, that's what I understand. (Male/20/Student)

The design of clothes worn by politicians is also captured by the prospective voters with different meanings but there could be difficulties arising from the choice of clothes. It also created competition over who was wearing the white shirt, which signified anticorruption. Jakowi also began to wear a sarong which is traditionally seen as a casual garment along with white shirt and a suit jacket accessorized with a *peci* (traditional Indonesian Muslim headwear) and *selops* (traditional slippers), which emphasized his traditional Javanese values (Wira 2017)

As if the uniform is capable of speaking, even Jokowi's black plaids at that time received criticism from the opponents that it symbolized discrimination instead of pluralism … then it changed into plain white to symbolize clean government. (Female/27/Civil Servant)

Each political candidate makes use of colors and design of clothes that are easily remembered by potential voters. The color and design of an iconic shirt makes it easy for prospective voters to capture the meaning of the created symbols.

Yes, that black (plaids) from Jokowi, and it is white safari for Prabowo. (Female/20/Student)

It was really popular, especially when Jokowi had his iconic black plaid shirt as the trigger. Then it encouraged Prabowo team to appear with his white safari. In addition to the programs and vision-mission they had at that time, it was an interesting phenomenon during 2014 and it became a jargon for people to place their sympathy, 'plaids!' meant Jokowi or 'white!' meant Prabowo. This was extremely interesting and possibly it made it easier for prospective voters to remember the figures they would choose. (Male/21/Entrepreneur)

The role of clothes, fabrics, colors, and accessories have always been a contributor to the candidate's persona such as Margaret Thatcher's power dressing (Rosenberg, Kahn, and Tran 1991). Colors and styles continue to be embedded with cultural references bound by tradition but can also signify innovation and difference.

Although some prospective voters may be able to assess the candidate's vision and mission, issues that are perceived by the citizen as trendy or of immediate importance need to be articulated by the candidates to prove that they understand the needs of their target audience. However, for some participants, there was a desire for something new or novel compared with the previous election. This reflects concerns that elections are viewed as entertainment (Franklin 2004; Alakali, Sambe, and Tondo 2014; Hall, Goldstein, and Ingram 2016) therefore required new and interesting issues. Moreover, there was little connection between what policies were offered and what the citizen wanted to hear:

> I don't think that the two parties for this year election have enough trendy issues to be fed to the public, or perhaps it's the public who are already fed up with it, considering that they already had similar notions during 2014 election. (Female/20/Student)

There was also a view that the candidates were keeping it too safe and thus making the election campaign boring. Political marketing strategy advocates an understanding of the needs of their target audience and present campaign promises in an engaging manner that resonate with the electorate. In the Indonesian Presidential election, there were few issues that resonated with the citizens that would galvanize or excite them to vote for either candidate.

> This year still tends to be boring, too serious, and extremely dragging. We remember in the 2014 presidential election, at that time Prabowo brought the problem of distribution which became a classic Indonesian problem, related to meat at that time, Prabowo offered a pattern of distribution of meat using frozen meat. Well, interesting issues like this needs to be brought up. Maybe not yet, but I hope that there will be more current issues raised during the political debate. If we really discuss this program campaign problem. (Male/19/Student)

Promises presented during the campaign in political marketing communications should resonate with the needs of the target voter. Moreover, these promises during the campaign should be delivered as tangible manifestations of the brand, which builds trust.

> How he leads and how he realizes what his vision and mission during his campaign. (Male/19/Student)

Therefore, campaign promises should be directly related to their brand vision, perceived as deliverable and at least some must be achieved and translated into policy:

> We call it as campaign promises, right? Of course, there are many that have not been realized, right? But there are also many that has been realized such as in education like free school, increase the teachers' support—not the salary itself—and other promises. (Female/19/Private Employee)

There were also concerns from one participant that some may forget the previous policy failures but there was disappointment that there was no innovation in either of the candidates.

> We know what our society is like? Political sin ten years ago can be erased by a day's rain, right? But, once again more striking and many visions, and promises, more campaign promises that are not fulfilled of course will be in the public spotlight to be taken into consideration. For this period, of course. Although people with low political understanding often pay little attention to the promises in detail, if in general the campaign promises are not realized, I think the vision and mission in this year's campaign will be a failed product for the incumbent Jokowi. (Male/21/Entrepreneur)

The notion that some citizens will not notice if campaign promises are not delivered depends upon how closely they match their needs and aspirations. However, if campaign promises are not converted to policy, over time trust starts to deteriorate and that will have an impact future voting intentions.

Political Trust and Participation

The Symbolic Political Branding Framework (Figure 1) has been developed from the findings of this research and shows how trust can foster engagement and participation in the electoral process. The extant literature has shown that trust can play an important role in increasing participation and how distrust can reduce engagement reflecting the work of Dermody and Hanmer-Lloyd (2004, 2005). This parsimonious model shows how the components of symbolic communication, embedded with cultural references are combined with the brand promise to build trust. The components of the symbolic communication style of the candidates including accent, voice tempo, vocabulary, presentation style, and the stories told are also a significant aspect of brand building as the embodiment of their personal characteristics. These personal characteristics combine with their chosen style of clothing, their connection with the media, and their campaign promises. The ability to convey their beliefs and values clearly, using cultural references, through the media is an important element of presenting their vision and mission. Thus, all the elements work to epitomize the

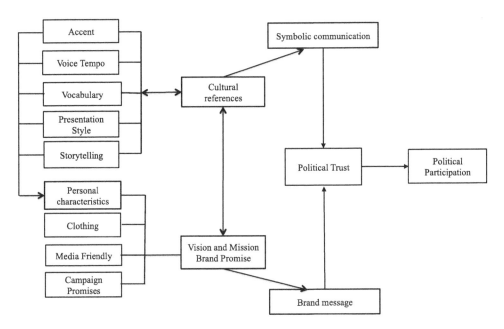

FIGURE 1 Symbolic political branding framework.

vision and mission of the brand, which help to build the brand and, in the process build trust.

In a political system where there is limited political literacy, the personal characteristics that convey symbolic meaning, derived from cultural references are crucial. The role of cultural references cannot be underestimated in any democratic election and the findings of this study highlight this.

Trust is characterized as the positive expectations and beliefs about other people's behavior. One interesting aspect of this study was that some participants claimed that the failure to achieve the vision and mission of the candidate's promise did not reduce their trust. Rather it appeared to "tar all politicians with the same brush."

> The failure to realize the vision of mission by those who are currently serving does not necessarily become an opportunity for their political opponents. It is possible for people to think that "meh, they will be the same" is what we worry about, and then they become apathetic. So, it is only the matter of how they manage the competition. (Male/21/Private Employee)

Thus, they still voted but voted for the same candidate they voted for in earlier elections. The Presidential election is a means to reach the hopes and aspirations of voters but for many participants there was nothing that was aspirational or interesting that set the candidates apart. Nevertheless, it was believed that citizens would still participate in the election.

> I think they will still participate. Most important, is to not act apathetically. Of course I will participate, as a voter, I will participate in the election. (Male/21/Private Employee)

This reflected the work by Susila, Dean, and Harness (2015) who revealed that in Indonesia, for some citizens, trust in the new democratic system is stronger than trust in the political candidate. In a similar vein, it is also in the interests of the incumbent candidate to keep the campaign uncontroversial, to keep it lackluster and uninteresting (Moore 2017) as citizens consider more of the same as being a safer option. Unless the incumbent has been seen to renege on their election promises or even worse, perceived to have deceived the electorate, then there is greater acceptance of the incumbent in contrast to the challenger who is an unknown quantity, untested and therefore, trust has not been built up over time. The limitations to the study relate to the difficulty of the male researcher interviewing female participants, further research could use a female researcher interview female participants but this research did not really find any gender differences. As a qualitative piece of work, this is not generalizable but provided rich insights to young Indonesian voters perceptions of the Presidential candidates and how trust is developed.

CONCLUSION

The aims of this study were to build an understanding how young voters in Indonesia perceive the political candidates' messages and imagery during the election campaign. Second, to understand how they relate to them and finally to evaluate if or how they build trust and thus influence their electoral behavior. This study contributes to the extant literature on political branding and shows how symbolic communications embedded in cultural references build the brand and thus help to build trust. This reflects the work of Holt (2010) who argues that brands emerge through social disruption. Jokowi emerged as a credible, honest Presidential candidate as a response to the corruption in the political environment. While Prabowo's credentials of strong, straightforward, and military background were based upon his experience in the Army, one of the most trusted institutions in Indonesia. Both these candidates built their brands through the cultural milieu and used metaphors, language and clothing to emphasize their connection to the citizens of Indonesia which help build trust. The accents and style of delivery were shown also to signify aspects of character, for Jokowi his Javanese accent and measured delivery indicated gentleness and importantly loyalty to the citizens, while Prabowo was direct, and emphasizing his "strong leader" values. Moreover, this study also shows how symbolic political communications are augmented by the candidates ability to communicate through the media and what they wear, clothing in terms of color and style which reinforce the brand values of each candidate.

This article also adds to the body of literature on trust in political marketing and election campaigning. Trust is built over time and reinforced by symbolic communication embedded within cultural references that the citizen is familiar with. Both Jokowi and Prabowo have distinct personal brands but both have emerged from Indonesian culture. They are consistent and for many citizens they are believable and therefore trustworthy. The election outcome was another term for Jokowi obtaining 55% of the vote precipitating a challenge by Prabowo who only gained 45%. This challenge was not upheld by the judiciary (The Guardian 2019). The study also adds to the body of literature on transitional democracies and political literacy and shows that political literacy is not just based on education and experience of the political system. Moreover, in contrast to many of the views on rational decision making this study reveals that affective intelligence does indeed engage young people as they respond to the symbolic communications of the political candidates and begin to make their judgements based on trust.

We hope that further research can build on this framework to build a deeper understanding of the cultural underpinning of trust in election campaigning and how political cultural brands emerge over time. As this research has revealed a relationship between affective intelligence and cultural referencing which helps to build a coherent brand leading to trust and electoral participation, we would like to see further research exploring this in other contexts.

REFERENCES

Alakali, T. T., S. S. Sambe, and A. W. Tondo. 2014. "Political Symbolism and Mass Mobilisation for Political Participation in Nigeria." *American International Journal of Humanities, Arts, and Social Sciences* 6 (1):44–49.

Berger, P., and T. Luckman. 1966-91. *The Social Construction of Reality: A Treatise in the Sociology of Knowledge*. London: Penguin.

Blumer, H. 1969. *Symbolic Interactionism: Perspective and Method*. London, UK: University of California Press.

Bunnell, T., M. A. Miller, N. A. Phelps, and J. Taylor. 2013. "Urban Development in a Decentralized Indonesia: Two Success Stories?" *Pacific Affairs* 86 (4): 857–76. doi: 10.5509/2013864857.

Burns, N., D. Kinder, and W. Rahn. 2003. "Social Trust and Democratic Politics." Annual Meeting of the Mid-West Political Science Association. Chicago, IL: Mid-West Political Science Association.

Cassel, C. A., and C. C. Lo. 1997. "Theories of Political Literacy." *Political Behavior* 19 (4):317–35. doi: 10.1023/A:1024895721905.

Chen, J., and E. A. Syailendra. 2014. "Old Society, New Youths: An Overview of Youth and Popular Participation in Post-*Reformasi* Indonesia." RSIS Working Paper Series No. 269, S. Rajaratnam School of International Studies, Singapore.

Cialdini, R. B. 2007. *Influence: The Psychology of Persuasion*. New York: William Morrow.

Clarke, H. D., D. Sanders, M. C. Stewart, and P. Whiteley. 2004. *Political Choice in Britain*. Oxford, UK: Oxford University Press.

Converse, P. 1964. "The Nature of Belief Systems in Mass Publics." In *Ideology and Discontent*, edited by D. Apter, 206–61. New York: Free Press.

Cunliffe, A. L. 2008. "Orientations to Social Constructionism: Relationally Responsive Social Constructionism and Its Implications for Knowledge and Learning." *Management Learning* 39 (2):123–139.

Cunliffe, A., and C. Coupland. 2012. "From Hero to Villain to Hero: Making Experience Sensible Through Embodied Narrative Sensemaking." *Human Relations* 65 (1):63–88.

Das, T. K., and B. Teng. 2004. "The Risk-Based View of Trust: A Conceptual Framework." *Journal of Business and Psychology* 19 (1):85–116. doi: 10.1023/B:JOBU.0000040274.23551.1b.

de Chernatony, L. 2002. "Would a Brand Smell Any Sweeter by a Corporate Name?" *Corporate Reputation Review* 5 (2–3):114–32. doi: 10.1057/palgrave.crr.1540169.

Dean, D. 2008. "The Lifeworld Mode Exploring the Vagaries in Political Consumption." In *Voters or Consumers: Imagining the Contemporary Electorate*, edited by D. Lilleker and R. Scullion, 209–29. Cambridge: Cambridge Scholars Publishing.

Dean, D., and R. Croft. 2001. "Friends and Relations: Long-Term Approaches to Political Campaigning." *European Journal of Marketing* 35 (11/12):1197–217. doi: 10.1108/EUM0000000006482.

Delli Carpini, M. X., and S. Keeter. 1993. "Measuring Political Knowledge: Putting First Things First." *American Journal of Political Science* 37 (4):1179–206. doi: 10.2307/2111549.

Dermody, J., and S. Hanmer-Lloyd. 2004. "Segmenting Youth Voting Behaviour through Trusting-Distrusting Relationships: A Conceptual Approach." *International Journal of Nonprofit and Voluntary Sector Marketing* 9 (3):202–17. doi: 10.1002/nvsm.248.

Dermody, J., and S. Hanmer-Lloyd. 2005. "Promoting Distrust? A Chronicle of the 2005 British General Election Advertising Campaigns." *Journal of Marketing Management* 21 (9–10):1021–47. doi: 10.1362/026725705775194210.

Dermody, J., S. Hanmer-Lloyd, and R. Scullion. 2010. "Young People and Voting Behaviour: Alienated Youth and (or) an Interested and Critical Citizenry?" *European Journal of Marketing* 44 (3/4):421–35. doi: 10.1108/03090561011020507.

Dillard, J. P., and L. Shen (eds). 2012. *The SAGE Handbook of Persuasion: Developments of Theory and Practice*. London, UK: Sage.

Duch, R. M. 2001. "A Development Model of Heterogeneous Economic Voting in New Democracies." *American Political Science Review* 95 (4):895–910. doi: 10.1017/S0003055400400080.

Easterby-Smith, M., R. Thorpe, and P. R. Jackson. 2008. *Management Research*. London, UK: Sage.

Edelman, M. 1964. *The Symbolic Uses of Politics*. Illinois: Illinois University Press.

Edvardsson, B., B. Tronvoll, and T. Gruber. 2011. "Expanding Understanding of Service Exchange and Value Co-creation: A Social Construction Approach." *Journal of the Academy of Marketing Science* 39 (2):327–339.

Eklof, S. 1999. *Indonesian Politics in Crisis: The Long Fall of Suharto 1996-9*. Copenhagen, Denmark: NIAS Press.

Fossati, D., H. Yew-Foong, and S. D. Negara. 2017. *The Indonesia National Survey Project: Economy, Society and Politics*. Singapore: ISEAS – Yusof Ishak Institute.

Franklin, B. 2004. *Packaging Politics: Political Communications in Britain's Media Democracy*. 2nd ed. London, UK: Bloomsbury.

Glaser, B. G. 2014. *Memoing: A Vital Grounded Theory Procedure*. Mill Valley, CA: Sociology Press.

Goddard, H. 2002. "Islam and Democracy." *The Political Quarterly* 73 (1):3–9. doi: 10.1111/1467-923X.00435.

Goulding, C. 2002. *Grounded Theory: A Practical Guide for Management, Business and Market Researchers*. London: Sage.

Grynaviski, J. D. 2010. *Partisan Bonds: Political Reputations and Legislative Accountability*. New York, NY: Cambridge University Press.

Hall, K., D. M. Goldstein, and M. B. Ingram. 2016. "The Hands of Donald Trump: Entertainment, Gesture, Spectacle." *HAU: Journal of Ethnographic Theory* 6 (2):71–100. doi: 10.14318/hau6.2.009.

Hamayotsu, K. 2015. "Indonesia in 2014: The Year of Electing the 'People's President'. " *Asian Survey* 55 (1):174–83.

Hardin, R. 2002. *Trust and Trustworthiness*. New York, NY: Russell Sage Foundation.

Harris, P., and A. Lock. 2010. "Mind the Gap": The Rise of Political Marketing and Perspective on Its Future Agenda." *European Journal of Marketing* 44 (3/4): 297–307. doi: 10.1108/03090561011020435.

Heath, A., and A. Park. 1997. "Thatcher's Children?" In *British Social Attitudes: The 14th Report, the End of Conservative Values?*, edited by R. Jowell, 1–22. Aldershopt, UK: Gower.

Henderson, J. V., and A. Kuncoro. 2011. "Corruption and Local Democratization in Indonesia: The Role of Islamic Parties." *Journal of Development Economics* 94 (2):164–80. doi: 10.1016/j.jdeveco.2010.01.007.

Holt, D. 2010. *Cultural Strategy: Using Innovative Ideologies to Build Breakthrough Brands*. Oxford, UK: Oxford University Press.

Indonesia Investments. 2017. Population of Indonesia. Accessed July 19, 2019. https://www.indonesia-investments.com/culture/population/item67?

Jevons, C. 2005. "Names, Brands, Branding: Beyond the Signs, Symbols, Products and Services." *Journal of Product & Brand Management* 14 (2):117–118. doi: 10.1108/10610420510592590.

Kapferer, J. N. 2008. *The New Strategic Brand Management*. London, UK: Kogan Page.

Knox, S. 2004. "Positioning and Branding Your Organisation." *Journal of Product & Brand Management* 13 (2):105–15. doi: 10.1108/10610420410529735.

KPU. 2019. Stages of the Program and Schedule for the Implementation of General Elections in 2019 (Tahapan Program dan Jadwal Penyelenggaraan Pemilihan Umum Tahun 2019). Accessed July 14, 2019. https://infopemilu.kpu.go.id/pileg2019.

Krauss, S. E. 2005. "Research Paradigms and Meaning Making: A Primer." *The Qualitative Report* 10 (4):758–70.

Kvale, S. 1996. *Interviews: An Introduction to Qualitative Research Interviewing.* London, UK: Sage.

Lakoff, G., and M. Johnson. 1980/2003. *Metaphors We Live By.* London, UK: University of Chicago Press.

Liddle, R. W. 2000. "Indonesia in 1999: Democracy Restored." *Asian Survey* 40 (1): 32–42. doi: 10.1525/as.2000.40.1.01p00462.

Lowrie, A. 2007. "Branding Higher Education: Equivalence and Difference in Developing Identity." *Journal of Business Research* 60 (9):990–99. doi: 10. 1016/j.jbusres.2007.01.024.

Luhmann, N. 2000. "Familiarity, Confidence, Trust: Problems and Alternatives." In *Trust: Making and Breaking Cooperative Relations*, edited by D. Gambetta, 94–107. Oxford, UK: Oxford University Press.

Marcus, G., W. R. Neuman, and M. MacKuen. 2000. *Affective Intelligence and Political Judgement.* London, UK: University of Chicago Press.

Maulia, E. 2019. "Capital Flows into Indonesia Slow Over Election Concerns." *Nikkei Asian Review*, April 12. Accessed July 14, 2019. https://asia.nikkei.com/Politics/ Indonesia-election/Capital-flows-into-Indonesia-slow-over-election-concerns

Mayer, R. C., J. H. Davis, and F. D. Schoorman. 1995. "An Integrative Model of Organizational Trust." *The Academy of Management Review* 20 (3):709–34. doi: 10.2307/258792.

McAdams, D. P. 1997. *The Stories We Live by: Personal Myths and the Making of the Self.* London, UK: Guildford Press.

Mietzner, M. 2014. "Indonesia's 2014 Election: How Jokowi Won and Democracy Survived." *Journal of Democracy* 25 (4):111–125. doi: 10.1353/jod.2014.0073.

Moore, S. 2017. "This Election Is Vitally Important. So Why Is It So Deathly Boring?" *The Guardian*, May 3. Accessed May 25, 2019. https://www.theguardian.com/commentisfree/2017/may/03/election-brexit-vitally-important-why-so-deathly-boring

Moran, D. 2000. "Heidegger's Critique of Husserl's and Brentano's Accounts of Intentionality." *Inquiry* 43 (1):39–66.

Morduchowicz, R., E. Catterberg, R. G. Niemi, and F. Bell. 1996. "Teaching Political Information and Democratic Values in a New Democracy: An Argentine Experiment." *Comparative Politics* 28 (4):465–476. doi: 10.2307/422053.

Muniz, A. M., and T. C. O'Guinn. 2001. "Brand Community." The *Journal of Consumer Research* 27 (4):412–432. doi: 10.1086/319618.

Newton, K. 2001. "Trust, Social Capital, Civil Society, and Democracy." *International Political Science Review* 22 (2):201–214. doi: 10.1177/0192512101222004.

Offe, C. 2001. "Political Liberalism, Group Right, and the Politics of Fear and Trust." *Studies in East European Thought* 53 (3):167–182. doi: 10.1023/ A:1011210918657.

Orr, K., and M. Bennett. 2017. "Relational Leadership, Storytelling and Narratives: Practices of Local Government." *Public Administration Review*, 77 (4):515–527.

Peñaloza, L., and A. Venkatesh. 2006. "Further Evolving the New Dominant Logic of Marketing: From Services to the Social Construction of Markets." *Marketing Theory* 6 (3):299–316. doi: 10.1177/1470593106066789.

Peng, N., and C. Hackley. 2009. "Are Voters, Consumers? A Qualitative Exploration of the Voter-Consumer Analogy in Political Marketing." *Qualitative Market Research: An International Journal* 12 (2):171–186. doi: 10.1108/13522750910948770.

Pich, C., and D. Dean. 2015. "Political Branding: Sense of Identity or Identity Crisis? An Investigation of the Transfer Potential of the Brand Identity Prism to the UK Conservative Party." *Journal of Marketing Management* 31 (11–12): 1353–1378. doi: 10.1080/0267257X.2015.1018307.

Potrafke, N. 2012. "Islam and Democracy." *Public Choice* 151 (1–2):185–192. doi: 10.1007/s11127-010-9741-3.

Rosenberg, S. W., S. Kahn, and T. Tran. 1991. "Creating a Political Image: Shaping Appearance and Manipulating the Vote." *Political Behavior* 13 (4):345–367. doi: 10.1007/BF00992868.

Rousseau, D. M., S. B. Sitkin, R. S. Burt, and C. Camerer. 1998. "Not So Different After All: A Cross-Discipline View of Trust." *Academy of Management Review* 23 (3):393–404. doi: 10.5465/amr.1998.926617.

Sarmazdeh, J. K. 2012. "Islam and Democracy." *Journal of American Science* 8 (1): 591–595.

Schiffman, L., S. T. Thelen, and E. Sherman. 2010. "Interpersonal and Political Trust: Modelling Levels of Citizens' Trust." *European Journal of Marketing* 44 (3/4):369–381. doi: 10.1108/03090561011020471.

Sebastian, L. C. 2004. "Indonesia's Historic First Presidential Elections." UNISCI Discussion Papers. Retrieved from http://www.redalyc.org/pdf/767/76711307006.pdf

Suryadinata, L. 2019. "Which Presidential Candidate Will Chinese Indonesians Vote for in 2019." *Perspectives*, February 13, 1–7.

Susila, I., D. Dean, and D. Harness. 2015. "Intergenerational Spaces: Citizens, Political Marketing and Conceptualising Trust in a Transitional Democracy." *Journal of Marketing Management* 31 (9–10):970–995. doi: 10.1080/0267257X.2015.1036768.

Tan, P. J. 2006. "Indonesia Seven Years after Soeharto: Party System Institutionalization in a New Democracy." *Contemporary Southeast Asia* 28 (1):88–114. doi: 10.1355/CS28-1E.

Tapsell, R. 2018. "The Smartphone as the "Weapon of the Weak": Assessing the Role of Communication Technologies in Malaysia's Regime Change." *Journal of Current Southeast Asian Affairs* 37 (3):9–29. doi: 10.1177/186810341803700302.

Tessler, M. 2002. "Islam and Democracy in the Middle East: The Impact of Religious Orientations in Attitudes." *Comparative Politics* 34 (3):337–54.

The Guardian. 2019. "Indonesia Election: Presidential Rival Challenges Widodo in Court." *The Guardian*, May 25. https://www.theguardian.com/world/2019/may/25/indonesia-election-presidential-rival-challenges-widodo-victory-in-court.

Thompson, M. R. 2001. "Whatever Happened to Asian Values?" *Journal of Democracy* 12 (4):154–65. doi: 10.1353/jod.2001.0083.

Veloutsou, C. 2008. "Branding: A Constantly Developing Concept." *Journal of Brand Management* 15 (5):299–300.

White, J., and L. de Chernatony. 2002. "New Labour: A Study of the Creation, Development and Demise of a Political Brand." *Journal of Political Marketing* 1 (2/3):45–52.

Wira, N. N. 2017. "Rocking Low-Maintenance Fashion, Jokowi Style." *The Jakarta Post*, January 11. Accessed December 16, 2018. https://www.thejakartapost.com/life/2017/01/11/rocking-low-maintenance-fashion-jokowi-style.html.

Index

accent 156–157, 159, 162, 164
accessibility 15, 30, 33, 36–37, 44, 112
agenda-setting 30–31, 33–34
anonymity 7, 59, 104–105, 108, 113, 117, 120, 124
applicability effects 30, 33, 36–37, 44
Armannsdottir, G. 4, 6
Atkin, D. 139
attitude change 33, 37, 40, 42
authentic political brand 91

Bargh, John 31
Belk, R. W. 137, 140
Bennett, M. 152
Bergan, Daniel E. 39
bitcoin 105–107, 109–110, 124
Bizer, George Y. 40, 42
Brake, T. 19
brand identity 55, 57, 72, 74, 82, 84, 88, 92,
    136–137, 139, 142–143; of personal political
    brands 77–78, 88, 93
branding/brand 5–6, 51–57, 59–61, 64–65, 74–76,
    78–79, 86, 88, 132, 134, 136–137, 139–143,
    148–149, 151, 155–156, 158–159, 161–164;
    communities 7, 132, 134, 136–137, 139–140, 143;
    creator 71, 73–74, 88–89; management 60, 81,
    85–86, 136; mantra 89; resonance 132, 137, 139
Brannon, Laura A. 34
Brewer, Paul R. 35
Bronn, P. S. 88
budget 135, 138
Butler-Kisber, L. 80

campaigns 2, 5–6, 8, 25, 38, 41, 54, 57–58, 61,
    155–156, 159, 161–162, 164
Carnell, S. 4, 6
case study approach 78
Chaum, D. 108
Chong, Dennis 31, 35
citizens 2–3, 6, 20, 24, 55, 58, 65, 71, 149–151,
    154–156, 158–159, 161–162, 164–165
Clawson, Rosalee A. 34
Cleveland, A. D. 75, 77, 90

coalition government 85–86
communities 55, 62, 64, 109, 125, 133, 136–137,
    139, 143
consumers 3, 13, 119–121, 134, 137, 139–140, 142
Converse, P. 150
core traits 16–17, 24
corpus 112–113, 117, 120
credibility 4, 6, 12–26, 56, 86, 134, 138;
    development of 15, 17, 21–22, 26; of political
    leader 13–14, 20; of scientists 138
cryptocurrencies 4, 6–7, 103–126
cultural authority of science 134–135, 137,
    140–141
cultural political branding 72
currencies 103, 109, 112–113, 118, 121, 123–126
Cwalina, W. 39

Davism, J. H. 152
Dean, D. 164
decisional privacy 123–124
democracies, established 149–150
Dermody, J. 151, 162
digital currencies 6–7, 104, 107, 126
Dodd, N. 109, 122
Druckman, James N. 31, 35, 38

Edelman, M. 156
education 82, 149–150, 162, 165
election campaign 61, 63, 150–151, 161, 164
elite interviews 79–80, 92
emotions 30, 32–33, 36, 38–40, 44
Esteves, Francisco 44
exploration 4, 73–74, 88–90
externalized traits 16–17, 23–25

Faber, Ronald J. 41
Falkowski, A. 5, 39–40
framing 5, 30–40, 42–44; effectiveness of 34–35,
    37, 43; effects 30–36, 38–40, 42–43;
    politicians 71
franchisees 53–54, 64
freedom 54, 63, 107–108, 117, 120

Gamson, William A. 32
Ganesh, B. E. 4, 6
Grynaviski, J. D. 151

Hanmer-Lloyd, S. 151, 162
Harness, D. 164
Harris, P. 2, 71
Hart, K. 109
Harvey, J. 6–7
higher political participation 38
Holt, D. 151, 164
human-politician brands 72

Icelandic Parliament 77–78, 91
identity creation 81, 89
India 2, 12, 20–23
Indonesia 2, 5, 148, 150, 152, 154, 156–157, 164
intended identities 71, 75–76
internal brand management 50, 55–56, 60
introspective evaluation 76, 87, 89–90
investigated political brand equity 72
Islamic political parties 153
Izberk-Bilgin. E. 140

Jabłońska, M. 5, 39, 40
Jain, V. 4, 6
Jokowi, Pak 156

Kahneman, Daniel 31
Kaid, Lynda Lee 41–42
Kapferer, J. N. 151
Keller, K. L. 139
Kosicki, Gerald M. 33
Krosnick, Jon A. 33–35
Kvale, S. 155

leader's credibility 19
Lecheler, Sophie 40
Lock, A. 2, 71
Lundqvist, Daniel 44

MacKuen, M. 150
March for Science 132–135, 137–141, 143
Marcus, G. 150
Marland, A. 5
Maurer, B. 107
Mayer, R. C. 152
McAdams, D. P. 149, 158
McDermott, Rose 38
Meiklejohn, S. 124
Miller, Joanne M. 33–35
Minsky, Marvin 32
Modi, Narendra 12–26

Na EK 37
Nabi, Robin L. 38, 40

Needham, C. 2
negative emotions 33, 38, 40, 44
Nelms, T.C. 107
Nelson, Thomas E. 34
Neuman, W. R. 150
Newman, B. I. 6
nontraditional political brands 2–3
Norvig, Peter 44

offline footprint 76, 83, 89–90
Ohman, Arne 44
Ohta, K. 108
Okamoto, T. 108
online footprint 83–84, 87, 89–90
Orlandi, C. 124
Orr, K. 152
Oxley, Zoe M. 34

Pan, Zhongdang 33
parliamentary systems 50–51, 53, 63–65
partisan politics 62, 64
party brand ambassadors 50–52
party branding/brands 5, 50–53, 55–56, 59–65,
    73–74, 91, 151
party discipline 5, 51–53, 55, 57–60, 62, 64
party leadership 51, 56, 60
party-political brand 70
performativity 15, 18
personal brand credibility 81
personal brand identities 72, 77, 88, 91
personal branding/brands 4, 56, 70–72, 75–77, 79,
    81, 83, 86–87, 91–93, 159
personal political brand identities 4, 70–72, 75, 81,
    88–90, 92; management of 71–72, 81
Personal Political Brand Identity Appraisal Framework 4
personal political brands 4–5, 56, 70, 76–78, 87–93
Peters, T. 75
Philbrick, J. L. 75, 77, 90
Pich, C. 4, 6, 73–74
political actors 3–4, 70, 133, 136, 139, 148
political behavior 44
political brand image 4–5, 30, 43, 72; management 44
political branding/brand 2–9, 13–15, 17–26, 31–41,
    43, 50–65, 70–89, 91–93, 103–113, 117–126,
    132–143, 148–161, 164–165; alternative 2–3,
    103–104, 110, 142; ambassadors 5, 56;
    communications 4, 6; communities 4, 6;
    environment 7; identity 71–72, 74, 79–80, 92;
    internal perspective of 72, 75, 77, 88; management
    3, 5, 30, 41; management process 5; nature of
    104, 110; personality 72; positioning 73; trinity 3;
    typologies of 4, 6–7, 73, 89, 91
political branding research 2–3, 7–8, 71–73, 110;
    diversity of 8, 72
political campaigns 21, 31, 72
political candidacy 58, 64

political candidates 21, 30–32, 41, 58, 133, 150–151, 159–160, 164–165
political communication 6, 59, 149
political cultural brands 165
political entities 2–3, 71
political groups 8–9
political ideologies 104, 122
political information 13, 149
political knowledge 34–35, 150
political leaders 12–21, 23–26, 132–133
political leader's ability 25
political leadership 20, 23–24
political leader's values 26
political literacy 149–150, 165
political marketing 2, 5, 9, 12, 14–15, 30–32, 34, 50, 52, 71, 136, 148–149, 151; communications 155, 161; research 4, 43
political marketplace 3, 132–134, 136, 139–141, 143
political motivations 7, 103, 113, 119
political organizations 110, 151–152
political participation 149, 155
political parties/candidates 149
political philosophies 7, 103, 106–107, 113, 122
political representations 52, 110, 137
political trust 155, 162
political values 64, 81, 133
politician brand identities 86
politician brands 72–73
politicization, of science 134–135
potential voters 42, 158–160
Price, Vincent 37
priming 5, 30–37, 42–43
privacy 103–110, 112–113, 117–126; claims 112, 117; functions of 113, 117
privacy coins 7, 103–107, 109, 117–118, 122–126
privacy coin whitepapers 103–126
prospective voters 149, 157–158, 160–161
Pura 117, 123

Risner, Geneviève 39
robust personal political brand identity 87
Russell, Stuart J. 44

Scammell, M. 13, 136
Schmitt, Kay G. 41
Schoorman, F. D. 152
Schuck, Andreas R.T. 40
science brand 6, 132, 139–141, 143
ScienceCounts 142
science issues 133, 135, 137, 141
scientific community 132, 134–135, 137–139, 142
Seele, P. 109
Semetko, Holli A. 34
Shepherd, I. D. H. 75
Smith, G. 2, 136
social media 14, 24–25, 55, 59, 84–88, 138, 149
Speed, R. 136
strong political brands 6
Suarez, M. 137
sub-political brands 8
Susila, I. 6, 164
Swartz, L. 107
symbolic communications 5, 148–150, 153, 155–156, 162, 164–165

target market 76–77, 83–84, 87–88
Tewksbury, David 37
Tims, Albert R. 41
Togeby, Lise 36
traits 12, 15–17

valence 39–40
Valentino, Nicholas A. 40
Valkenburg, Patti M. 34
Varman, R. 140
voters 4–5, 12–18, 20–26, 50–51, 62–64, 83, 133, 136, 149–151, 163–164; credibility 14; engagement 20
Vreese, Claes H. de 40

Wagner, A. 5
Washington 138, 141
Westin, A. F. 107–108, 113, 117
whitepapers 104, 112–113, 117, 119–121, 124–125
Widodo, Joko 153, 156

young voters 5, 14, 148, 150, 154–155, 157, 164

For Product Safety Concerns and Information please contact our
EU representative GPSR@taylorandfrancis.com Taylor & Francis
Verlag GmbH, Kaufingerstraße 24, 80331 München, Germany